UNDERSTANDING
SCHOOL BULLYING

SAGE has been part of the global academic community since 1965, supporting high quality research and learning that transforms society and our understanding of individuals, groups and cultures. SAGE is the independent, innovative, natural home for authors, editors and societies who share our commitment and passion for the social sciences.

Find out more at: **www.sagepublications.com**

UNDERSTANDING SCHOOL BULLYING

Its Nature & Prevention Strategies

Peter K. Smith

Los Angeles | London | New Delhi
Singapore | Washington DC

Los Angeles | London | New Delhi
Singapore | Washington DC

SAGE Publications Ltd
1 Oliver's Yard
55 City Road
London EC1Y 1SP

SAGE Publications Inc.
2455 Teller Road
Thousand Oaks, California 91320

SAGE Publications India Pvt Ltd
B 1/I 1 Mohan Cooperative Industrial Area
Mathura Road
New Delhi 110 044

SAGE Publications Asia-Pacific Pte Ltd
3 Church Street
#10-04 Samsung Hub
Singapore 049483

Editor: Michael Carmichael
Editorial assistant: Keri Dickens
Production editor: Imogen Roome
Copyeditor: Audrey Scriven
Proofreader: Leigh Timmins
Marketing manager: Catherine Slinn
Cover design: Wendy Scott
Typeset by: C&M Digitals (P) Ltd, Chennai, India
Printed in Great Britain by Henry Ling Limited at
The Dorset Press, Dorchester, DT1 1HD

MIX
Paper from
responsible sources
FSC
www.fsc.org FSC™ C013985

Library of Congress Control Number: 2013951824

British Library Cataloguing-in-Publication Data

A catalogue record for this book is available from
the British Library

ISBN 978-1-84787-904-2
ISBN 978-1-84787-905-9 (pbk)

Contents

Acknowledgements

The research area around school bullying, and more recently cyberbullying, has been growing so rapidly, that it is difficult for any book to do justice to it. Like the Red Queen in *Alice in Wonderland*, I felt I had been running as fast as I could to keep up with the research, and meanwhile the book stayed where it was (half completed). A mixture of patience and cajoling from the publishers, and my own desire to finally finish it, has helped bring about a conclusion. I would like to thank a number of colleagues and friends who have contributed to or commented on drafts and excerpts, or answered queries, including Cristina del Barrio, Antonella Brighi, Hilary Cremin, Rosario del Rey, Jevetta Doyley, Erika Fox, Carrie Herbert, Alana James, Seung-ha Lee, Conor McGuckin, Ersilia Menesini, Mona O'Moore, Dan Olweus, Rosario Ortega, Debra Pepler, Tiziana Pozzoli, Christina Salmivalli, Muthanna Samara, Shu Shu, Ruth Sittichai, Barbara Spears, Fran Thompson and Michael Turner. Inevitably, some things will be omitted, and some material will be superceded as research moves on, but I hope not too many errors have been made. Working in this area of social science has been satisfying and rewarding, both through having so many helpful colleagues, and through the knowledge that we appear to be having at least some success in reducing the impact of school bullying and improving children's well-being. I hope this book can also contribute to this wider endeavour.

Peter K. Smith
January 2014

ONE

School bullying as a personal issue, a practical issue and a research programme

As a psychologist, I have spent over twenty years researching bullying in schools. As a person, I have my own recollections of bullying at school. And I have met and talked to many teachers, pupils and parents for whom this is a vital practical issue. It is an issue that transcends just schools, and also transcends 'bullying' in a narrow sense, if we take it to reflect the abuse of power in relationships. But in this book, the focus is on bullying in schools, which is where the term probably originated and where very much research has been carried out, and policy change in many countries has occurred. I attempt to describe the extensive research on this topic, and the relationship between research and practice. Hopefully, changes in practice will improve the quality of relationships and experiences in school of many pupils.

Bullying as a personal experience

I can remember being bullied in secondary school. It was verbal bullying, and it was unpleasant. It went on for some time, and I am sure teachers were aware of it. In fact one teacher – who was himself taunted by a lot by pupils, as he was unable to keep any discipline – once actually joined in himself, probably to curry favour with the other pupils; an act I despised him for. The school had no policy as such on bullying, and nothing was done to prevent it, except that it more or less went away as I entered sixth form.

I can also remember bullying someone else at this school. The victim was in my class and was very studious and a bit lacking in social skills. He was the brunt of a lot of verbal teasing. I quite liked him, and did not usually join in. But I remember once I did, and he was very upset. (In fact he retaliated by punching me very hard on the nose – it bled a lot, and is still slightly bent as a result!). I think this illustrates at least three things. One is the power of the peer group, as I probably wanted to 'join in' with the majority. A second is the temptation to show one's power, or get pleasure from hurting a more vulnerable person, that most of us are vulnerable to, at least to some extent.

The third point is that being a victim, or a bully, can happen to most people, and has happened to most people at some point in their lives. Surveys that ask 'have you ever been bullied?' or 'have you ever bullied someone else?' typically get a considerable majority responding 'yes'. Abuse of power is in itself a powerful temptation, and often happens, in all kinds of relationships. Someone who has never been involved as a victim or bully may have led a rather sheltered existence! And of course virtually everyone will have witnessed bullying. That means that (if they did not join in) they did nothing, or else helped the victim in some way – which researchers call 'defending'. In this broader sense, all of us have been involved in bullying, and all of us have a stake in understanding it and preventing the worst forms of abuse.

Table 1.1   Shows a few other personal experiences of school bullying

1. *VICTIM* (from England)

I was born in Vienna, to East European Chassidic Jews. When the Nazis took over and it gradually became apparent that Jewish lives were in peril, those members of my family who managed to escape did so and I was left alone with only my mother for quite a long time because obtaining a visa was by then well-nigh impossible. Eventually we succeeded and boarded a flight to London in July 1939. My grandfather, three uncles and one aunt, my mother and I lived together in a house which was adapted as a synagogue, in London's Swiss Cottage. During the Blitz my mother and I were evacuated to Leeds where we lived first in a house for refugees and then for some months only, probably because there was nowhere else available, a home for orphaned Jewish girls. During the whole of my early childhood schooling was very sporadic, and sometimes seemed almost non-existent.

I have given this short résumé of my background to throw some light on events, a few of which I shall describe, although it is perfectly possible that personal circumstances have little or even no bearing on one's propensity to be bullied, a phenomenon in which I have always been interested. As far back as I can remember, both as a young child and to a certain extent throughout my entire life, I seem to have been subjected to one or other of its various manifestations.

Almost as soon as I went to school I became aware of being entirely ostracised and 'on my own'. There was no way I could, however hard I tried, be accepted among my peer group and make friends. I tried, of course, in ways that were entirely 'wrong'. For instance, an uncle of mine obtained (probably on the black market!) a box of very nice chocolates as a present for me. I approached a group of children playing together at break time and offered them the box, which they immediately devoured at great speed. I expected them to give me at least one, but they did not, nor did they offer any thanks. When I asked whether I might play with them they looked at me as though I were stupid to even ask such a question, and walked away.

Another time, the girl I was sharing a desk with threatened to 'take me to the headmaster' (seen as a dire punishment for only the most serious misdemeanours, none of which I was, nor would have dared to be, guilty). I recall being very afraid and holding on to her arm with all my might, to try and stop her from 'taking' me to this dreaded person! When she did not move I asked her why she wasn't carrying out her threat, and I remember being amazed when she answered 'because you're holding my arm!' I had become, by that time, completely cowed and unable to believe I had any power at all.

There was another occasion when a boy in my class approached me in the playground and, putting a scarf around my neck, said he was going to kill me. He did indeed pull so tightly that I all but passed out, but managed to struggle free. Again, although I was bewildered by the fact that others seemed to wish to harm me, I had begun to think that I was fated to be some kind of victim, and felt helpless in the face of that. The feeling of continuous fear and isolation gave rise to physical symptoms, and I began to tell my mother I was too ill to attend school. She believed me, not only because it would, at that time, not have occurred to me to tell lies, but also when she took my temperature, I actually had a slight fever. These bouts of fever continued and doctors were unable to find a cause. As a last resort, my mother took me to see Anna Freud (at that time living and practising as a child psychotherapist in what is now the Freud Museum in North West London), who diagnosed that I was suffering from '*Schulangst*' (a German term meaning simply 'fear of school')!

At her wits' end my mother came to the school with me to explain matters to my form teacher who said 'I don't know about "*schulangst*", she is just being mercilessly and continually bullied!', and proposed to sit me at a desk next to herself and to 'keep an eye out', after which the fevers subsided. What did not change, however, nor was it likely to, with me now being seen as 'teacher's pet', was any hope of my joining the ranks of normal, gregarious children.

It was not until well into my secondary schooldays, during which I established a 'niche' of my own, as someone interested and quite gifted in music, that I began to find any sort of acceptance among my peers.

2. VICTIM/BULLY (from South Korea)

Victim experience

When I was 11 years old (in fifth grade), I had an experience of being a victim. One day I received a slip of paper from a group of girls (around seven of them), in which they wrote down several points about how I had to change. I did not know what to do, how to get along with these girls (for example, they said I should change how I walked). I was very depressed and did not feel any motivation in school life. I recognised that one of the girls who sent the slip of paper was my friend who used to walk with me together on the way back home everyday. After I received the slip, she did not walk back with me, so I had to go back home alone, thinking 'how can I change my walking?', and I actually tried to walk in a different way but didn't think it would really be different. I still find it strange that I did not tell anyone such as my mother, or another friend. I guess that I was very lacking in confidence about myself and thought that it was me who had a big problem. However, the victimisation did not last long. One week after I had received the slip, the girl (who had been my friend) began to keep company with me on the way home again. I was embarrassed and asked 'why do you come with me again?', and she said 'because you changed yourself'. I was a bit surprised because I did not think I changed anything. (What I can guess now is that I was a kind of a teacher's pet. I was very compliant and used to do the teacher's errands. My depressed mood may have affected my behaviour toward the teacher, and the other girls might have considered it as a change.)

Bully experience

My experience as a bully was more complicated than my experience as a victim. At the age of 12 (a year after the victim experience happened, in my sixth grade), I had a close friend, M, at the beginning of the first semester. But in the middle of this semester, I intentionally excluded her for two to three months. In my class, the teacher encouraged classmates to get along and help each other. He organised the class into several small groups of children. Each group consisted of four children, who varied in their academic achievement and school lifestyle. We had to sit as a group. There was a leader in the group: a child who was a leader had to help other members and the leader usually had high academic achievement and was regarded as an exemplary student; the leader had a helper who usually had the lowest academic achievement in the group. Thus, the leader should assist other members during class time if required. I guess that the teacher's intention was basically a good one.

I was a leader in my group and the academic achievement of my helper, another friend P, was not good. M was also in our group (and had the second highest achievement among our four members). I don't remember why and when I began to exclude her but I do remember a couple of things related to the exclusion.

One day, M yelled at and then ignored P. P did not reply to her at all. I realised why M ignored P (dirty clothes, low academic ability). I was very upset but did not say anything that time. Also I am not sure whether the event triggered the exclusion toward M or not.

I excluded M when we had lunch and a talk. I cannot forget her depressed look. The severity of exclusion escalated over time. I disliked even her hairstyle and was picky about that (it is much the same thing as changing walking style!). Other members in the group might have thought I had gone too far, but nobody told me that. She must have been very lonely and I did not give any space for her to escape. I tried more and more mean ways to hurt her, and tried to justify everything of hers as wrong. At some point, I stopped the exclusion (I don't know why).

(Continued)

Table 1.1 (Continued)

Around one to two years later (we had graduated from elementary school and entered into different middle schools), I made a phone call to her house and asked her to meet me and apologised: 'I didn't know why I teased you that much, and I am really sorry.' She smiled but I don't remember what she said. I still feel sad when I think of her and the hurt which I gave to her. Although I apologised to her, I cannot forget her hurt and those bad memories.

3. *VICTIM* (from England)

'You bullied me at school.' I was sitting in her car opposite the station where I was to catch my train back to London. She was my 'best' friend from secondary school, whom I had met, ironically enough, at an anti-bullying conference. I had delivered a presentation and when it was finished, she came and sat beside me: 'I know you.' I recognised her immediately. I needn't have addressed it so soon, but I had needed to say that for decades. The impact was dramatic and immediate. She cried and cried: 'I'm so sorry; I didn't mean to bully you. I was so young and wanted more friends and I didn't know what to do.'

We had had one of those intense friendships only girls have – the same sense of humour (laughing until we cried) and similar interests (music, boys). But our relationship became claustrophobic for her. She needed to change and, as my adult self knows, change can be painful even if handled carefully. Change affected by ostracism and rejection was the worst. I was excluded from both her friendship and my friendship group, as they took sides. Whereas before I had had a close group of friends, now I was utterly alone. I wasn't included in any social events inside or outside school. No-one spoke to me. They often exchanged smiles when I spoke, as though sharing a private joke. I felt shunned, spending breaktimes alone, marginalised and miserable.

I remember crying in my Mum's lap and her stroking my back, unable to say anything to make it better. My 17 year old self was heart-broken. For one term it was hell. I felt lost and didn't understand what I had done to deserve this. It wasn't all bad though because I went on to make a new set of friends and became more academic and ambitious. She was limiting for me too but I hadn't realised it. We went on to be friends again, but although she had admitted to Mum that she had treated me badly at school, I never received an acknowledgement of the relational bullying, nor an apology. So when her Christmas cards started arriving about seven years ago, my feelings were deeply ambiguous. I didn't know what I wanted to do. The larger part of me just wanted to leave the past alone. A smaller part saw the possibility of closure. And this is what I got, forty years after the event: 'I'm sorry I bullied you.' When we parted, we hugged and she was still visibly upset and crying: 'You didn't damage me for life – I'm fine.'

So what was the impact of the bullying? On the negative side, I don't trust people easily. On the positive, I went on to become more of myself, to grow and change in ways I'd never thought I could and now leave plenty of air around my relationships. And the impact of the apology? It feels like an incomplete circle has been completed. She must have been aware something needed to be put right, so had tried to re-establish contact. And she was generous. I told her and she listened. The good memories of our friendship are now at the forefront of my mind and the painful ones are in perspective.

4. *VICTIM* (from Australia; written by a mother, whose daughter made a serious suicide attempt following severe bullying)

My daughter was threatened, harassed, physically assaulted, taunted, had things stolen, broken, and was isolated and rejected throughout her primary schooling. I watched her change from a bright, happy child, to an angry, sad, confused teen. Apart from having fake birthday party invitations sent to our home, where someone thought it would be funny to have her turn up for a birthday that didn't exist, her teenage years brought other horrors. After rejecting a particular 'popular' boy's sexual advances in her final years of school, she became the centre of attention by his cronies, and they would race up to her daily, screaming in her face, and then they would pretend to gag and vomit over her. Every day. She made a decision that she just couldn't take it any longer, and put a suicide plan into place.

In 2001, the internet was still new, and my daughter liked going to gigs, hearing bands play, and joined 'band' chat rooms to talk about them with other fans. She orchestrated her music/band chat lines so that no-one would think her behaviour unusual. She arranged music lists for her funeral via her chat group, telling them that she was doing an English assignment and gathered lists of everyone's favourites, so that they could be played on the day. She left the list as part of her detailed set of wishes.

Unknown to me, that last weekend before she attempted suicide, she arranged a trip interstate to see her favourite band play. This was all organised on the internet. I thought she was having the weekend at the beach with friends.

Her chat group knew she was going to the gig, but she left a cryptic message about 'going off the air' and them 'not seeing her around for a while, but hoped to meet up with them again one day'. No-one realised she was saying goodbye.

In the notes the police gave me that she had left in her back pack, she had left me her password, and whilst she had deleted much on the chat group, I went on as M, but wrote a message and asked the group for help to understand why she had done what she had done: and kids and adults in their hundreds turned up to the hospital and intensive care, to talk with me, and to show support for her.

Before the principal had been able to get in touch with me, to tell me what had happened, the news had already spread via sms/mobile phone to schools across the city. The night before, M sms'd about 100 kids with a cryptic goodbye message: but they thought it was a chain mail message ... and so no-one responded. Three friends who would have tried to find out what was going on, either had a problem with their phone (no battery), or she deliberately didn't send it to them.

M survived, but has a permanent life-altering disability as a result of her suicide attempt. Her life will never be the same. I recall saying at the time (2001), that the internet and mobile phones had changed the ways kids were interacting/communicating around their friendships/relationships, so in a way M's story was a window to the future. A future where the bullying has gone online.

Bullying as a practical issue

As the personal experiences above have illustrated, it is often the case that school actions about bullying have been non-existent, or unplanned and ineffective – at least, in the past! And to be fair to schools and teachers, for many decades there was limited awareness about the consequences of bullying, and little or no resources to help them.

When I started doing research on school bullying in England, around 1989 and in the early 1990s, there were no resources for teachers, and no specific expectations for schools concerning bullying. Everyone knew the term, and there was general agreement that it was a nasty kind of behaviour, although there was also a view that it was 'part of growing up' and perhaps a necessary rite of passage to go through. For example, in January 1996, the Member of Parliament for Hammersmith (London), Clive Soley, said in a House of Comments debate that 'He had been to an inner city comprehensive where violence and bullying had been the norm and it had helped him cope with life, in a way privileged schools did not' (*Guardian*, 25 January 1996, p. 5). Furthermore, few schools were even willing to admit that it was a problem for them. A likely response to enquiries would be that 'we know what bullying is, and we know that it is a problem in some schools, but we don't have it here'.

All of this has changed, certainly in England, but also in many other countries, over the last two decades. On enquiry, a school in England is now likely to say 'we know what bullying is, and of course it can happen in our school as in any other school. We have a policy on bullying and this is what we do when it happens ...'. This is a much more realistic and useful kind of response. There are good reasons to be concerned about the issue of bullying in schools. It is immediately damaging to those persons involved. Also, it can create insecurity and fear that work against the purpose of the school: a climate of bullying in school is the opposite of the 'education for citizenship' that we broadly aim for, and it goes against the rights of children and young people (as in the UN Convention on the Rights of the Child: United Nations, 1991) to live free from fear and intimidation.

Many countries now have legal requirements and expectations about what schools should do about bullying. And this is supported by many resources for teachers – handbooks, practical exercises, web-based materials. Although not as yet an integral part of teacher training in most countries, these resources and opportunities for in-service training, plus support from local education authorities or educational psychology teams, plus school inspections, mean that responses to school bullying have changed from near-denial and inaction, to – at least in better organised schools – a prompt, co-ordinated and often effective response.

These changes have come about because of media interest and research. In many countries the media have played an important part in raising awareness through publicising cases – personal experiences, some tragic that resulted in suicide. For example, in England, in 1992, the BBC *That's Life* programme pursued the topic of school bullying vigorously, following the suicide of an adolescent girl due in part to bullying at school. Questions were asked in Parliament about what action the government was taking on bullying, contributing to an expansion of national action on the topic.

Because everyone has some experience of bullying, and because very many parents of school-aged children are likely to be concerned about it, it is a media-worthy issue, and also one that politicians are likely to take note of. But research has a vital role too. Most basically, research has shown how prevalent school bullying can be, and how severe the effects of it can be. If we are concerned about human rights and human happiness, it is not something that can be ignored. Going beyond this, research is telling us a lot about the nature of bullying, and why it happens. This of course is essential if we are going to develop effective intervention policies and actions. And research on school bullying has grown enormously, from small beginnings in the 1970s and 1980s.

Bullying as a research programme

In this book I describe research on school bullying as a *research programme*. This term comes from a philosopher of science, Imre Lakatos (1970). He described a scientific research programme as encompassing a set of theories and methods, which can change over time. However, there is a *hard core* of very basic theoretical assumptions which do not change (for example, in chemistry, this could be atomic theory). This hard core would not be questioned by adherents of the research programme; indeed, they would defend the hard core assumptions vigorously – a process called *negative heuristics*. However, the hard core would have generated a range of *auxiliary hypotheses*. These are considered much more open to question.

These auxiliary hypotheses are the frontiers of the research programme, ideas which are being tried out and tested for their range and explanatory power. If they prove successful, well and good. If they do not, they will be jettisoned, or changed to accommodate anomalies or falsifications, without threatening the hard core. These *positive heuristics* of active testing and questioning complement the negative heuristics used to protect the hard core assumptions.

Lakatos also described research programmes as *progressive* or *degenerating*. Rational criteria are available to decide whether a particular research programme is progressive or degenerating. A progressive programme anticipates novel facts and produces novel theories, which have *heuristic power*: changes in the auxiliary hypotheses are productive. A degenerating programme, by contrast, patches up anomalies in ad hoc ways which do not generalise to other situations: changes in the auxiliary hypotheses are unproductive. Nevertheless, Lakatos conceded that there is necessarily some subjectivity in these judgements, and also that over time what had seemed a degenerating programme may become progressive again (or vice versa).

These ideas have been applied to the social sciences. For example, van IJzendoorn and Tavecchio (1987) discussed attachment theory in this way. Gholsen and Barker (1985) described traditional learning theory in psychology as a degenerating research programme. This is basically the idea that learning is through positive or negative reinforcement of behaviours. This approach is in fact more about controlling behaviour than explaining it. It is useful for circus trainers who want to persuade a lion to jump through a hoop, but tells us little about how humans (or many animals) learn in most real-life situations. The 'cognitive revolution', plus the recognition of social factors in learning (Kendal, 2008), provide newer research programmes that have largely displaced the traditional learning theory research programme.

I believe that these ideas of Lakatos can be applied to the research on school bullying. The hard core of this programme is that *bullying* can usefully be distinguished from *aggression*, in terms of specific criteria (repetition and the imbalance of power). This has generated many auxiliary hypotheses. Some examples are given in Table 1.2. The advent of cyberbullying has reinvigorated the area,

Table 1.2   Bullying as a research programme

Hard core	As a subset of aggression (intent to harm a person), 'bullying' is a useful concept (defined by repetition and imbalance of power)
Some auxiliary hypotheses	1. the term 'bullying' is understood by older children and adults 2. there are different roles in bullying, which can be measured 3. even if much bullying is one-to-one, the peer context is important 4. there are attitudes to bullying which can be measured and which show some relation to behaviour 5. there are definite psychosocial correlates and consequences of involvement in bullying (different from or more severe than those to aggression in general) 6. school-based interventions against bullying can reduce its incidence
Signs of a progressive research programme	Advances in one area (e.g. roles in bullying) make coherent or successful predictions about another area (e.g. attitudes, psychosocial adjustment) Knowledge about roles in bullying, attitudes, peer group influences, helps design more effective school-based interventions
Signs of a degenerating research programme	Continuing unresolved debates about definition Interventions based on knowledge advances have little success.

but also potentially threatens the hard core of the programme, as it has reignited debate about the hard core assumptions regarding repetition and power imbalance.

Plan of the book

In this book I try to pull together these various strands. The emphasis is on the research, which is by now very extensive. It covers three decades of work, carried out in very many countries. But the relevance to practice and policy is a recurrent theme.

In Chapter 2, I discuss definition(s) of bullying and related terms such as harassment and abuse. Although this book is about bullying in school, I do give a brief overview here of corresponding literature in other child contexts (in the family, as abuse; in institutional children's homes; and in the community), and of bullying in a lifespan perspective (workplace, prison, armed forces, elder abuse). Moving on to focus on school bullying, I then give a summary history of how research in this area has developed, starting from its origins in Scandinavia and having now become a vigorous international research programme with many applications to practice.

In Chapter 3, I discuss how we can find out about bullying. There are various methods, including questionnaires, nominations (peer, self, teacher, parent), observations, interviews, focus groups, incident reports, and retrospective data. Issues of reliability and validity are considered here.

In Chapter 4, I look at some of the basic knowledge about school bullying that these methods have uncovered. Topics include the kinds of involvement in bullying and participant roles, and the various types of bullying (physical, verbal, indirect, relational, cyber). What has been called 'identity-based' or 'bias bullying' (homophobic, faith-based, racist, sexist, disability-based) is an important topic. So too is cyberbullying – this has developed over the last decade and presents new features, and challenges to intervention.

Examples from surveys in several countries are given, to get an idea of the incidence of these various types, and age and gender trends, as well as other aspects such as the location and duration of bullying and attitudes to it.

Two aspects of time changes are considered next. One is the stability of roles over time – how likely is it that a child who bullies, or is a victim, will still be in that role some time later? The second is historical changes in incidence rates, with evidence of some decline in the last two decades. The final topic is cultural differences, especially comparing individualistic societies (North America, western Europe) to more collectivist societies (such as Japan and South Korea).

In Chapter 5, I consider who is at risk of involvement in bullying and what the effects are. Trying to disentangle causes and correlates is difficult and longitudinal studies are important. Many psychological studies have focused on individual or family factors, and risk factors have been identified for being a victim of bullying, and for taking part in bullying others – and to a lesser extent for other roles such as bully/victims (those who are both bullies and victims) and defenders. The peer group has increasingly been seen as important. Classroom norms, school climate and related school factors are aspects of the broader environment that can affect the benefits/costs of bullying behaviour, norms for bystanders, and support for victims. Influences from the community, and wider society (such as the media and economic inequality), are also considered.

In Chapter 6, I look first at what coping strategies pupils use to deal with being a victim and how successful such strategies typically are. After considering the role of parents, most of the chapter focuses on school-based actions. This starts with reactive interventions: how others can respond when a child is actually bullied, ranging from direct (sometimes punitive) sanctions, through to restorative approaches, and support group or Pikas procedures which are distinctly non-punitive. Controversies and evidence in this area are examined.

I next consider more preventative work in schools, that may make bullying less likely to happen in the first place: proactive and peer support interventions via the school, classroom, playground and peer group. These include whole school policies; classroom interventions such as curricular approaches; role play, drama and video, and quality circles; playground interventions, such as playground design; and the training and role of playground supervisors and other school staff. In addition, peer support schemes have expanded greatly in recent years. The chapter discusses types of peer support, and the role of peer support systems in empowering defenders and helping change school ethos and rates of bullying – together with what evidence there is for their effectiveness.

Finally, I describe a number of large-scale intervention studies that have taken place in a number of countries. These have incorporated both reactive strategies and proactive and sometimes peer support strategies. The range of success for these interventions, and possible explanations and ways forward, are considered.

In Chapter 7, I reflect on the need to take action on bullying, including evidence on its long-term effects into adult life. I conclude with some reflections on bullying as a research programme, its success and future directions.

TWO

What we mean by 'bullying' and a history of research on school bullying

What is 'bullying'? How does it differ from aggression, harassment, intimidation, abuse or violence? These very basic questions about the definition of terms raise important issues that are discussed in the first part of this chapter. An understanding of what 'bullying' is can vary by age and historical period, and of course the word itself is an English term, so must be translated into other languages which may not have an exact equivalent. A consideration of definitions leads to describing a cartoon task, developed to investigate these various nuances and differences in understandings.

The second part of the chapter puts bullying in context. Although the book is focused on school bullying, bullying can occur in many other contexts than school, and it can occur throughout the lifespan, not just in childhood. Here some attention is paid to these wider issues, and the connections with bullying in school.

The final part of the chapter gives an overview of how the school bullying research programme has developed. Over a period of some thirty years, it has grown from small beginnings to a large enterprise involving many researchers, and linking strongly with public policy and educational initiatives – themes that are taken up again in the final chapters.

Issues of definition

Definitional issues can be seen as a dry matter. However, certainly in this area, looking at definitions is important in several ways. It is obviously necessary for precise research and action – for a worthwhile research programme. But also, the origins and changes in meanings of a term like bullying, and of similar terms, can give us some insight into attitudes, how we see the world to some extent, and how other people see it.

Table 2.1 gives some definitions from the *Encarta World English Dictionary* (1999), for *aggression, bully(ing)*, and some similar terms: *harassment, intimidation, abuse*, and

Table 2.1   Definitions of terms (from *Encarta World English Dictionary*, 1999)

Aggression	1. Attack – hostile action, especially a physical or military attack, directed against another person or country, often without provocation. 2. Hostile attitude or behaviour – threatening behaviour or actions [Early 17thC. Directly or via French, from the Latin stem *aggression*, from *aggress*-]
Bully	n. Aggressive person – an aggressive person who intimidates or mistreats weaker people. v. Intimidate – to intimidate or mistreat weaker people [Mid-16th century origin uncertain; probably from Middle Dutch *boele* 'lover'. Originally 'sweetheart', then 'fine fellow', 'blusterer']
Harass	1. Keep bothering or attacking somebody – to persistently annoy, attack or bother somebody … . [Early 17thC. From French *harasser*, from *harer* 'to set a dog on' (by crying 'hare'; ultimately of uncertain origin; perhaps from Old High German *haren*]
Harassment	Behaviour that threatens or torments somebody, especially persistently
Intimidate	1. Persuade or dissuade by frightening – to persuade somebody to do something or dissuade somebody from doing something by means of violence or blackmail. 2. Daunt – to create a feeling of fear, awe, or inadequacy in somebody. [Mid-17thC. From medieval Latin *intimidare*, literally 'to put in fear', from Latin *timidus* 'fearful']
Abuse	1. Maltreatment – the physical, sexual, or psychological maltreatment of a person or animal … . 3. Insults – insulting or offensive language … . [15thC. Via French *abus* from Latin *abusus* …]
Violence	1. Physical force – the use of physical force to injure somebody or damage something; 2. Illegal force – the illegal use of unjustified force, or the effect created by the threat of this… .
Violent	[14thC. From Latin *violentus* 'forcible, vehement', of uncertain origin]

violence. One thing to notice here is that whereas *bully* has a Dutch origin (probably), all the other words have their origins in Latin or French (which comes from Latin). This is significant when we look at words for *bully* in different languages, as there is no closely corresponding word in the Latin-based languages. Another point is that *bullying* is defined in terms of aggression and intimidation, but of a weaker person. Generally, *bullying* is seen as a subset of *aggression*. So, let's start by defining *aggression*.

Aggression

In the psychological literature, *aggression* is generally taken to be a purposeful act that is intended to cause harm to somebody. That 'somebody' is usually another individual, although of course people can self-harm. As the first definition in Table 2.1 indicates, aggression can be against a country or an institution, but our focus is on inter-personal aggression – aggression *by* a person *against* another person.

The aggressive act may cause harm, or may just threaten to cause harm. The Encarta definition is clear on that, and it is consistent with psychological usage. But that definition is not entirely clear about another issue – behaviour versus attitudes (see definition 2 under Aggression in Table 2.1). Generally, an internal attitude would need to be expressed in some way, through some kind of behavioural threat perhaps, to count as aggression. It is one thing to harbour evil thoughts in our mind, another to actually put these into effect.

Finally, most researchers would say that the act should be intentional, as accidental harm is not usually considered aggressive. As an example, I remember running to catch a train, jumping into the carriage as it was about to go, and inadvertently treading hard on someone's foot! The person made a rude remark to the person he was talking to on his mobile ('Ow! – some stupid twat just trod on my foot!'), but basically he knew that this was not an aggressive or provocative act.

Types of aggression

The most obvious types of inter-personal aggression are direct physical attacks (such as hitting, kicking, punching) and direct verbal attacks (such as threats, taunts or insults). These are direct or face-to-face kinds of aggression. During earlier decades, the psychological literature on aggression focused on these. But in the early 1990s the work of two groups of researchers – with Kaj Björkqvist in Finland, and then with Nicki Crick in the USA – focused attention on other kinds of aggression.

Björkqvist, Lagerspetz and Kaukiainen (1992) introduced the concept of *indirect aggression*. This is aggression not aimed directly at someone, but via a third party: for example, spreading nasty rumours about someone. Although not face-to-face, there is the intent to harm another person, and this was soon accepted as a valid extension of the concept of aggression: an interesting one, as they and many subsequent researchers have found that – at least relative to direct aggression, where boys and males generally are more involved – girls, and women, are more represented in assessments of indirect aggression.

Crick and Grotpeter (1995) proposed the term *relational aggression* to refer to aggressive behaviour that is intended to damage someone's relationships. This can often be indirect: for example, spreading rumours targets someone's relations and reputation with others. But it can be face-to-face as well: for example, social exclusion from normal group activities can be seen as another form of relational aggression ('You can't play with us'). Galen and Underwood (1997) introduced the similar term *social aggression* as aggression intended to damage another's self-esteem or social status. It is now generally accepted that aggression should include the indirect and relational forms, as well as the more direct hits and insults studied in earlier decades.

Especially in adult life, aggression can also occur institutionally – for example, by setting someone totally unrealistic goals and thus undermining their confidence and work satisfaction.

In this century primarily, cyber-aggression has become noticeable. This includes many forms of attack using mobile phones and the internet. It is generally not face-to-face, so it can be seen as having some similarity to indirect aggression, but with other features which are discussed later with respect to cyberbullying.

Origins of the term 'bullying': *bullying* and *mobbing*

The concept of *bullying* first came to prominence in England through Thomas Hughes's (1857) book *Tom Brown's School Days*, in which Tom and some of his friends are tormented by Flashman and his gang at Rugby school: 'Flashman was about 17 years old, and big and strong of his age ... a formidable enemy for small boys' (p. 178); 'What your bully really likes in tossing, is when the boys kick and struggle, or hold on to one side of the blanket, and so get pitched bodily on to the floor; it's no fun to him when no one is hurt or frightened' (p. 134). The Head of House says: '... there's a deal of bullying going on. . . . Bullies are cowards ...' (p. 123).

In Europe, the scientific study of bullying had its main origins in Scandinavia, and especially in the work of Dan Olweus. A school doctor, Heinemann, had introduced the Swedish term *mobbning* in a book *Mobbning – Gruppvåld bland barn och vuxna* [Mobbing – Group Aggression Against Boys and Girls] (1972). This term was borrowed from the ethological sense of *mobbing*, or 'all against one', describing a collective attack by a group on an individual (here, often of another species). Olweus then used the term in his book *Forskning om skol-mobbning* [Research on school mobbing] (1973), later translated as *Aggression in Schools: Bullies and Whipping Boys* (1978). His subsequent book, *Mobbning – vad vi vet och vad vi kan göra* (1986), uses the same term, and was the basis of his most well-known book *Mobbning i skolan* (Swedish version), *Mobbing i skolen* (Norwegian version) and *Bullying at School: What We Know and What We Can Do* (English version) (all 1992/1993), which has since been translated into many languages.

Mobbing carries the connotation of the 'group vs. one'. However, Olweus soon rejected this. He wrote (1973/1978: 5):

> It is ... questionable how common all-against-one situations really are in a school setting ... it is perhaps rather unusual for the whole class (the boys or the girls) to be united in an intense collective activity ... mobbing by very small groups is the more frequent type in our schools.

and later (1999a: 10):

> Data from our Bergen study ... indicate that, in the majority of cases, the victim of bullying is harassed by a small group of two or three students, often with a negative leader. A considerable proportion of victims, some 25–40 percent, report, however, that they are mainly bullied by a single student.

Although the term *mobbing* still has some currency in Scandinavian countries, it is not now confused with *bullying*.

Quite separately, in Japan, there had been much concern about physical acts of violence in schools in the 1970s. By the end of the 1970s there began to be attention paid to *ijime* (Morita, Soeda, Soeda & Taki, 1999). During the 1980s and 1990s, *ijime* came to be recognised as a distinctive phenomenon and research on it gathered pace. Morita (1985) defined *ijime* as:

> A type of aggressive behavior by which someone who holds a dominant position in a group-interaction process, by intentional or collective acts, causes mental and/ or physical suffering to another inside a group.

Ijime has come to be seen as the Japanese term most closely corresponding to bullying, although it was only in the later 1990s that Japanese and western researchers got together and discussed the commonalities in research and intervention. As discussed further in Chapter 3, the definition does place somewhat more emphasis on group processes than is usually found in modern definitions of *bullying*.

Bullying

What do we now mean by *bullying*? Although there is no universally agreed definition, there is some consensus, at least in the western research tradition, that bullying refers to repeated aggressive acts against someone who cannot easily defend themselves (see Olweus, 1999a,b; Ross, 2002).

Not all definitions have made this clear. For example Tattum (1989: 10) wrote that:

> Bullying is a willful, conscious desire to hurt another person.

However, most people would not count a desire to hurt someone as aggressive (let alone bullying) unless that desire is turned into action. As another example, Randall (1997: 4) stated that:

> Bullying is the aggressive behaviour arising from the deliberate intent to cause psychological or physical distress to others.

Here we do have actual behaviour, but no further criteria to distinguish bullying from aggression in general.

Two further distinguishing criteria were introduced by Olweus, and have come to be widely adopted. Olweus (1999a: 10) wrote that:

> A student is being bullied or victimized when he or she is exposed, repeatedly and over time, to negative actions on the part of one or more other students.

But also added (1999a: 11) that:

> In order to use the term bullying, there should also be an imbalance of strength (an asymmetric power relationship); the student who is exposed to negative actions has difficulty in defending himself or herself and is somewhat helpless against the student or students who harass.

This definition is embedded in the Olweus questionnaire, which states:

> We say a young person is being bullied, or picked on, when another young person, or a group of young people, say nasty and unpleasant things to him or her. It is also bullying when a young person is hit, kicked or threatened, locked inside a room, sent nasty notes, when no-one ever talks to them and things like that. These things can happen frequently and it is difficult for the young person being bullied to defend himself or herself. It is also bullying when a young person is teased

repeatedly in a nasty way. But it is not bullying when two young people of about the same strength have the odd fight or quarrel.

A similar definition is that bullying is a 'systematic abuse of power' (Smith & Sharp, 1994: 2; see also Rigby, 2002). This has a broader remit, however, as it need not refer to young people or student–student bullying.

The earlier work on bullying only mentioned physical and verbal kinds of bullying (reflecting the main kinds of aggression described at the time). However, contemporary definitions stress a broader range of forms that bullying can take. Only in the 1990s was attention drawn explicitly to indirect, psychological and relational forms of aggression, and also of bullying. And in the 2000s, research on cyberbullying has developed rapidly.

Within most of the research literature then, bullying is taken as:

- an aggressive act (intent to cause harm);
- perpetrated via any of the forms of aggression – physical, verbal, cyber; direct or indirect;

but with two further defining criteria:

- there is an imbalance of power (the victim finds it difficult to defend him-/herself);
- it has some element of repetition (these things can happen frequently).

These two further defining criteria mean that all bullying is aggression, but not all aggression is bullying. This is an important issue in two respects.

First, these criteria define the research programme on bullying as (largely) separate from the research programme on aggression. Research published on bullying should be using these criteria. This, however, is not always the case. Further, if a separate research programme on bullying is to be justifiable, then some of the correlates and consequences of bullying should be distinct from those of aggression generally. This is considered further in the final chapter.

Second, the repetition and imbalance of power are likely to lead to particular outcomes, such as fear of telling by the victim, and low self-esteem as well as depression. The relative defencelessness of the victim to repeated attacks implies an obligation on others to intervene, if we take the democratic rights of the victim seriously. Olweus (1993: 48) argued that it is a 'question of fundamental democratic rights' not to be bullied. The increase in international concern about school bullying over the last thirty years appears to reflect an increase in concern for rights issues throughout the twentieth century and continuing into this century (Greene, 2006). This has been evidenced by an awareness of, and legislation against, forms of discrimination due to (for example) sex, race, age, religion, disability and sexual orientation – a process that is still continuing. *Bullying* can embrace discrimination on a more individual basis, although the terms *bias bullying, identity-based bullying* or *prejudice-driven bullying* refer to bullying on the basis of group rather than individual characteristics, and would include racial harassment, faith-based bullying, sexual harassment and homophobic bullying.

Nevertheless, the two criteria of repetition and power imbalance are still not universally accepted, and face particular issues regarding cyberbullying; and even the intent to cause harm criterion can raise issues.

Issues around the criteria for defining bullying

Intent

Almost all definitions of bullying refer to it as an intentionally aggressive act. However, what is intentional – the act itself, or the outcome of hurting another? Certainly bullying should be considered intentional in the sense that it is not accidental! But does the person bullying intend to actually hurt the victim? This is indeed sometimes the case, when the bully laughs at the victim's distress and chooses ways to hurt them most effectively. However, Horton (2011a,b; 2012) has challenged this view of bullying as individual aggressive intentionality. In a study of schools in Vietnam, he describes *bat nat* – the nearest equivalent term to bullying in Vietnamese – as repeatedly making someone do something that they would not otherwise have done. Focusing in this way on power relationships, he argues that power is not held but is exercised in strategic situations. For example, one child may make another child go to the canteen to get them a snack; this means the first child (bully) saves time and avoids possible attacks to him- or herself in an unsupervised canteen setting. This in turn leads Horton to question whether a bully is necessarily intentionally wishing to hurt the victim, rather than responding to the institutional power structure in the school. He similarly examines the actions of teachers, ways in which pupils may bully teachers and teachers may bully pupils, and interprets this in relation to power relations within the immediate context of the school and the wider society.

Imbalance of power

The imbalance of power criterion is usually taken in a more individualistic sense. It means that a fight between equals (although aggressive) is not bullying. This is quite explicit in the Olweus definition (earlier) used in his questionnaire. Thus in bullying, it is difficult for the victim to defend him- or herself. Some indicative criteria for this are:

- being physically weaker (for example, for physical attacks);
- being verbally less fluent (for example, when teased);
- lacking confidence or self-esteem;
- being outnumbered;
- lacking friends or social support;
- being in a low status or rejected position in the peer group
  (Smith, del Barrio & Tokunaga, 2013).

In an empirical study, Hunter, Boyle and Warden (2007) compared questionnaire responses by Scottish 8–13 year old pupils to items concerning both aggressive behaviour and bullying behaviours (where there was a perceived imbalance of power through physical strength, group size and/or social popularity). Their study showed that victims of bullying, as opposed to victims of peer aggression more generally, felt less control over the situation and were more depressed.

Repetition

The repetition criterion implies that a hurtful action happens more than just once or twice (and thus, implicitly, is an intentional picking on or harassing of someone). But, some commentators have argued that even one threat or nasty stare can imply a long-term bullying attitude and should be construed as bullying (Guerin & Hennessy, 2002). There are difficulties in deciding what is 'just once'. A threat, such as 'I am going to kill you!', even if uttered once, could be regarded as a continuing threat unless it is actually rescinded or apologised for. Also, who has to do the repetition? If a victim is repeatedly attacked or threatened, but each time by a different person, is that bullying?

To some extent the issue of repetition interacts with intent to harm. Repetition of a harmful action clearly is a very strong indication that the harm is intended by the perpetrator. The issue is not fully resolved: Smith et al. (2013) argued that while an important criterion, repetition is not an essential one for bullying in the way that imbalance of power is central; it is more of a probabilistic indicator.

Additional bullying criteria

The distinction of bullying from more general aggression has been an important and widely accepted aspect of traditional bullying research, and despite some issues still being discussed, the criteria of repetition and imbalance of power are quite widely accepted, certainly for traditional (offline) bullying. But they might be on less firm ground as regards cyberbullying (Dooley, Pyzalski & Cross, 2009; Smith, et al., 2013). How useful is it to distinguish between cyberbullying and cyber-aggression? This issue is considered further in the next section.

Finally, imbalance of power and repetition are not the only additional criteria proposed. A very full definition comes from Rigby (2002: 51):

> Bullying involves a desire to hurt + a harmful action + a power imbalance + (typically) repetition + an unjust use of power + evident enjoyment by the aggressor and generally a sense of being oppressed on the part of the victim.

The concept of unjust use of power is also captured in 'a systematic abuse of power' (Smith & Sharp, 1994). In other words, there can be just use of power, and it can hurt others. For example, repeatedly putting someone in prison because they commit offences, or – for the school situation – a teacher repeatedly putting a pupil in detention because of indiscipline – could count as bullying, unless we somehow incorporate this idea of what is 'just' or 'legal' in the context. Thus, it may be important to add this criterion, even though it is often neglected (as it is in the Olweus definition).

Rigby's final qualification(s), on the enjoyment by the bully and the sense of oppression by the victim, are more debatable as they may be difficult to ascertain. Some victims may deny being bullied, even though an 'outside observer' would describe it as such. Also, such perceptions might change. A victim might not feel victimised at the time, but – through later awareness-raising – come to realise that they were indeed bullied. Does this really change whether we call the original behaviour 'bullying'? Beyond the 'intent to hurt', it seems best not to second-guess the feelings of the perpetrator and the victim, but to go with what a reasonable third party or outside observer would judge to be bullying, using the other agreed criteria.

The definition of cyberbullying and application of traditional bullying criteria

An early and oft-quoted definition of cyberbullying was 'the use of information and communication technologies … to support deliberate, repeated and hostile behavior by an individual or group that is intended to harm others' (Belsey, 2004: 3). This definition includes the criterion of repetition, but not imbalance of power. A similar definition was used by Sourander et al. (2010).

Another much quoted definition follows the Olweus approach, defining cyberbullying as 'An aggressive, intentional act carried out by a group or individual, *using electronic forms of contact*, repeatedly and over time against a victim who cannot easily defend him or herself' (Smith, Mahdavi et al., 2008: 236). Li (2007) used a similar definition.

Tokunaga (2010) lists these and other definitions, which vary as to whether repetition and imbalance of power are included, and also in other respects (for example, types of bullying mentioned). However, a number of authors have pointed out problems with defining cyberbullying (or online bullying) as analogous to traditional (or offline) forms of bullying (Dooley et al., 2009; Vandebosch & van Cleemput, 2008).

An imbalance of power is more difficult to define in cyberbullying. Here, any imbalance of power does not obviously refer to physical strength or numerical strength. There may nevertheless be an imbalance of power either through the anonymity of the perpetrator(s), if present, or if the perpetrators are known, then relative (physical, psychological or numerical) strength offline may still be a factor in the victim's perception of the situation. Cyberbullying actions, such as taking someone else's identity to send false messages, may also imply some imbalance of power in technological skill in cyberspace.

There are also problems with using the repetition criterion in a simple way for cyberbullying: a single act by an aggressor, such as posting a nasty website comment, may be seen, commented on and forwarded by many others, so that in effect the others involved (and not the original perpetrator) undertake the repetition (Slonje, Smith & Frisén, 2012). For example, if something abusive is uploaded onto a webpage, every hit on that page could count as a repetition. Consequently, the use of repetition by the initial perpetrator as a criterion may be less reliable for cyberbullying.

The cyberbullying literature has been somewhat inconsistent in the use of these criteria. Some studies on cyberbullying have used items of mobile phone or internet aggression, together with a repetition scale: see, for example, the work by Calvete, Orue, Estévez, Villardón and Padilla (2010), and Cassidy, Jackson and Brown (2009). But in these and similar studies, analysis often focuses on those 'involved' – that is, not replying *never*, which may of course mean just once or twice. Hinduja and Patchin (2010: 211) noted that their 10 cyber bullying and victimisation items 'might better be characterized as "online harassment"' but restricted analysis to repeated incidents. But Wang, Iannotti and Nansel (2009: 370) explicitly examined only *once or twice or more* because 'it is not uncommon in the literature of cyber bullying to count a single incident as an experience of cyber bullying', although this study did include imbalance of power in the definition.

It is also an issue as to whether children/young people themselves use or recognise the term *cyberbullying*, or indeed what terms they do use (Grigg, 2010). Nevertheless, the term is now widely used in the media and research. Just as *bullying* has come to be a well-understood term across ages and cultures (Smith & Monks, 2008), *cyberbullying* may come to be understood similarly, even if there is some confusion over the variety of terms at present. In studying how 11–17 year olds in six European countries understood the term *cyberbullying*, Menesini, Nocentini, Palladino, Frisén et al. (2012) examined how they categorised a wide range of scenarios that differed by specific criteria. Adolescents gave most weight to imbalance of power in judging whether a scenario was a case of cyberbullying (except in France, where the term *cyberviolence* is used), followed by intentionality, and anonymity as a substitute for imbalance of power: repetition or the public/private nature of the context was less important.

At present, opinion remains divided as to whether cyberbullying can basically be defined and considered in a similar way to traditional bullying (Olweus, 2012a; Smith et al., 2013), or whether linking it to other forms of cyber-aggression is more useful (Bauman, Underwood & Card, 2013).

Other terms related to bullying

How about some other related terms? Some definitions from the *Encarta World English Dictionary* are given in Table 2.1, and how various criteria may be thought to apply to them in Table 2.2.

Table 2.2 Criteria as applied to bullying and related terms

Term/criteria	Cause harm	Intent	Repeated	Power imbalance	Only physical	Only person to person	Only if unjust
Aggression	x	x				x	
Bullying	x	x	x	x		x	x
Harassment	x	x	x	x		x	x
Intimidation	x	x		x		x	
Abuse	x			x		x	x
Violence	x				x		

Violence

The English word *violence* has linguistic cognates in the Latin languages (for example, in Spanish *violencia*, Portuguese *violência*, Italian *violenza*, French *violence*), but other terms in European languages have quite different linguistic origins (as in German *gewalt*, Greek βία or Icelandic *ofbeldi*). The English term *violence* is open to different interpretations. Besides the two given in Table 2.1, Olweus (1999: 12) defines violence or violent behaviour as:

> Aggressive behaviour where the actor or perpetrator uses his or her own body or an object (including a weapon) to inflict (relatively serious) injury or discomfort upon another individual.

The World Health Organisation (WHO) has defined violence as:

> The intentional use of physical and psychological force or power, threatened or actual, against oneself, another person, or against a group or community, that either results in or has a high likelihood of resulting in injury, death, psychological harm, maldevelopment, or deprivation. (see www.who.int/violenceprevention/approach/definition/en).

These definitions share some features but differ on others. Shared features are normally that (as with aggression) violence is harmful or damaging (or at least threatens such harm or damage) and is also intended. But there are several dimensions of difference. Some are similar to issues in defining *bullying* – does violence actually have to be manifested as behaviour that damages someone or something, or is just the threat of this sufficient (as stated in *Encarta* (2) in Table 2.1, and the WHO quotation)? Is violence still violence if it is legal (cf. *Encarta* (2))? However, two other issues are distinct.

First, is violence necessarily physical? It is, according to *Encarta* (1, in Table 2.1) and Olweus, but not according to *Encarta* (2) or the WHO. Restricting violence to physical acts makes it more restricted in focus, and perhaps easier to measure. It makes *violence* different from *aggression*. However, while some researchers and writers are happy with this definition, others are not.

Second, does violence necessarily involve people? Does violence have to be done by somebody (Olweus), or can it be done more impersonally by a social group or an institution? The term *institutional violence* suggests the latter, and allows us to consider the possibility of a school inflicting violence on its pupils, because of certain actions or policies. Also, is violence necessarily against a person? Not according to *Encarta*, but this is the case according to Olweus, and possibly the WHO. In other words, does vandalism (such as graffitti on the school walls, or intentional damage to school books or equipment) count as violence?

There are too many personal, disciplinary, cultural and linguistic differences for these definitional issues around violence to be fully resolved, but some at least do not concern us in defining bullying. Bullying need not be physical, and (in normal usage) must involve people as perpetrators and victims.

Harassment

Harassment is a term quite similar to *bullying*, especially in terms of the criterion of repetition or persistence (see Table 2.1). It tends to be used more in cases of bias bullying, especially as in *sexual harassment* and *racial harassment*, discussed later.

Abuse

The term *abuse* is also similar to *bullying*, and in the maltreatment sense (see Table 2.1) implies an imbalance of power. It tends to be used more in the family context, as in *child abuse*, which can be physical, sexual or by neglect.

Convivencia

It may be helpful to consider a concept opposite to *bullying* – the Spanish term *convivencia*. It does not have an exact translation into English, but Ortega, del Rey and Fernandez (2003: 136) describe it as follows:

> The Spanish term *convivencia* could be translated as coexistence, but it signifies not merely sharing time and space, nor merely tolerance of others, but also a spirit of solidarity, fraternity, co-operation, harmony, a desire for mutual understanding, the desire to get on well with others, and the resolution of conflict through dialogue or other non-violent means.

As the Spanish lack a cognate term to *bullying* (see later), they have sometimes imported the English term to describe such behaviours in Spanish schools. It would be appropriate if we can import from them the term *convivencia*, as indeed was done in a Council of Europe report (Gittins, 2006).

Actual understandings of bullying

Whichever definition researchers decide on, children and young people, and even parents and teachers, may not necessarily share that definition. How can we study this? Two main approaches have been used in the study of how bullying is defined outside the research community: basically, 'recall' and 'recognition' tasks.

In 'recall' tasks, participants are asked to define bullying, say what they think it is, and/or give examples of bullying. For example, Madsen (1996) asked participants aged 5–6, 9–10, 15–16 and 18–29 years 'What do you think bullying means?' and 'Can you give me some examples of bullying?'. Children primarily gave adjectival descriptions, for example 'It's being nasty and they're hurting people and don't even know what they are doing' (9 year old). Examples were mainly of physical or verbal kinds of behaviour. Citing examples of indirect bullying was absent in the 5–6 year olds and only found in 20% of the 9–10 year olds, but rose to 44% for 15–16 year olds and 71% for 18–29 year olds.

A similar approach was used by myself with colleagues in a study with English pupils 11–14 years old, in 1999–2000 (Smith, Talamelli, Cowie, Naylor & Chauhan, 2004). Children were interviewed individually and asked 'What do you think bullying is?'. Altogether 54% included physical behaviour in their definition, and 58% verbal behaviour, but only 4% included social exclusion, and only 2% indirect verbal bullying such as rumour spreading.

While such procedures tell us what participants readily call to mind, they do not necessarily represent their full range of knowledge. For example, indirect kinds of bullying are rarely recalled by children, even though in recognition studies most will agree that indirect examples can be bullying. Recall tasks are also not efficient at showing important age changes, such as the greater breadth of definition in younger children (see below).

The cartoon test

For these reasons, many researchers have used 'recognition' tasks: for example, a participant is given a vignette and asked if this is bullying. A methodology specifically developed for this purpose is the cartoon test (Smith, Cowie, Olafsson & Liefooghe, 2002). The test uses a set of 25 cartoons, illustrating various social situations that might or might not be bullying. The situations differ in terms of their relevant definitional parameters, such as type of aggression, number of aggressors, relative power, intent of the perpetrator, provocation of the victim, repetition, and negative effect on the victim. Themes such as racism, sexism and discrimination on the basis of disability or sexual orientation are included. There are also a few neutral or prosocial cartoons as controls. Stick figures are used so as to avoid issues of clothing, which might vary by culture, and also avoid suggesting any particular ethnic group or skin colour. Examples are shown in Figure 2.1 (the last being a neutral cartoon).

Figure 2.1 Examples of six stick figure cartoons

To give the test, each term is taken in turn, and the participant is required to either include or exclude each cartoon as examples of the term they are presented with, by scoring, or sorting in a pile, under a heading: for example, 'this is X' or 'this is not X' (where X is the term being currently considered, such as *bullying, harassment, teasing*). For each cartoon, the percentage of participants who include it as part of their 'definition' of each term is calculated. A meaning profile for each term can then be constructed, based on which cartoons are scored highly as being an example of it. The cartoon test can be used to give an empirically-based understanding of how words such as *bullying* (or similar words in English or other languages) are applied, and it facilitates comparisons across age, gender or experience, as well as across cultures, since the cartoons are stick figures with universal applicability.

Smith et al. (2002) found that there was little gender difference in the understanding of terms on the cartoon task, even though other evidence shows that the style of bullying behaviours between males and females differs (see Chapter 3). However, there were substantial age changes (see below), and also variation of meaning amongst the terms used in different countries.

Age changes in the understanding of bullying

There is good evidence of age-related changes in the understanding of *bullying*. A number of studies show that until around 8 or 9 years of age, pupils use the term quite broadly to cover all nasty kinds of behaviour, even when no imbalance of power is involved (Smith & Levan, 1995; Smith, Madsen & Moody, 1999). This appears to reflect a simple 'good–bad' evaluative dimension used by younger children.

Smith et al. (2002) compared 8 and 14 year olds on the cartoon task. Examining the structure of the cartoon set using multidimensional scaling, the solution for the 8 year olds produced only two clusters: Non-aggressive and Aggressive items. The solution for the 14 year olds showed five clusters: Non-aggressive; Physical Aggression (an even-handed dispute or a provoked retaliation); Physical Bullying (with a power difference between the disputing parties in terms of size, strength, number and consistency); Verbal Bullying (direct + indirect); and Social Exclusion.

So how about adults? Children may tell an adult (parent, teacher) something about bullying, but how do adults understand this? This may depend, at least in part, on the significance adults give to children's words like 'hurt', 'calling names' and 'bullying'. It is therefore very important to assess what adults understand and mean by 'bullying', in order to evaluate what probability children have to be clearly understood.

Monks and Smith (2006) compared the definitions of *bullying* held by children (4–6 years old and 8 years old), adolescents (14 years) and adults (parents) in England, using a shortened version of the cartoon task (omitting extortion, sexual or racial discrimination, homophobic bullying or bullying about a disability, considered inappropriate for use with young children). The findings, some of which are included in Table 2.3, show that the two child groups (4–6 years and 8 years) had a similar understanding of the term *bullying*, but were over-inclusive in their definition of it. For example, in the first two data lines of Table 2.3, most 4–6 and 8 year olds thought that fighting (without an imbalance of power) and that not letting someone play on one occasion was bullying, but fewer adolescents and adults thought this.

These age-related changes in understanding might be developmental (for example, related to changing cognitive capacities and greater experience in older children or adults), or perhaps historical (for example, reflecting the predominant usage at the time a person was growing up and at school). Looking at the lower three data lines in Table 2.3, all age groups agree that physical aggression with an imbalance of power is likely to be bullying, but adults were less likely to consider social or relational aggression as bullying. Fewer adults than pupils considered never letting someone play, or spreading nasty stories, to be bullying. This may be

Table 2.3 Some age differences in use of the term 'bullying' (data from Monks and Smith, 2006)

Cartoon	4–6 yrs (N = 99)	8 yrs (N = 40)	14 yrs (N = 40)	Adult (N = 40)	Chi-square (3df)
Helen and Jo don't like each other and start to fight	81.8	90.0	15.0	7.5	111.76***
Matt won't let Lenny play today	72.7	87.5	45.0	27.5	41.03***
Mary starts a fight with Linda, who is smaller	72.7	92.5	97.5	92.5	19.52***
Sebastian never lets Rob play	65.7	90.0	75.0	45.0	19.78*
Fran tells nasty stories about Melanie	76.8	90.0	85.0	52.5	18.34***

related to the work in schools in recent decades to include these forms of bullying within anti-bullying programmes. Parents' understanding of *bullying* may still often derive from when they were at school, at a period when bullying was mainly viewed as describing verbal or physical aggression.

Using the full cartoon set, Smorti, Menesini and Smith (2003) examined the understanding of *bullying* held by parents in England, as well as similar terms in four other countries. They found that parents tended to focus on physical acts of aggression and viewed bullying as meaning severe physical aggression, and they were unlikely to consider severe social exclusion as bullying. Menesini, Fonzi and Smith (2002) compared teacher and pupil responses to the cartoon task in Italy. There was high agreement on physical acts, but pupils were more willing than teachers to include social exclusion and gender-based exclusion as aggressive or bullying acts.

These findings highlight the potential for miscommunication between teachers/parents and pupils who do not have a shared understanding of the concept of 'bullying'. This may lead, on the one hand, to teachers/parents being seen by children as not responding to or even condoning certain types of bullying, and to children being seen by teachers or parents as over-reporting bullying, on the other.

Cultural differences in the terms used for bullying

When one tries to translate the term *bullying* in other languages, there is generally no equivalent word that covers its meaning fully. This can even be the case in other English-speaking countries, such as the USA, where the term *victimization* has mainly been used, at least until recently. In Latin languages (for example, French, Italian, Spanish, Portuguese) several terms exist, but none of these are a very good match. In Poland, Janowski (1999: 265) commented that 'The Polish language has no exact equivalent of "bullying" … one has to talk about "acts of aggression", "violence" or "oppression"'. This is quite a general issue.

In fact, as the research area on bullying expanded, and public concern has grown, in some countries the English word *bully* or *bullying* has been adopted or adapted: in Germany the term *bully* is now used as well as *täter*; in Spain *bullying* is an increasingly recognised term; and in Italy the term *Il bullismo* has been introduced, as evidenced in Fonzi's *Il Bullismo in Italia* (1997); Menesini's *Bullismo: Che Fare?* (2000) and Genta's *Il Bullismo* (2002).

Smith et al. (2002) used the cartoon task in an empirical attempt to study the meaning of terms in different languages, cognate to bullying. A survey of children's definitions of bullying across 14 different countries was carried out. Identical pictures were used across all cultures. Each cartoon had a caption in the native language, with the English captions constituting a reference set. In each other country, these captions were translated into the native language used by participants, and back-translated to ensure fidelity of meaning. Then the terms for *bullying* and *social exclusion* were selected, and checked with focus groups of pupils to ensure these were widely used and understood. The sorting task was then given to a minimum of 20 boys and 20 girls each at 8 and 14 years, in Austria, China, England, France, Germany, Greece, Iceland, Italy, Japan, Norway, Portugal, Spain, Slovenia and Thailand.

In each country, one to five terms were examined in relation to the cartoons, and specifically to the five main clusters of cartoons described earlier. The meaning of each term could be expressed as average percentage scores within each cluster of cartoons (rather than 25 individual scores). Table 2.4 gives some examples. The similarity or difference in meaning between any two terms could then be assessed by comparing their percentage profiles across the five clusters.

Table 2.4 The loading of some different terms from five countries, on five cartoon clusters (mean percentage of 14 year olds who included the cartoons in each cluster as part of their 'definition' of the term; data from Smith et al., 2002)

	Non-aggressive	Physical aggression	Physical bullying	Verbal bullying	Social exclusion
ENGLAND					
Bullying	4	34	94	91	62
Harassment	10	42	88	84	49
Intimidation	7	42	78	82	46
Tormenting	14	59	76	84	64
Teasing	15	43	35	83	51
GERMANY					
Schikanieren	6	20	58	80	55
FRANCE					
Violence	3	56	83	60	26
ITALY					
Prepotenza	10	71	92	86	90
Violenza	10	93	96	63	59
Aggressivita	10	91	96	68	63
PORTUGAL					
Rejeição	1	8	38	54	81

A hierarchical cluster analysis was conducted over a total of 67 terms, in order to show which of these had similar meanings. Six main groups or clusters of terms were identified:

- Nineteen terms that were generally higher on physical bullying, verbal bullying and social exclusion than on physical aggression; these terms tended to be closest to the definition of bullying, and did indeed include the English terms *bullying* and *picking on*, and the Italian term *prepotenza*.
- Six terms that scored most highly on social exclusion, for example the Portuguese *rejeição*.
- Seven terms that all scored much more highly on verbal bullying (direct + indirect) rather than physical bullying or social exclusion, including the English term *teasing*.
- Nineteen terms that were weighted most highly on verbal bullying (direct + indirect), but moderately on physical bullying, and less on social exclusion, including the English terms *harassment, intimidation* and *tormenting*.
- Three terms that were only weighted highly on physical aggression and physical bullying.
- Thirteen terms that were loaded highest on either physical aggression or physical bullying, but moderately on either verbal bullying (direct + indirect) and/or social exclusion, including the Italian terms *violenza* and *aggressivita*.

The cartoon methodology proved easy to administer and to be a relatively interesting task to do, but obviously the results were limited by the situations presented. In particular, the set of 25 cartoons did not represent some situations found in eastern countries such as Japan or South Korea, including severe or whole class-based social exclusion, and nor did it include cyberbullying – an increasingly common form. An expanded set of 40 cartoons has been developed and piloted in England, Iceland, Canada, Japan, mainland China, Hong Kong, Pakistan, South Korea and Turkey. For example, Ucanok, Smith and Karasoy (2011) used this test to examine age and gender differences in a Turkish sample.

Bullying in different contexts

In school it is mainly pupil–pupil bullying which has been the focus of research, but there can also be teacher–pupil and pupil–teacher bullying, as well as teacher–teacher bullying (which although in school would be an example of adult workplace bullying). Indeed bullying can happen in many contexts – such as the workplace generally, prisons, family homes, children's homes, dating relationships and homes for the elderly. Wherever there are reasonably stable social groups which a person cannot easily exit from, then the possibility of bullying is present. However, the study of this has to some extent been fragmented. A systematic comparison of research on bullying in various contexts was made by Monks et al. (2009), and chapters in Monks and Coyne (2011) give more detailed expositions.

Workplace bullying

The systematic study of workplace bullying started in the 1990s, especially in Scandinavia, where the term *mobbing* was used (for example, Leymann, 1996). As this area has developed, terms such as *workplace bullying* or *workplace harassment* have become common (Coyne, 2011). The definitions generally emphasise frequent negative acts directed against someone, with a power imbalance (often from a higher-ranking person in an organisation). This is similar to the definition used in school bullying, and there are similar issues around the use and importance of each of these criteria.

The types of workplace bullying identified include personal abuse (such as insults), physical intimidation, social ostracism, and work-related abuse (such as unfair work pressure or deadlines). Mainly based on self-report data, prevalence rates within Europe have been estimated at around 1–4% for serious bullying and around 20% for occasional experiences (Zapf, Einarsen, Hoel & Vartia, 2003). Victims experience a range of psychological and psychosomatic effects. Risk factors studied include individual personality and coping strategies, organisational factors and leadership styles, and group-level processes such as cohesion and scapegoating (Coyne, 2011).

Bullying in prisons

Research on bullying in prisons has gathered apace since the mid-1990s, and there is now a substantial volume of work (Ireland, 2011). Some earlier research used Olweus-type definitions to assess prevalence rates. Ireland (2011), however, argues against using a traditional bullying definition, due to the nature of prisons being so different from schools – including a larger but more transient peer group, and the existence of some specific aggressive behaviours (such as *baroning*, where goods are provided to someone at a high rate of interest – a kind of extortion, but one that is entered into 'voluntarily').

In fact, Ireland challenges the use of all the traditional criteria for bullying. First, she believes that prison bullying need not be intentional: some of this may be 'ill-considered actions' (2011: 138), but she argues that these 'can be considered bullying if the victim believes that they have been aggressed towards' (2011: 139) – essentially, taking the victim's perspective. This does, however, have some problems, as noted earlier.

Second, she argues that bullying need not be repeated (one threat may have powerful effects): 'An individual is being bullied when they are the victim of direct and/or indirect aggression happening on a weekly basis, by the same perpetrator or different perpetrators. Single incidences of aggression can be viewed as bullying, particularly where they are severe and when the individual either believes or fears that they are at risk of future victimisation by the same perpetrator or others' (2011: 139). However, this definition suggests that repetition of aggression is the norm, and that individual instances need to be severe to count – a position that many school bullying researchers would also accept.

Third, Ireland argues that bullying in prisons need not be based on an imbalance of power, as in 'baroning' above, although she in fact modifies this by stating that 'It can also be bullying when the imbalance of power between the bully and his/her victim is implied and not immediately evident' (2011: 139). There are certainly difficulties in defining an imbalance of power, but it appears that Ireland is not entirely dismissing it. Thus, while she presents a noticeable revision of the definition of bullying for use in prisons, it is arguably not so radically different from that used in school bullying as it might first appear.

Ireland suggests that a four-fold classification of bullies, victims, bully/victims and not-involved is useful in prison populations, but not so much the other participant roles developed by Salmivalli (see Chapter 3), due both to difficulties in obtaining such peer nomination data in prisons and the larger and more fluid nature of the peer group. However, interesting findings regarding the bully and victim groups in prisons are a substantial overlap of roles, and also that such behaviours may in some circumstances be quite functional: bullying behaviour can bring material benefits, and victim behaviour can mean increased monitoring by staff and segregation or transfer to another unit – thus providing a face-saving way of reducing the chances of being bullied in future.

Bullying in family homes

Within the family home, there can be bullying between adults (as in *intimate partner violence*, or IPV), from adults to older adults (see elder abuse, later), from adults to children (as in child abuse), between children (as in sibling bullying) and from children to adults (although this appears relatively rare due to the different power dynamics). In their review of these topics, Naylor, Petch and Ali (2011) discuss how IPV is found worldwide and experienced by many adults, although with wide cultural variations. Generally, males perpetrate more violence to females than vice versa, especially physical violence. Children's exposure to IPV by adults is also a significant issue. This, along with some work on sibling–sibling bullying, is discussed further in Chapter 4.

Abuse of children and adolescents by adults can take the form of neglect, emotional abuse, physical abuse or sexual abuse (or combinations of these). The World Health Organisation has defined *child maltreatment* as:

> All forms of physical and/or emotional ill treatment, sexual abuse, neglect or negligent treatment or commercial or other exploitation, resulting in actual or potential harm to the child's health, survival, development or dignity in the context of a relationship of responsibility, trust or power. (Butchart & Kahane, 2006: 59)

These and similar definitions of abuse are very similar to definitions of bullying, as they imply or specify repeated intentional harm by those in power. Nevertheless, the very extensive literature on child abuse has largely been separate from the research literature on bullying.

The extent of child abuse is difficult to determine, as naturally parents are secretive about it, and children are often too young or too frightened to seek help. It can also be very difficult and distressing for the victims of child abuse to speak out, as they may not be believed and interviews by police and judges can seem very intimidating. Some large-scale studies have used retrospective interviewing of young adults, asking about specific experiences, but embedded in other more general questions about childhood. Using this approach in the UK, May-Chahel and Cawson (2005) reported data in the categories of severe physical abuse (caused injuries, or continued for years), serious absence of physical care (food, clothing, cleanliness), serious lack of supervision, emotional maltreatment and contact sexual abuse. In the USA, Hussey, Chang and Kotch (2010) used similar categories of supervision neglect (left home alone when an adult should have been present), physical assault (slapped, hit or kicked), physical neglect (basic needs not taken care of, such as keeping clean, providing food or clothing) and contact sexual abuse (touched in a sexual way, forced to touch another in a sexual way or to have sexual relations). Females were more at risk for sexual abuse, but males were more at risk for the other three categories.

Child abuse can have severe and sometimes devastating long-term effects. Hussey et al. (2010) found that each of their four types of maltreatment was associated with a range of adolescent mental health factors, including depression, obesity, drug use and involvement in violence. In a study in the south of England (Isle of Wight), Collishaw et al. (2007) had available detailed interview data from adolescents when they were 14–15, and re-interviewed as adults aged 44–45. Those who retrospectively reported serious physical and sexual abuse up to age 16 had a higher rate of psychiatric disorder in adolescence, and as adults had high rates of adult psychopathology (for example depression, suicidal thoughts or attempts). Nevertheless, some of these adults were judged as resilient: for them, the abuse had often been less serious or sustained, but other protective factors appeared to be personality (not neurotic) and having some good relationships (one caring parent, and/or peer relationships, and/or a stable partner relationship).

Bullying in residential children's homes

Children in residential care often have had difficult histories of family and/or peer abuse, and it is not surprising that the levels of bullying and violence in residential children's homes can be high. In her review, Barter (2011: 67) writes that 'overall levels of "bullying" in residential children's homes seem comparable to, and indeed often substantially higher than, those in other non-residential settings, such as schools'. She is concerned about using the term *bullying* and prefers to discuss issues around violence. Besides peer violence, there can be programme abuse or institutional violence, as in excessive use of techniques such as pindowns and exclusion by staff. Staff abuse of children in care may be facilitated by the negative perceptions often held of such children.

Young people in care do regard bullying and violence as major concerns. So far as peer violence was concerned, Barter's own research derived four major forms: direct physical assault; physical 'non-contact' attacks such as threats, damaging belongings; verbal abuse; and unwelcome sexual behaviours (sexual gestures and remarks, grabbing private body parts, through to rape). Consistency of staff response is one important aspect of dealing with these forms of bullying and violence, and the use of restorative justice, and other strategies taken from the work on school bullying, are described as promising approaches.

Bullying in juvenile dating

Romantic relationships and dating start in the adolescent years and become more steady and serious as young people move into early adulthood. Although founded on a basis of interpersonal attraction, violent behaviours can occur in such relationships. Ortega and Sánchez (2011) describe these as ranging from verbal violence (insults) to psychological violence (threats, emotional blackmail), physical violence (slaps, punches, beatings) and sexual violence (pressure to have sexual contact, rape). Forms of indirect relational violence may appear within dating relationships and are aimed at controlling the behaviour, attitudes and feelings of the partner. Although there is often a power imbalance involved, measurement scales in this area are typically based on behavioural acts, so the imbalance of power may not be assessed (Foshee & Matthew, 2007). 'Dating violence' is thus an appropriate term, although much of this could be seen as bullying.

Although the common presumption is that males perpetrate more dating violence, in fact self-report surveys do not show this, and indeed some show greater involvement by females. This may interact with the severity of the violence and the age of those involved: also, some violence will be in self-defence. Although experience of interparental violence can be a predictor of adolescent dating violence, the peer network, and related phenomena such as drug abuse, appear to be stronger factors (Foshee & Matthew, 2007).

Elder abuse

A House of Commons report in the UK on elder abuse (2004: 5) commented that a small but significant proportion of older people experience abuse from those who care for them, in the context of either informal care (by family and friends) or formal care (by health and social care staff). A commonly used definition for elder abuse is cited as a single or repeated act or lack of appropriate action occurring within any relationship where there is an expectation of trust, which causes harm or distress to an older person. As this document also makes clear, there is a presumption here that older people may often be vulnerable (due to their physical or psychological infirmity), such that there is likely to be an imbalance of power in these relationships. Elder abuse can occur in family contexts, but also in residential homes for the elderly.

The main types identified in the House of Commons report, and in much of the subsequent literature (Walsh, D'Aoust & Beamer, 2011), are physical, sexual, psychological, financial or material neglect and acts of omission, and discriminatory (such as racist, sexist or based on disability). Distinctive here is the inclusion of financial/material as a special category: older people may, for example, be pressured into giving money or making changes to their will. Also neglect/acts of omission is a separate category, given that some older people have very definite medical or physical care needs which caregiver(s) are entrusted with.

The 'older-old' groups (those aged 80 years and above) appear more vulnerable to elder abuse, as do those in poorer physical or mental health and those in minority groups. As with family abuse generally, and child abuse, the detection of elder abuse is not always straightforward and is probably under-recognised by many professionals. Elderly people experiencing abuse may be afraid to tell others, or may not conceptualise their experiences as abuse. Greater awareness of the issue, and alleviating the social isolation of older adults through social support networks, are seen as important primary intervention strategies (Walsh et al., 2011).

History of research on school bullying

Returning to the main focus on school bullying, starting with research in Scandinavia, Japan and the UK, there is now active research in most European countries, Australia and New Zealand, Canada and the USA, and Japan, South Korea, Hong Kong and mainland China (Jimerson, Swearer & Espelage, 2010; McGrath & Noble, 2006; Smith et al., 1999; Smith, Kwak & Toda, in preparation). In fact the research programme on school bullying can be thought of as going through four rather distinct waves or phases (Smith, 2011).

First wave of research: origins 1970s–1988

Probably the first article on bullying published in a scientific journal is that of Burk on bullying and teasing published in the *Pedagogical Seminary* in 1897. This is worth looking at for the range of anecdotally observed behaviours he includes in his overview. However, the topic was then virtually neglected for many decades. The systematic study of school bullying can be dated from the 1970s, mainly in Scandinavia with Heinemann's (1972) book described earlier, which Olweus credits as first seriously raising awareness of the issue. The first important scientific work on the topic was the book by Olweus (1973, English translation 1978) which defined bullying in terms of physical and verbal behaviours.

Throughout the 1980s Olweus developed a self-report questionnaire to assess bullying, which proved an important tool in subsequent work. Also, in parallel with the first Norwegian National Anti-Bullying campaign, launched in 1983, he developed a school-based intervention programme (see Chapter 6). His evaluation of the original version of the Olweus Bullying Prevention Programme (1983–1985), with reports of reductions in bullying of around 50%, encouraged researchers and inspired the next wave of research. A meeting in Stavanger in 1987 brought together a number of European researchers to discuss bullying and intervention strategies. As noted earlier, there was a separate tradition of *ijime* research in Japan, of which western researchers appear to have been unaware.

Second wave of research: establishing a research programme: 1989–mid-1990s

The work by Olweus, and the Stavanger meeting, marked the start of a phase when bullying suddenly began to be noticed more widely in some western countries. This was something I noticed personally, as I began to be seriously interested in the topic in 1989. From that time, a number of books and journal articles were appearing (for example, Besag, 1989; Roland & Munthe, 1989; Tattum & Lane, 1989). Also, often using the Olweus questionnaire, surveys in other countries beyond Scandinavia were starting to be carried out (for example, Ahmad, Whitney & Smith, 1991). Besides self-report surveys, some studies began to use peer nominations methodology. In addition, some intervention campaigns took place, partly inspired by the Norwegian campaign: early large-scale interventions were in England (Smith & Sharp, 1994), Canada (Pepler, Craig, Zeigler & Charach, 1994) and Flanders (Stevens & Van Oost, 1994).

A key change in this period was the broadening of the research definition of *bullying*, to include indirect and relational bullying (such as rumour spreading, social exclusion), following the similar broadening of the understanding of *aggression*. In addition, work on bullying was becoming more international. Contacts were taking place between researchers in Europe and North America, and towards the end of this period, with researchers in Japan. Studies on *ijime* dated back at least to the 1980s, but this separate research tradition only made substantial contact with the western research tradition following a Monbusho/ UNESCO study in the later 1990s (see Smith et al., 1999).

Third wave of research: an established international research programme: mid-1990s–2004

In this period, research on bullying had become an important international research programme. Many more publications appeared, and research featured substantially in European and international conferences. Surveys, and interventions, took place in many countries (see the 21 country reports in Smith et al., 1999, and the 11 country reports on interventions in Smith et al., 2004). A notable methodological step was the introduction of participant roles in bullying from Salmivalli's work in Finland (Salmivalli, Lagerspetz, Björkqvist, Österman & Kaukiainen, 1996). Researchers in the USA substantially developed research on victimisation and bullying during this period, as evidenced by edited collections from Juvonen and Graham (2001) and Espelage and Swearer (2004). Significant work was also being undertaken in Australia and New Zealand: for example, see Rigby (2002) and Sullivan et al. (2004).

Fourth wave of research: cyberbullying: 2004–the present day

A substantial shift and new impetus in the bullying research programme has been brought about by the advent of cyberbullying. Significant awareness of cyber-bullying, and press reports, appear to date from around 2000–2001. In England, for example, the Department for Education (DfE) resource pack for schools *Don't Suffer in Silence* (1994) did not mention cyberbullying, but a revision published in 2002 mentions 'sending malicious emails or text messages on mobile phones' (2000: 9). Indeed, early forms of cyberbullying seem to have been mainly text messages or emails, at least judging from the extant research: for example, Rivers and Noret (2010) surveyed 11,000 English pupils from 2002 to 2005, asking about who had 'received nasty or threatening text messages or emails'. But since then, social networking sites such as Facebook have gained hugely in popularity, and the forms of cyberbullying have diversified greatly.

Starting from a small number of articles in the first few years of this cen-tury (although rather more on websites), academic publications in the cyber-bullying area have increased rapidly in the last few years. Notable publications in the area are books by Willard (2006), Shariff (2008), Kowalski, Limber, and Agatston (2008), Hinduja and Patchin (2008a), Mora-Merchan and Jäger (2010), Bauman (2011), Li, Cross and Smith (2012), Patchin and Hinduja (2012), Bauman, Walker and Cross (2013) and Smith and Steffgen (2013), along with many spe-cial journal issues, including the *Journal of Adolescent Health* (2007: 41 (2)), the *Zeitschrift fur Psychologie/Journal of Psychology* (2009: 217 (4)), the *Australian Journal of Guidance and Counselling* (2010: 20 (2)), the *European Journal of Developmental Psychology* (2012: 9 (2)), *School Psychology International* (2012: 33 (5)), *Emotional and Behavioural Difficulties* (2012: 17 (3/4)) and the *Journal of Community & Applied Social Psychology* (2013: 23 (1)).

Of course, work on what has come to be called 'traditional' bullying has continued in this latest wave of studies, including developments in social network analysis (see Chapter 3), and increasing numbers of meta-analyses as publications in certain areas accumulate. But methodologies (such as questionnaires) have had to be adapted to include new forms of bullying. Cyberbullying also brings some new challenges and opportunities to the bul-lying research programme. Besides the definitional challenges discussed ear-lier, the opportunities include a greater disciplinary breadth and a chance to extend the focus beyond the school context alone, and beyond just the school age range (Smith, 2012).

Summary

The term *bullying* has come to occupy a certain privileged position in the scientific community, due to the dominance of English-language journals and publications. In fact in various languages there is a range of terms with both subtle and sometimes obvious differences in meaning. Nevertheless, *bullying* has come to have a relatively well-defined meaning as behaviour that intentionally harms another person, typically with repetition and an imbalance of power. Rather less well specified, but often assumed, is that the harm must be in some sense unjustified. The criteria of repetition and power imbalance separate bullying into a subset of aggression of a particularly nasty kind. This notion of bullying also forms the hard core of a research programme, which in the case of school bullying has expanded and consolidated tremendously since its origins in the 1970s. To varying extents, the definitions and approaches used in school bullying have some similarity to bullying-type behaviours in other contexts, although in family contexts especially the term *abuse* is preferred, and the research programme in this area has been largely separate. In this century the research programme on school bullying has been affected by the advent of cyberbullying, which provides not only opportunities in new directions but also some challenges.

THREE

How we can find out about bullying

I think that is such stuff that you keep to yourself.

Well I don't trust her because she says that it is confidential but I don't believe her.

We reported it to the school ... so it stopped in the end.

(quotes from Swedish pupils, aged 14 years, from Slonje, Smith & Frisén, 2013)

It is not always easy to access information on school bullying, but it is important, as the above quotes illustrate. These come from interviews made by an experienced researcher and youth worker (Robert Slonje) with nine pupils with experience of bullying and cyberbullying. Interviews are time-consuming, and questionnaires are most commonly used for gathering data on large samples. There are a number of issues in designing questionnaires appropriately, and they are not always well used, but they do possess obvious advantages. Some questionnaires are retrospective, while some are not pupil-based but teacher-based, and merge into incident report forms. But in fact there are a variety of ways of finding out about school bullying, and many other methods can provide useful information. The rows in Table 3.1 show different methods of doing so. These include nominations, interviews and focus groups, diaries, blogs and drawings, and observations. All assessment methods raise issues of reliability and validity. In addition, all assessment methods raise ethical issues.

The columns in Table 3.1 show different types of informant, with an X indicating a common and feasible combination of method and informant (or in the case of observations, who is being observed): the informant might be the pupil him- or herself; a peer (usually someone in the same class, or year group, at school); an adult at school (usually the class teacher, or perhaps a pastoral care teacher, school nurse or counsellor); or a family member (usually a parent or carer, or perhaps a sibling or other relative). Self-reports by pupils have been widely used in questionnaires, and both self- and peer reports in nomination procedures. Adult (teacher and parent) reports may have more limited value for pupil–pupil bullying, as adults are often only aware of a fraction of what is going on in a peer group.

Table 3.1 Summary of some main methods of obtaining data on school bullying

Method/Informant	Self	Peer	School staff	Parent/carer/family member
Questionnaire	X	X	X	X
Nomination	X	X	X	X
Interview	X	X	X	X
Focus group		X	X	X
School incident reports/audits			X	
Diary/blog	X			
Drawings	X	X		
Observations	X			

All these procedures, but especially questionnaire surveys, are often combined with measures of possible correlates of bullying experiences or roles, such as attitudes (see Chapter 4), effects (see Chapter 5) or coping strategies (see Chapter 6).

Types of informant

Self-report

Self-report has been the most widely used informant source: for example, someone is asked whether, or how often, they have been bullied or have bullied others, perhaps over some recent time period such as the previous term. Getting self-reports has some face validity, in that only the actor really knows what they intended (in hurting someone) or how they felt if someone attacked them, and they probably know best how often these things happened to them. This may be particularly important for some of the less 'public' kinds of bullying that can be experienced, such as social exclusion, or certain types of cyberbullying. A disadvantage is the reliance on one informant, and that informant may not be totally reliable. Answers may be affected by social desirability and a self-serving bias, which can particularly affect 'bully' responses: for example, children may be unwilling to self-report as being a bully, despite assurances of anonymity, for fear of the consequences. 'Victim' responses may also be subject to other biases. On the basis of a comparison with peer reports, Juvonen, Nishina and Graham (2001) argued that some pupils may be 'paranoids' – that is, saying they are a victim even though the peer group does not report this. Conversely, some pupils may be 'deniers' – that is, they say they are not victims, even though many peers think that they are.

Peer report

Peer reports are also frequently used in research studies, especially those focused on a relatively small number of schools and classes. These are normally gathered on a class basis. Some advantages of peer reports are that classmates are often well aware of pupil–pupil bullying in their class, and if reports are obtained from most classmates, then one has multiple informants and some measure of reliability amongst them. A disadvantage, however, is that some children may be 'labelled' by the peer group as a 'bully' or 'victim', and that this label may persist even after some behavioural change in the pupil concerned. This problem may then be exacerbated in that peer nomination procedures usually ask generally about 'who gets bullied?' or 'who bullies others?', rather than asking about a specific time period such as the previous term, as is usually the case in gathering self-reports.

Comparing peer and self-reports

Ladd and Kochenderfer-Ladd (2002; their study one) compared self- and peer reports of victimisation for US children recruited in kindergarten (around 5 years old) and followed for five years up until they entered fourth grade. The correlations between self- and peer reports were near zero in kindergarten, but increased steadily up to around .50 in fourth grade. Initially, from kindergarten to second grade, the self-reports were modestly stable and showed some relationship to measures of social adjustment, but the peer reports showed little (non-significant) stability and little relationship to the adjustment measures. From third to fifth grade, both the self- and peer reports became equally stable and predictive. Thus peer reports seemed to be increasingly useful by around 8 years of age.

Cole, Cornell and Sheras (2006) compared self-reports of bullying others (from an anonymous questionnaire) and peer reports of bullies (through nominations) in a middle school in the USA. They reported very low correspondence between the two methods. Self-reported (but not peer-nominated) bullies also reported more positive attitudes to aggression; however, peer-nominated (but not self-reported) bullies had had more disciplinary referrals, detentions and suspensions by the school.

Bouman et al. (2012), reviewing a number of studies comparing peer with self-reports, suggested that overall peer ratings correlated more with measures of social adjustment (such as peer liking and popularity, which are aspects of standing in the peer group), and self-reports correlated more with internalising problems (such as depression, which is something perhaps most accurately reported by oneself). They tested this out systematically, in a sample of 1,192 Dutch children aged 9–12 years. The correlations between peer and self-report were .35 for victimization and .32 for bullying, and therefore rather modest. Some further results are shown in Table 3.2. Looking at the scores for being a victim, these tend to go with poorer social adjustment and greater internalising problems, whether peer or self-reports are used, but clearly the relations are stronger for peer reports with social adjustment, and for self-reports with internalising problems. Looking at the scores for bullying others, the pattern is a bit more complex. For social adjustment, bully scores correlate with perceived popularity (a measure of social prestige), but negatively with likeability (whether individual children like them), but the relationships are stronger for peer reports than self-reports. By contrast, the relationships with internalising problems

Table 3.2 Correlates of peer and self-reports of bullying, and being bullied, with measures of social adjustment and internalising problems (data from Bouman et al., 2012)

Outcome measure	Peer-reported victimisation	Self-reported victimisation	Peer-reported bullying	Self-reported bullying
Social adjustment measures				
Perceived popularity	−.38*	−.24*	.44*	.15*
Likeability	−.45*	−.24*	−.37*	−.18*
Social acceptance	−.32*	−.32*	.18*	−.03
Internalising problems				
Anxiety	.08	.24*	−.04	.10*
Depression	.15*	.24*	−.04	.09*
Self-worth (negative)	.17*	.21*	−.02	.10*

are much smaller but only significant for self-reports. The authors conclude that which method is adopted may depend on the outcome measure the researcher is most interested in, but that a fuller picture comes from using both methods.

Teachers

Although teachers are part of the school community, according to victims they may only be told about bullying in one-third to one-half of incidents (or less for cyberbullying), as discussed in Chapter 6. Also, bullying behaviours tend to take place out of sight of the teacher, such as in the playground or corridors rather than in the classroom (see Chapter 4). Teacher reports may be more valuable for younger children (especially preschool children; see later in this chapter) and less so for older children. Teachers may have less contact with individual students at older ages, and also bullying becomes more complex and covert.

Comparing teacher, peer and self-reports

Leff, Kupersmidt, Patterson and Power (1999) evaluated teacher identification of bullies and victims in US elementary and middle schools, through a nomination procedure. Agreement with peer nominations was modest, although better if several teacher nominations were combined. Compared to peer nominations, teacher nominations were more accurate in elementary than in middle schools. Totura, Green, Karver and Gesten (2009), in a study in US middle schools, found very limited agreement between self-reports and teacher reports on bullying and being bullied. Self-reports were more frequent for being bullied, whereas teachers were more likely to report bullying of others (perhaps as it was more obvious to them, or perhaps if students were less willing to admit to bullying). Psychological and behavioural difficulties were greatest for those children concordant for self- and teacher ratings of involvement.

Parents

Parents may be told about bullying, and sometimes more often than teachers (see Chapter 6), but their knowledge of bullying in school is likely to be limited. On a practical level it may be difficult to recruit parents/guardians to provide information (whereas one teacher can provide information on a whole class of pupils), and in particular, parents of children involved in bullying others may be less inclined to complete questionnaires about their children's behaviour.

Comparing parent and self-reports

In a study in England and Wales, Shakoor, Jaffee, Andreou et al. (2011) used mother nominations of their child being a victim, and child self-reports through interview. There was modest agreement, with kappa coefficients of 0.20 in primary school and 0.29 in secondary school. However, parent and self-reports did correlate similarly with emotional and behavioural problems, so the authors considered that mothers' reports were useful, although multiple informants would be best.

Parent interviews might be especially useful for children with disabilities, who are often in special schools: parents may be particularly involved in their welfare, and the children may be less able to communicate their experiences accurately themselves. Christensen, Fraynt, Neece and Baker (2012) used parent (usually mother) interviews in a study in California, USA, of bullying in children with learning difficulties (IQ below 85 at age 13). They also interviewed the young people themselves. There was substantial agreement between mothers and adolescents on the occurrence or not of victimization (kappa coefficient 0.38), but little agreement on its frequency or severity.

Comparison of multiple informants

A number of studies have compared several informants. Ladd and Kochenderfer-Ladd (2002; their study two) compared self-, peer, teacher and parent reports of victimisation, from grades 2–4 (ages 7–9 years) in US classrooms. Short rating scale questionnaires (combined with some nomination assessment for peers) were used. This was a longitudinal study over three years, and all four informant measures showed some stability. Concordance estimates were modest but statistically significant in most cases: correlations were typically in the .20–.40 range. Agreement between self- and peer reports increased by grade level, especially for boys (up to .50 at fourth grade). Teacher reports agreed more with peer reports (around .50) than with self-reports (around .20). Agreement of parent reports with the other three informants remained modest throughout (around .30). Peer and teacher reports were correlated more strongly than self- or parent reports to separate measures of social problems, rejection and loneliness, but a composite multi-informant measure was the best predictor.

Cornell and Brockenbrough (2004) compared self-, peer and teacher reports of bully and victim in a US middle school. They gave pupils a self-report questionnaire, while peers and teachers used a nomination procedure. For victims, they found some agreement between peer and teacher nominations (a correlation of .28), and less for self-report with peers (.17) or teachers (.12). For bullies, the corresponding correlations were .52 (peer–teacher), .10 (self–peer), and .05 (self–teacher). The findings led the authors to raise concerns about the reliance on self-report, especially for identifying bullying (where the self-report frequencies were noticeably low).

Cullerton-Sen and Crick (2005) compared teacher (ratings), peer (nominations) and self-reports (questionnaire) of relational and physical victimisation in fourth-grade US pupils. Correlations were generally around .2–.3 for all informant pairings and both kinds of victimisation.

Pellegrini and Bartini (2000a) compared self-report (through both structured diaries and an Olweus questionnaire), peer nominations, and direct observations of aggressive behaviour and victimisation, in a US middle school, plus teacher ratings for aggression only. For measures of aggression/bullying, all the informants correlated positively, but the correlations with direct observation were very low. For victimisation, again the correlations were positive: observation had very low correlations with both self-report methods, but moderate correlations with peer nominations. Self-report and peer nominations had moderate agreement. The authors recommended a multi-informant (and multi-method) approach as the most useful.

Summary of informant methods

Agreement between different informants as to bully and victim status is typically modest, which is disappointing. Self-reports have their own intrinsic value, but clearly do not always accord with the perceptions of others. Peer reports appear to become more valuable as children get older (from the US third grade or around 8 years old), and teacher reports perhaps less valuable. There is a general consensus that, where possible, multiple informants should be used to gain a fuller and more reliable assessment.

The choice of informant(s) is particularly crucial when data on bully and victim roles are correlated with other measures (for example, of adjustment). Even if only one informant source is used for bully or victim status, it is highly desirable to use a different informant source for other correlate measures. If the same informant is used for both sets of measures, then this would incur the issue of shared method variance. For example, if someone tends to be paranoid and sees themselves as a victim they may also tend to report themselves as depressed, or if peers have labelled a child as a victim they may similarly label them as unpopular. As Bouman et al. (2012) demonstrated, correlations of bully or victim status with other variables will give a fuller picture when different informants are used for the various sets of data.

Methods: Questionnaires

In a questionnaire, a set list of questions will be answered. These typically are about experiences related to bullying, as well as demographic questions (age, sex, background) and other questions such as emotional responses, coping strategies, knowledge and attitudes. The most widely used approach has been to use pupil self-report questionnaires, but questionnaires can be used with teachers and parents as well. Often questionnaires are anonymous to encourage accurate reporting, and individual bullies or victims cannot be identified.

The questionnaire method is particularly suited to large-scale surveys, for example, when surveying an entire school, or a number of schools across a region or country. Questionnaires have the important advantage that different researchers can use the same instrument and then compare findings rather precisely, or the same research team may use it at two (or more) time points to assess changes and the effects of a school-based intervention. Besides incidence, questionnaires can give information on related matters such as where bullying happens, attitudes to bullying, what pupils have done about it, and other correlates or outcome measures.

Questionnaires can similarly be useful for schools if they wish to find out how effective their anti-bullying work is. Although a school may devise its own questionnaire there are a lot of pitfalls in questionnaire design, so it may be best using an established version. Besides those mentioned below, examples of pupil, teacher and parent questionnaires are available from the Anti-Bullying Alliance website (www.abatoolsforschools.org.uk/default.aspx).

Many questionnaires have been developed, and a number are discussed in Furlong et al. (2010). A compendium was produced by Hamburger, Basile and Vivolo (2011) and is available at www.cdc.gov/violenceprevention/pub/measuring_bullying.html.

In this century the advent of cyberbullying has led to the development of new questionnaires as well as revisions of established ones. Berne et al. (2013) and Frisén et al. (2013) carried out a systematic review of measuring instruments used for cyberbullying, up until October 2010. Altogether 44 different instruments were identified!

Two main variants of questionnaires are *definition-based* and *behaviour-based*.

Definition-based questionnaires

Some questionnaires give a definition of what is meant by bullying, at or near the start. Four examples are discussed below.

The Olweus Bully/Victim Questionnaire (OBVQ)

The Olweus Bully/Victim Questionnaire (see Solberg & Olweus, 2003) was developed in Norway, in the context of assessing the effects of the nationwide campaign in Norway in the 1980s. In a fully developed form it has been used widely since the 1990s, translated into many languages, and is available for purchase from Dan Olweus at the University of Bergen. It starts with a definition of what is meant by bullying (see Chapter 2). After a few demographic items, it then asks a couple of key questions about how often you have been bullied (usually, over the previous term), and how often you have taken part in bullying others. These have five standard frequency response options: never, only once or twice, several times, about once a week, several times a week. There are subsequent questions where experiences of different types of bullying (physical, verbal, etc.) are listed. There are then further questions such as where this happened, how many other pupils were involved, whether anyone was told of the bullying – the exact number and form of these questions have varied in different versions. Altogether the questionnaire has some 25–35 questions to answer and takes about 30 minutes to complete. It has been used very widely and translated into many languages. For example, Eslea et al. (2003) reported similar data from seven countries (China, England, Ireland, Italy, Japan, Portugal and Spain) using the OBVQ.

Kyriakides, Kaloyirou and Lindsay (2006) examined the psychometric properties of the OBVQ in a Greek Cypriot sample. They found good internal consistency of items for physical, verbal and indirect bullying (since then, the OBVQ has incorporated items for 'electronic' or cyberbullying).

The Health Behavior of School-aged Children (HBSC) survey (Currie et al., 2012), given across over 30 countries world-wide, uses what is effectively a short version of the Olweus questionnaire. It provides an older version of the Olweus definition (it does not specifically mention indirect bullying such as exclusion and rumour spreading) and asks four questions: two about bullying others and two about being bullied, either in school or away from school during the current term. The standard five frequency response categories are used.

The Rigby and Slee Peer Relations Questionnaire (PRQ)

The Peer Relations Questionnaire (Rigby & Slee, 1993), developed in Australia, has been widely used as a short and convenient instrument. It starts with a standard definition of bullying. It then has six items on tendency to be victimised (for example, 'I get called names by others') and six items on tendency to bully others (for example, 'I tell false stories or spread rumours about others'). Responses are on a four-point scale: never, once in a while, pretty often and very often. Responses over the six victim and six bully items are normally summed for a composite score.

The PRQ acronym is, confusingly, sometimes used for the quite different Participant Role Scale, or PRS, developed by Salmivalli (see later).

The Forms of Bullying Scale (FBS)

Shaw, Dooley, Cross, Zubrick and Waters (2013) designed an instrument to use with 12–25 year old adolescents. It starts with a definition similar to that of Olweus, plus one for cyberbullying adapted from Smith, Mahdavi et al. (2008). It then has 10 victim items and a matching 10 perpetrator items. These do not explicitly cover cyber forms, but physical, verbal, relational and social forms on whether they occur offline or online (for example 'I was hurt by someone trying to break up a friendship'). Confirmatory factor analyses confirmed the usefulness of two scales, FBS-V (victim) and FBS-P (perpetrator), and good evidence for validity was found based on correlations with mental and social health outcomes. The authors recommended the instrument as an efficient way of measuring victimisation and perpetration with equivalent scale items, although they also acknowledged that not all kinds of cyberbullying behaviours may be captured by these scales.

The DAPHNE II bullying questionnaire

Another example of an anonymous definition-based questionnaire was designed as part of a European-funded DAPHNE II project and used in Italy, Spain and England (Genta et al., 2012; and see http://www.bullyingandcyber.net/media/cms_page_media/44/Questionario%20EQCB%20english_4.pdf). This questionnaire has sections on demographic aspects, and on loneliness and self-esteem, followed by questions regarding bullying and cyberbullying. Brief definitions of bullying and cyberbullying are given so that pupils have a clear understanding of the behaviours classified as bullying and cyberbullying and do not confuse these with other aggressive behaviours; questions are then asked about four kinds of bullying, two traditional (direct and indirect) and two cyber (via mobile phones and the internet).

Behaviour-based questionnaires

An alternative approach is not to give a definition and instead ask about experiences of specific types of behaviour, such as being hit or insulted or excluded. Five such examples of behaviour-based questionnaires are mentioned below.

The Life in Schools Questionnaire

This questionnaire was developed by Arora at the University of Sheffield, England (Arora, 1994; Arora & Thompson, 1987). It asks pupils about whether they have experienced various behaviours over the previous week. Altogether there are about 30 items, of which six (tried to kick me, threatened to hurt me, demanded money from me, tried to hurt me, tried to break something of mine, tried to hit me) were identified as measures of being bullied. This questionnaire has been used in a number of studies in England.

The School Life Survey

A similar kind of questionnaire, called the School Life Survey, was developed by Chan in England (see Chan, Myron & Crawshaw, 2005). This asks about experiences during the last four weeks at school, with nine bullying scale items (for example, 'I told lies and stories about other students to make them look bad') and 15 victim scale items (for example, 'This student hurt me by hitting or beating me up'). The student is asked the number of times it happened, and who did this.

The Reynolds Bully-Victimization Scale

This scale (Reynolds, 2003), developed in the USA, assesses physical and verbal forms of aggression and is appropriate for secondary school age pupils. It has 23 items in the bully scale and victim scale and takes about 15 minutes to complete. Sample items are 'I picked on younger kids' and 'I teased or called other kids names', and pupils check how often they have adopted such behaviours over the past month.

The Personal Experiences Checklist (PECK)

The PECK was developed in the USA by Hunt, Peters and Rapee (2012) to provide a convenient battery of items that included not just physical bullying and relational-verbal bullying, but also 'bullying based on culture' (such as 'other kids make fun of my language') and cyberbullying (such as 'other kids say nasty things to me by SMS'). Altogether there are 32 items, which confirmatory factor analysis showed to comprise the four scales mentioned. Good internal consistency and test-retest reliability were reported.

The E-Victimization and E-Bullying Scales

These scales were developed by Lam and Li (2013), initially with adolescents in mainland China. They started with six items each for electronic victimisation and bullying scored on six-point frequency scales. Confirmatory factor analysis led to a final five-item victim scale (for example, 'How many times did someone threaten you using emails, texting, short messages, or a website such as Renren [Chinese social networking site], etc?'), and to two, three-item bully scales – one for mild forms (teasing, calling bad names, saying mean things) and one for more serious forms (saying you were going to hit/hurt, threatening, making something up about someone to make others not like him/her anymore).

Issues in designing and giving questionnaires

Definition

As seen above, some questionnaires, such as the Olweus and DAPHNE questionnaires, give a full definition of what is meant by bullying in the context of answering the questionnaire, usually introducing the ideas of intentional hurt, repetition and imbalance of power (in suitable language). By contrast, some questionnaires assume that pupils will know what *bullying* is, and simply go straight into asking questions about it. But giving a definition can help to standardise responses, as otherwise pupils may use their own personal definitions of *bullying* which may vary and not conform to the researcher's own definition. Nevertheless, relying on giving a definition does assume that pupils actually read and consider it, and keep it in mind for the 20–30 minutes they spend filling in the questionnaire.

Difficulties with definition are circumvented by behaviour-based question-naires, such as the Life in Schools Questionnaire and School Life Survey, but these can run into other problems if they are taken to measure *bullying*. They can assess actual experiences, such as being hit or insulted, but is this more than just *aggression*? One distinctive criterion is repetition: this can be accommodated if pupils say how often these things have happened to them. The other distinctive criterion is imbalance of power, and here these surveys appear to lack discrimination. Someone who has been in several fights with an equal strength peer will have been hit lots of times, but this would not normally be considered bullying.

Kert, Codding, Tryon and Shiyko (2010) looked at the effects of giving a definition of bullying, and using the word 'bully', on response rates in a sample of 114 pupils aged 10–15 years, from three US schools. They used the Reynolds Bully-Victimization Scale and assessed rates of self-reported bullying behaviour. When a definition of bullying was given, and it was made clear that items such as 'I picked on younger kids' and 'I teased or called other kids names' were referring to bullying, response rates were significantly less (almost half) than when just the behavioural items were used with no reference anywhere to bullying. Thus giving a definition may help pupils to discriminate bullying from more general aggressive behaviours.

This issue was also clearly demonstrated by Hunter et al. (2007). They asked pupils between 8 and 13 years old from 10 schools in Scotland about their experiences of various aggressive behaviours, and in addition about both the intent of the perpetrator, the frequency, and the perceived power imbalance (in terms of physical strength, number of children and relative popularity). Out of 1,429 pupils surveyed, 438 (30.7%) reported being attacked repeatedly, but only 167 pupils (11.7%) also reported intent to hurt from the perpetrator plus an imbalance of power on at least one of the three criteria.

Sawyer, Bradshaw and O'Brennan (2008) also compared a definition-based and behaviour-based measure in a very large (over 24,000) sample of students from 107 US schools. They compared responses to a single item ('How often have you been bullied in the last month?') with a prior definition of bullying, with responses to experiencing 10 different behaviours (such as pushing/shoving, email/blogging). The behaviour-based measure gave higher prevalence rates. Their definition of bullying was flawed in not including the imbalance of power criterion, but nevertheless this study also shows the influence of assessment measures on prevalence rates.

Ybarra, Boyd, Korchmaros and Oppenheim (2012) carried out two online survey studies with young people aged between 6 and 17 years in the USA: each study had over 1,100 participants. In the first, participants were randomly assigned to one of four conditions, which varied by whether an Olweus-type definition of bullying was given, and separately by whether the word 'bully' was used. The prevalence rates were then compared – those quoted here are for monthly or more often. They were lowest when the word 'bully' was included, either with the definition (34%) or without (35%), and were higher if the word 'bully' was not mentioned, either with the definition (39%) or without (40% – this last condition merely asked if certain behaviours had been experienced). The researchers concluded that using the word 'bully' did cut out some behaviours that would go beyond the normal definition, probably with the word 'bully' being well understood now as regards meaning. However, actually giving the definition (or not) did not make much difference, possibly because it was not read or remembered carefully. Their second study looked at the effect of adding 'harassment' to 'bullying', but this was negligible. In addition, using follow-up questions, it examined whether the experience of those bullied satisfied three criteria (repetition, power imbalance and occurrence over time): only about one-third of those reporting being bullied also satisfied all three criteria.

Anonymity

Most questionnaires are anonymous. The Olweus Questionnaire (and many others) are explicitly so, stating that the respondent should not put their name on the questionnaire and no-one will know what they said. Quite apart from ethical issues, it is widely thought that both victims of bullying and especially perhaps those involved in bullying others, will feel more confident about recounting such experiences without revealing their identity. At most, they need tick their age, gender and school class (and possibly, ethnicity). However, one disadvantage is that it is not easy for researchers, or school personnel, to follow up on an individual basis – for example, in order to understand who is bullying whom, to assess the effects of an intervention on particular pupils, or to direct help to particular victims or action to change the behaviour of those involved in bullying others. To do this, they or the pupil must provide a code or pseudonym to identify and match up with a later questionnaire – a process that may compromise the confidence that anonymity is supposed to give.

Ahmad and Smith (1990) carried out a small study comparing the incidence of bullying obtained from an anonymous Olweus questionnaire to that from individual interviews. For taking part in bullying especially (not so much for being a victim), fewer admitted to this in the interview than in the questionnaire. This might suggest that the anonymous questionnaire does indeed facilitate the admission of what most adults see as undesirable behaviour, namely bullying another student. However, this conclusion was questioned by Chan et al. (2005). They pointed out that Ahmad and Smith's conclusions were based on the assumption that a denial (of bullying behaviour) was the main source of error. They argued that, in contrast, pupils might exaggerate or give irresponsible answers in a questionnaire but take a personal interview more seriously.

Chan et al. (2005) carried out a study with 562 students from 30 classes in two elementary schools in Toronto, Canada. On a class basis, students filled in the School Life Survey either anonymously or non-anonymously (asked to write their name on the questionnaire). The mean bullying and victimisation rates were similar under both conditions, and the small differences (bullying rates slightly higher but victimisation rates slightly lower in the non-anonymous condition) were not statistically significant. The authors thus questioned whether anonymity was really necessary.

Context of administration

Who gives the questionnaires? Especially when anonymity is stressed, it is best if these are given out by a researcher, who can make it very clear that the filled-in questionnaires will be put directly into an envelope, sealed, and taken back to the university or research institute. Independence from the school is clearly demonstrated. Nevertheless, especially in large surveys, this may not be feasible, and class teachers may administer the questionnaire. Little is known about the effects of this: indeed, probably much depends on how a teacher handles this, and the trust pupils have in him or her.

The importance of the context of giving a questionnaire survey was vividly illustrated by Frey (2005). Unless carefully supervised, students may watch what others are writing and then try to influence them. In one classroom she observed, 'I saw one student "dictate" survey answers to a classmate by covertly pointing to particular responses. The exchange was clearly intimidating, even though it occurred in a supervised setting. The targeted classmate pretended to circle the demanded response, and then covertly circled another option' (2005: 411).

It is sometimes the case that questionnaires are obviously filled in carelessly or irresponsibly, and these should be removed in the initial stage of screening the data obtained. These usually make up only a small percentage of the total, but can be much higher in some circumstances. Cross and Newman-Gonchar (2004) reported on surveys on antisocial behaviour at two US high schools, given by a range of trained and untrained administrators in different classrooms. Looking at the proportion of obviously inconsistent or implausibly extreme responses, these were around 1 to 4% for classrooms with trained administrators, but rose to an alarming level of 28% when untrained administrators were used. These were very sensitive surveys including questions on gang membership and drug use, but questions on bullying and victimisation are quite sensitive too, and careful instructions for the briefing and preferably training of administrators, as well as adequate assurance of confidentiality, are clearly important.

Online surveys

As schools and classrooms become better equipped with computers, it is increasingly feasible to provide questions online. Online data entry has a great advantage in that the data can be entered easily into a statistical analysis package such as SPSS, saving a lot of data transcription time.

Offline questionnaires can be adapted for online use, or questionnaires can be designed with the internet in mind. One example of the latter is the Survey of Bullying at Your School, used by Perkins, Craig and Perkins (2011). This is a behaviour-based questionnaire with eight behaviours (such as 'teasing in an unfriendly way'): students say how often they have adopted each behaviour in the previous 30 days. This survey also asks how often students think other students have done these things at school – a measure of 'perceived social norms' for bullying.

As another example, Wachs (2012) gave an online definition-based questionnaire to high school students in Germany. This was the Mobbing Questionnaire for Students, which gave a definition of bullying and asked *'How often have you been bullied?'* (or cyberbullied, or have bullied others, or cyberbullied others) over the previous 12 months. Wachs used a Computer Assisted Personal Interview (CAPI) method to improve validity: a researcher/interviewer is present in the computer room with the students and oversees the entry of responses, remaining available to answer any queries.

Length

Pupil questionnaires are often given in a class or form period, and this suggests they should not take more than 30 minutes to complete, as some time is needed to distribute and introduce the questionnaire and collect it at the end. Also, pupil concentration is unlikely to last longer than 30 minutes, even for older pupils. The amount of information potentially to be obtained from longer questionnaires must be balanced against the quality of information, as bored or tired pupils are unlikely to give valid or well thought-out responses. For younger pupils, questionnaires should be shorter.

Format

To maintain pupil interest, understanding and involvement, questionnaires should be accessible and the instructions easy to understand. For any new instrument, piloting with an initial pupil sample will be essential. Formatting should be clear and consistent (for example, for scales, using the same number of scale points for each question). Sometimes an issue arises if pupils who have not been involved in bullying experiences at all simply tick 'no' a few times and then have nothing to do; this can be avoided if the format of some questions is hypothetical, for example, as well as asking *'What did you do when you were bullied?'* having as an alternative *'What would you do if you were bullied?'*.

Language

The language used in questionnaires needs to be suitable for the age, background and vernacular of the pupils responding. Younger pupils, for example 8–11 year olds, really need simple words and sentences. This is especially important in multi-ethnic classrooms with a wide range of reading ability. Also, besides issues around equivalent words in languages other than English (see Chapter 1), there can be national or regional variants within a language. For example, the Australian term *dobbing,* and the corresponding English term *snitching,* might not be comprehensible in other English-speaking countries.

Multiple choice or open-ended questions

The most usual format in questionnaires is to have multiple-choice responses. These may just be yes/no (for example, *Have you been bullied during the last term?*), or on a frequency scale (for example, *How often have you been bullied in the last term?*, with standard response options such as never, only once or twice, several times, about once a week, several times a week). Multiple-choice questions are easy to score, and scaled responses can be used for parametric statistics.

Open-ended questions allow a respondent to write in detail, giving personal experiences. Sometimes these can be appended to multiple-choice questions. For example, commonly in lists of types of bullying (hit, called names, etc.) there is a final multiple-choice option *'Other (please specify) …'.* This gives the respondent the opportunity to mention some other type of bullying experience that they felt was not included in the list given. Or after a multiple-choice question such as (for victims) *'Did you tell anyone you were bullied?'* there might be an open-ended question *'What happened?'.*

Open-ended questions need to be content analysed, and responses can then be converted into quantitative data if this seems desirable. However, their inclusion in questionnaires can be of great value from a qualitative point of view. An inevitable shortcoming of questionnaires is that you only find out about what you ask, which is limited by the range of options provided. Open-ended questions give the possibility not only of getting more detail, but also of accessing information outside of the 'expected' range used in the multiple-choice options – for example, new or different types of bullying. When some colleagues and I started doing surveys of cyberbullying in English schools, we included a range of open-ended questions about the kinds of cyberbullying experienced, and these were interesting and informative about what was at the time a relatively new phenomenon (Smith, Mahdavi et al., 2008).

Frequency and severity

Usually, questions about bullying experiences are asked on a scale. In the Olweus questionnaire and many others, the scale is one of frequency, such as given above.

This reflects the repetition criterion in defining bullying, so a response 'only once or twice' is usually put together with 'never' as not having experienced bullying. However, frequency is only one measure of the overall intensity or impact of being bullied. Another might be severity. Just responding that you have been 'teased' or 'hit' on a weekly basis does not discriminate how serious that actually was. How serious does the harm have to be to count as bullying? Every day most of us experience minor hurts. So, should bullying be limited to quite serious blows, or very hurtful insults or social provocations? Or can it include what some French researchers have called 'micro-violence' or 'incivilities', namely relatively minor kinds of impoliteness (Debarbieux, Blaya & Vidal, 2003)?

The seriousness of being bullied is, however, more difficult to assess than the frequency: frequency has an obvious objective scale, but severity does not. Researchers may resort to subjective ratings of seriousness as the most feasible option. Another, slightly indirect, way of looking at seriousness is how many types of bullying a pupil has been involved in.

Types

Besides asking if a pupil has been bullied, or has taken part in bullying others, most questionnaires ask further about what kind of bullying took place. Some may make broad-brush distinctions: for example, in the cross-national comparison using the DAPHNE II questionnaire (Genta et al., 2012), questions were asked about four types of bullying: direct, indirect, using mobile phones and using the internet. (The distinction between mobile phones and the internet was useful in 2007–2008 when these data were collected, although less useful now with the spread of 'smart phones'.)

Quite often a longer list of more specific kinds of behaviour is given, for example:

- *Physical*: hitting, kicking, punching, taking or damaging belongings (sometimes damaging or taking belongings is taken as a separate Property category).
- *Verbal*: teasing, taunting, insulting, threatening.
- *Social exclusion*: systematically excluding someone from social groups ('you can't play with us').
- *Indirect relational*: spreading nasty rumours, telling others not to play with someone.
- *Cyberbullying* (perhaps split further, for example, email bullying, text message bullying, on social network sites).
- *Bullying due to race, ethnicity or religion.*
- *Bullying due to disability.*
- *Sexual bullying.*

These lists are not straightforward: some items are types of action (hit, spread rumour), but others may be more related to the cause of bullying. For example, racial bullying might be an actual racial slur, but might also be other kinds of behaviour (such as social exclusion) that the pupil sees as racially motivated – similarly for other kinds of bias or prejudice-based bullying (see Chapter 4).

Roles

The obvious roles obtained from questionnaires are those of *bully* and of *victim*. It is easy to calculate the data for two other roles. *Bully/victims* are those who score on both bully and victim, and *non-involved* or control pupils are those who score on neither. Thus, this yields four role categories.

This is only the bare bones of a more complicated dynamic, however. Pikas (1989) and others had long distinguished two types of victim: the so-called passive victim, who has not directly provoked the bullying, and the provocative victim, who can be thought to have contributed to their being bullied by having acted in an annoying, provocative way to peers (thus, this group may overlap considerably with the bully/victims). Salmivalli, Lagerspetz et al. (1996) identified further roles in bullying, using peer nominations (discussed below). Questions about these more complex roles can be asked in questionnaires, but lend themselves more readily to peer nomination methods.

Scales or one item

Judgements about the frequency of bullying and assignment to roles (bully, victim, bully/victim, not-involved) are often made on the basis of single items. The Olweus questionnaire has two main items, on how often you have been bullied and how often you have taken part in bullying others, which have often been analysed as single items (although it is also possible to use a scale, with other items in the questionnaire). The large-scale HBSC surveys (Currie et al., 2012; Molcho et al., 2009; see also Chapter 4) have used similar single item responses from an Olweus-type questionnaire, one for bullying and one for being a victim, as a basis for comparing bullying rates across countries.

In questionnaire design generally, however, single items tend to be avoided as less reliable, and scales are preferred. This is very much the case for measuring attitudes, personality traits, etc. Obviously it is not the case for factual information such as age and gender, or even family background. Are bullying experiences more like these factual items, or are they more like opinions and traits? Arguing that bullying is a latent construct, that is something that is indirectly assessed, Bovaird (2010) argued that a minimum of three separate items is desirable for their assessment.

Time reference

Bullying experiences can happen at any point in the lifespan. It is a lucky or an unusual adult who can say they have *never* been bullied, or have *never* taken part in bullying someone else. Questions that simply ask if you have ever been bullied generally get very high response rates. For example, in a study of 11–16 year olds in English schools (Smith et al., 2008) we found the incidence of bullying to be 13.5% within the previous month, 14.1% over the previous six months, but rising to 49% if pupils were asked if they had ever been bullied in school.

It is usually more useful to ask about a recent time period such as one month or one term, or six months, perhaps anchoring it to a memorable time point such as Christmas. For example, in one cross-national study (Morita, 2001), the key question was *'How often have you been bullied at school since Christmas?'*, with questionnaires given in June. This time period is long enough to ensure reasonably high response rates, without unduly taxing memory demands and without getting the ceiling effects that are likely if no time period is given.

Time of year

The time of year when questionnaires are given is often determined by practical considerations. It interacts with the issue of time reference (above), and the end of a school term is often a preferred time, so that pupils can think back over the previous term or perhaps two previous terms. Equally, a less-preferred time would be the start of a school year, after a long summer break and before pupils have settled into experiencing a new class and year group, and thus perhaps a relatively new peer group.

Time of year, however, also means a season such as spring, summer, autumn, winter. Time of year may affect mood, opportunities for outdoor play, different kinds of activities, etc. Little is known on whether these in themselves might affect rates of bullying and victimisation.

Sample size and representativeness (individuals, schools)

Many large-scale survey studies attempt generalisations about rates of bullying, or related characteristics, in a region or a country, or even comparing different countries. How valid this is will depend on the sample(s) obtained. Obviously there need to be enough individual pupils sampled to allow meaningful statistical comparisons. Since the base rate for more than occasional bully or victim experiences may be around 5–20% (see Chapter 3), and if as a rule of thumb we take a sample size of 50 as sufficient in a particular role (for example, bully, victim), then this suggests around 1,000 pupils need to be sampled. If we are going to analyse the sample further (by age, or gender, or type of bullying experienced) then we need a correspondingly larger sample.

Pupils are in classes, however, and classes are in schools, and schools are in regions of a country. Bullying rates show some variation according to all these factors (see Chapter 5). For country-level generalisations, we really need to gather samples from a considerable number of schools, ideally of different types and from various regions of the country. Many studies understandably fall short of this ideal. Consider three examples, all from the same edited book on cyberbullying by Li et al. (2012).

Aoyama, Utsumi and Hasegawa (2012) reported a comparison of cyberbullying among high school students in Japan and the United States. Their samples were 142 students from one school in Tokyo, and 133 students from one school in Texas. A number of significant differences were found, and the authors summarise, for example, that 'Overall, the Japanese participants reported less experience of cyberbullying than was found in the US' (2012: 195). They then rightfully add that 'A limitation of this study is the small sample size – only one school in each culture' (2012: 197). This study is not untypical of many small-scale comparisons, some of which do not so clearly acknowledge the sample limitations. They are useful for generating hypotheses, but cannot give us generalisable country or culture differences.

Genta et al. (2012) reported on comparative aspects of cyberbullying in Italy, England and Spain. Here, the samples were 1,964 (Italy – from 39 schools in Emilia Romagna), 2,227 (England – from 14 schools in different parts of the country) and 1,671 (Spain – from seven schools in Andalucia, around Cordova). These are reasonable size samples, so it seems fair enough to make some tentative statements about cultural differences. Note, however, that the study samples only one region in Italy and one region in Spain. The sample in England is more representative of the country, but it does not represent the UK (no schools in Scotland, Northern Ireland or Wales were sampled) – hence any generalisation to the UK would not be warranted.

Salmivalli and Pöyhönen (2012) reported on bullying (including cyberbullying) in Finland. Their data came from a nationally-funded KiVa project (see Chapter 6). The sample providing data was 17,627 students, from 156 different schools representing all five provinces of mainland Finland. Clearly this is a very satisfactory sample, and can really allow generalisations to be made about rates and types of bullying in Finland, at the time of the study (2007–2008). Such a comprehensive study requires large-scale funding, indeed more than is usually available, and the authors could not make corresponding cross-national comparisons to any other data set.

Year of study

Many research reports do not report the year or date at which the data were collected. This illustrates the ahistorical way in which many psychologists think. In 2010, I was invited to comment on a special issue on peer victimization for the *Merrill-Palmer Quarterly* (Smith, 2010c). Of the eight target articles, only two initially reported the year in which data were collected, although this was remedied by the editors when I pointed out the importance of stating this. As I commented there:

> Victimization has a historical context in many ways. This is so even for definition (e.g. indirect and relational victimization became incorporated only in the later

1980s). But on a more short-term basis, it is especially important for cybervic-timization. Not only is this relatively recent, but the preferred forms of cyber-bullying seem to be changing rapidly, from initially mainly text messages and emails, though to instant messaging and social networking (Smith et al., 2008). Historical context is also important if we take the impact of large-scale interventions seriously. In Finland, the Kiva project is rolling out an anti-bullying intervention program across the country, and one that so far is having considerable success (Salmivalli et al., 2010). So it is desirable to know if a study in Finland is done before or after Kiva .... the point is a more general one, as school-based interventions have taken place in many countries. (2010c: 451)

Unfortunately this problem continues. For example, in a special issue on 'Cyberbullying in schools' in the journal *School Psychology International* (2012: 33 (5)), only two out of seven empirical articles gave the date of data collection. Similarly, when guest editing a special issue of the journal *Emotional and Behavioural Difficulties* (2012: 17 (3–4)) on 'Bullying and cyberbullying', I had to ask or remind many authors to add in the date of data gathering. It is not adequate to rely on the date of publication – in one article in this 2012 journal issue, data was gathered in 2003–2004.

Retrospective data

In a sense, all data is retrospective – respondents are typically asked to think about the previous term or year. However, the term *retrospective* is normally reserved for thinking back over a previous period of life – for example, adults thinking back to their school years. This has a potential advantage that an adult can put things in a more mature and distanced perspective, and also report on aspects such as in which phases of school life they were most involved in bullying episodes. A drawback is that there are likely to be more memory distortions in recalling events from some time ago. Nevertheless, examining retrospective reports in general, Brewin, Andrews and Gotlib (1993) found that when reporting facts from childhood, most adults are reasonably accurate and stable in their recollections; reports were especially likely to be reliable for highly salient and emotionally charged events, such as experiences of victimisation could be expected to be. Looking specifically at reports of school victimisation by adults (in this case, gay/lesbian and bisexual adults), Rivers (2001) established quite reasonable degrees of test-retest reliability when giving a retrospective questionnaire twice, 12–14 months apart: reliability was high for placing important events chronologically as well as for recalling specific types of bullying occurring in specific locations, although recollections of subsequent outcomes were less accurate.

Schäfer et al. (2004) devised a Retrospective Bullying Questionnaire (RBQ), designed to ask about experiences of six types of victimisation (two physical, two verbal, two indirect), separately for primary school and secondary school. Questions asked about frequency, seriousness and duration in each case, together with questions about short-term effects (suicidal ideation, intrusive memories) and victimisation experiences in adulthood. The authors gave the RBQ to adults from two occupations (teacher, student) and three countries (Spain, Germany, the United Kingdom). Meaningful relationships were found with current relationship quality measures (self-esteem, attachment style and friendship quality).

McGuckin, Lewis, Cummins and Cruise (2011) gave retrospective questionnaires to undergraduate students in Ireland (both Northern Ireland and the Republic). They were asked to list the extent of different traumatic events that had happened to them at school. Almost all reported some experience of being teased, yelled at, left out, and having a story made up about them, although often only on a few occasions. Of males, 13% said that 'being beaten up' was their single worst experience, while for females, 11% described 'I was teased' in this way. Some of these behaviours might be aggression rather than bullying, but they were clearly remembered as distressing.

Retrospective methods have been used with those who may have experienced prejudice-related bullying at various times. Hugh-Jones and Smith (1999) analysed questionnaires from members of the British Stammering Association. The questions covered the nature of the individual's stammer, school friendships, extent and form of bullying experiences, teacher and family awareness of bullying, and any short- and long-term effects of being bullied. Rivers (2011) has carried out retrospective studies of homophobic bullying with former victims, looking at the nature of the experiences and the likely effects.

Incident reports and school audits

An incident report is generally filled in by a teacher or other member of school staff, soon after an incident has happened. In the UK, schools are not obliged to keep such records, except for cases of racial harassment, but it is considered good practice to do so. In its guide for school governors, the Anti-Bullying Alliance (ABA) stated:

> ... we would recommend that schools have a system to record all bullying incidents, however minor. The system should include a record of action taken following an incident and the outcome of this action. Such a system has a number of advantages, including tracking whether incidents are recurring, and if certain pupils have repeated involvement. It also provides schools with a historical account of incidents including previous action the school has taken – this is crucial should there be formal meetings with parents, outside agencies or a formal investigation. (2011: 15)

In a survey of 56 schools in the UK, OFSTED (2012) found a wide variety of practice in recording methods. Only one school kept no records of bullying at all, while in 12 schools records were just kept in pupils' files. In 18 schools, records were kept in a central log together with other kinds of incidents, and in 25 schools records were kept centrally in a dedicated log on bullying. The survey found that whereas these incident records often recorded who was involved and where, and gave some indication of the action taken, there was often little attention paid to the types of bullying that occurred or to following up the initial action taken and whether it was effective.

Recording systems are often paper-based, but there are also computer programs available for these purposes. An efficient centralised recording system can monitor behaviour, target students for additional support (for example, peer support), and provide evidence for the effectiveness for a school's anti-bullying work. Information provided by feeder primary schools can assist secondary schools with identifying vulnerable students at intake.

An example of an Incident Report Form is given in Appendix A. This was used in connection with research in England on anti-bullying work in schools (Thompson & Smith, 2011).

Official statistics

Some relevant statistics on bullying can be found in many countries. These are usually based on questionnaire surveys. All the issues discussed above about questionnaires apply here. In order to be valuable, these surveys should be carried out at a national level with a representative sample. A clear definition of bullying should be provided, as some surveys are about violence rather than bullying (Smith, 2003).

In England the government-sponsored Tellus surveys produced nationwide figures, based on reports by pupils. The first two years of these were small-scale and exploratory, but in 2008 a more comprehensive and large-scale Tellus 3 survey was made. However, in a survey the following year Tellus 4 used a different metric (results of these surveys are discussed in Chapter 4). The Tellus surveys were then discontinued with a change in government.

In Japan, national surveys have typically relied on teacher reports. For example the Japanese Ministry of Education, Culture, Sports, Science and Technology (2012) issued a national survey on *ijime* as part of an Annual Fact-Finding Survey on Problematic Behaviour in School covering primary (6–12 years), lower-secondary (13–15 years) and upper-secondary schools (16–18 years). The statistics were an accumulation of data originally compiled by local boards of education based on teachers' reports. These indicated a steady decrease in occurrences of *ijime* since 2006, although with a slight increase in 2010. However, as pointed out for similar kinds of teacher-based surveys in the 1990s, these trends may not be validated by pupil-based surveys (Morita et al., 1999).

Methods: Nomination procedures

In a nomination procedure, an informant is asked to nominate self or others (for example, classmates) for involvement in roles such as bully or victim. This can be used with teachers or parents, but is most commonly adopted on a class basis with pupils, namely peer nominations. The procedure may involve a paper- or computer-based survey, or individual interviews.

Peer nominations are probably best gathered by someone from outside the school so that pupils can respond in confidence. Children typically work through a list of classmates, or are shown names or photos of all classmates, and are then asked to select or point to those in a certain role. This procedure usually also picks up self-nominations: the researcher can make it explicit whether pupils should include themselves in the nomination procedure or not.

Nomination procedures are clearly good at identifying individuals in roles. Multiple informants can provide good reliability in identifying bullies or victims. They are less useful for large-scale prevalence studies for two reasons. First, they are relatively time-consuming and more suitable for class-based studies, and second, they do not normally give an idea of frequency – nominating a classmate as a victim, for example, does not in itself give an idea of how often this victimisation happens or over what time period. Nevertheless, nomination data can be used in before-and-after studies of the effects of class-based interventions.

Salmivalli Participant Role Scale

A widely used instrument has been the Salmivalli Participant Role Scale or PRS (Salmivalli, Lagerspetz et al., 1996). Salmivalli and colleagues took things further than the conventional roles of *Bully* and *Victim*, by splitting up the roles involved in bullying. Through peer nomination procedures they identified the roles of *Ringleader* bullies (who take the initiative), *Follower* bullies (who then join in) and *Reinforcers* (who encourage the bully or laugh at the victim). They also identified *Defenders* (who help the victim) and *Outsiders* (who stay out of things), as well as the *Victims* themselves. Each of these roles has a number of items to identify them. Subsequently some investigators have distinguished *Bystanders*, who see the bullying but do not act in any way, from *Outsiders*, who simply have not witnessed what was happening.

The research by Salmivalli, Lagerspetz et al. (1996) was with young adolescents. Sutton and Smith (1999) successfully used a similar procedure with 8–11 year olds. Monks, Smith and Swettenham (2003) adapted the participant roles for use with younger children, aged 4–6 years, using cartoon pictures. The roles of *Bully* (or *Aggressor*), *Victim* and *Defender* could be identified with some reliability, but other roles were not clearly understood at these younger ages. Goossens, Olthof and Dekker (2006) used a revised version of the PRS in the Netherlands with 10 year olds, including an improved victim scale; the five scales (leader bully, follower bully, outsider, defender, victim) had good reliability and moderate test-retest stability.

Social network analysis

The Participant Role Scale asked for nominations of individual pupils to various roles. A step further is to ask for who is involved in dyadic relationships. Veenstra et al. (2007), working with children around 11 years old in the Netherlands, asked in addition 'Who do you bully?' and 'By whom are you bullied?'. The answers were analysed in terms of how dyadic bully–victim relationships are related to dominance, liking, and same or opposite gender. Sainio, Veenstra, Huitsing and Salmivalli (2010) extended this to defenders, using data from a large sample of 10–12 year olds in Finland related to the evaluation of the KiVa project (see Chapter 6). Any pupil who reported being victimised at least two or three times a month was asked to nominate who (if anyone) in their class defended them. Defended and non-defended victims were compared, and victim–defender dyads analysed for gender and sociometric characteristics. Huitsing and Veenstra (2012), using data from 10 year old children in the Netherlands, asked for dyadic information on all the main participant roles – ringleader bully, assistant, reinforcer and defender – as well as gathering sociometric data. This enabled them to carry out a social network analysis on a class basis, looking at specific kinds of networks involved in such relationships.

Cut-off in nomination procedures

Just as questionnaires have to decide a frequency cut-off to get to prevalence rates, so nomination methods have to decide on a proportionality cut-off, at least when multiple nominations are obtained, as is typical for class-based peer nominations. So what proportion of pupils should nominate someone as a bully or victim (or other role), to assign them to this category? It is possible to use standardised scores (by class, or by total sample), but these will vary from one study to another. Another option is to take a certain percentage of nominations as a criterion. For example, Bowers, Smith and Binney (1992) used a 33% cut-off (that is, one-third of classmates nominating someone as a bully or victim): this in fact corresponded to about one standard deviation above the average score. Mahdavi and Smith (2007) looked at several criteria: 25% (seen as a 'lenient' criterion), 33% and 50% (seen as a 'tough' criterion).

Methods: Other approaches

Interviews

In-depth interviews usually focus on personal experiences, although they can also ask about aspects such as knowledge concerning others, or responses to bullying within a school generally. They can focus on recent events, or be more retrospective, looking back over a school career for example. Rivers (2011) used in-depth interviews with victims of homophobic bullying, and quotations from some of them in his book provide a vivid illustration of their experiences and coping strategies.

Duncan (2002) carried out semi-structured interviews with seven girls from two English secondary schools who were in trouble for bullying. These explored the reasons they perceived for what happened. Although Duncan had expected an emphasis on indirect bullying and social exclusion (common in girls bullying), in this sample he uncovered a great deal of direct physical aggression as well.

Lam and Liu (2007) interviewed eight boys aged 12–17 years in Hong Kong secondary schools. All had been bullying other pupils. The semi-structured interviews asked about how they perceived bullying, when they started doing it and why, and the consequences. Besides getting interesting narrative excerpts from the interviews, Lam and Liu used the data to construct a process model for how the boys became involved in bullying, and why it might continue or terminate.

Sawyer, Mishna, Pepler and Wiener (2011) carried out interviews with 20 parents of children who had self-reported (in an adapted Olweus questionnaire) as being frequently bullied. These interviews were semi-structured and lasted about 60–90 minutes. They were tape-recorded, transcribed, and analysed to create categories and themes. Key themes emerged about how parents defined bullying behaviours, their awareness of and reactions to their child being bullied, how it affected their child and how they responded.

Focus groups

Focus groups usually bring together some five to eight students to discuss a particular topic such as bullying in a school. A skilled facilitator leads the group and takes notes, and/or the discussion is recorded or videotaped. The discussion amongst participants can be enlightening, revealing agreements and disagreements; likewise, it can spark off other ideas or insights that might not come from the individuals if interviewed separately, and this approach is more economical time-wise than individual interviews. However, there is a danger that a few individuals dominate the discussion, and some experiences (such as being a victim) may be withheld in this more public forum compared to a private interview. The composition of the focus groups and their management are important factors.

Smith, Mahdavi et al. (2008) reported the use of focus groups with seven or eight pupils aged 12–15 years in English secondary schools. Here, part of the aim was to present some survey findings on cyberbullying (about incidence, age and gender differences, coping strategies) and see if pupils agreed with them. The method was useful in highlighting some areas of disagreement, which were then discussed, such as how prevalent cyberbullying was and what could be done about it.

Guerra, Williams and Sadek (2011) used 14 focus groups with pupils in US elementary, middle and secondary schools. This study also used focus group findings to complement survey findings with a different population. A range of themes came from the focus groups, covering why some pupils bully others and why some pupils are victimised, and for the adolescents, provided insights into the dynamics of bullying and its relationship to issues of sexuality and social identity.

Children's diaries, blogs and drawings

Pellegrini and Bartini (2000a) described using diaries, with US adolescents aged around 12–13 years. They were asked to fill in the diary once a month, over a school year, saying how they had spent their time over the previous 24 hours, and answering specific questions such as 'Did anyone tease or hit you?' and how this was done, with a list of standardised response options (such as 'kicked', 'called a name') provided. In this format, the method is rather like a repeated questionnaire. It is also possible to gather more unstructured narrative diaries, which could give a greater depth of information but which may be more difficult to quantify. More recently, online blogs provide another way of accessing diary-type information.

Pictorial representations of bullying provide a different kind of insight. Bosacki, Marini and Dane (2006) asked 8–12 year old children in the USA to draw an incident of bullying and tell a brief story about it. Similarly, Andreou and Bonoti (2009) asked 9–12 year old children in Greek schools to 'Draw a scene of peer victimisation taking place in your school. In case that you participate in the scene, please, mark yourself with an arrow'. They also completed some self-report measures. Girls tended to draw more verbal victimisation scenes, and boys more physical aggression scenes. Girls more often indicated themselves as a defender, and boys more often as a bully, victim or outsider. There was little relationship to the answers on the self-report questionnaires. As the authors suggest, drawings may be influenced by stereotypes about bullying, but might also be a useful additional methodological tool.

Observations

Direct observations could avoid many of the problems of self-, peer, parent or teacher reports, as what 'actually happens' can be recorded. Observers need to be well-trained and able to conduct observations of children over a substantial period of time. Even then, observational methods do have disadvantages. Children taking part in bullying may choose to do so where it is not easy to see them, and they may behave differently if they know they are being watched by an adult. It can also be intrusive and time-consuming to undertake sufficient observations to gather reliable data. In addition, while physical bullying may be relatively easy to detect, more subtle and verbal forms such as rumour-spreading would seem much more difficult.

Boulton (1999) made extensive playground observations in two UK middle schools, using scan sampling to record details of playground activities and companions. Nevertheless, he resorted to a peer nomination procedure to gather data on bully and victim roles. Pellegrini and Bartini (2000a) made observations of aggression and victimization in 12–13 year olds in a US middle school. They used focal child methodology: for example, following a chosen child for three minutes and recording their behaviour continuously on a check sheet, then moving to the next child on a list. Observations were made by trained observers in the cafeteria, during break-time and in the hallways. Over a school year, each child was observed a minimum of 40 times, with observations coded according to a predetermined schedule.

Pepler and Craig (1995) developed a sophisticated methodology to observe aggressive and bullying behaviours, using remote audiovisual observations. A camcorder with a telephoto lens filmed children during the playground break, from a classroom overlooking the playground. A target child or a number of children were asked to wear radio microphones, with that of the target child being switched on to combine with the visual recording. A focal child was typically observed for 10 minutes before switching to another child. The filmed records could be replayed as often as needed, and were scored using a predetermined category list (Pepler, Craig & Roberts, 1998). Tapper and Boulton (2002) used a similar combination of wireless microphone and video recording, this time with a micro-recorder that fitted into a rucksack worn by the observer.

Observations may be subject to bias. Pellegrini et al. (2011) compared observations of aggressive behaviour in preschool children made by male and female observers. All observers had been well trained previously using videotapes to high reliability. Nevertheless, male observers scored much more aggression in their observations and especially in boys. The authors speculated that this may be due to males having more experience of the physical aggression that is common at this age. There can be other problems in observational work as well, including 'observer drift' where observers change their internal definitions and criteria over time (Martin & Bateson, 2007).

Assessment of bullying-like behaviours in preschool children

Traditional methods used to find out about bullying such as the Olweus questionnaire, or peer-nomination procedures such as the Participant Role Scale, are not appropriate for use with pupils below about 8 years old. This is because younger children do not have the same level of reading skills and concentration. In addition, care has to be taken as they generally have a broader understanding of terms such as *bullying* (see Chapter 2). Some questionnaires, using a simple format and pictures, and suitable for individual administration, have been devised: for example, Smith and Levan (1995) designed a questionnaire for use with children around 6 years old, and von Marées and Petermann (2009) devised a bullying and victimisation questionnaire (originally in German) for use with 4–10 year olds.

To gather information from preschool children using self-report or peer nomination, it may be best not to ask the children directly about their experiences and awareness of *bullying* (which is likely to be interpreted as 'nasty things that happened'). An alternative approach is to use direct examples of bullying behaviours and to ask children about their knowledge of this having occurred within their peer-group. Monks et al. (2003) developed a cartoon methodology using this type of questioning to find out about children's experiences of bullying-type behaviours in kindergarten. The cartoons were used within an individual interview setting which overcame issues surrounding young children's more limited reading and writing abilities, as well as their slightly different understanding of the term *bullying*. The methodology used four stick-figure cartoons modelled on those adopted by Smith et al. (2002). The cartoons depicted four main types of bullying-type behaviour: direct physical (one child hitting, kicking or pushing another); direct verbal (one child calling another nasty names); direct relational (a child telling another in a face-to-face encounter that they cannot join in); and indirect relational (a child spreading rumours about another behind his/her back) (see Figure 3.1). Using this methodology, children were asked to provide peer and self-nominations for involvement in these behaviours.

Monks and Smith (2010) compared 5 and 8 year olds on peer-nominations for a number of roles. They obtained peer-nominations (including self-nominations), on a class basis, for participant roles of aggressor, reinforcer, assistant, defender, outsider, passive and provocative victim, and similar nominations from their teachers. The younger 5 year olds could make nominations for all the roles, but were most reliable for aggressor and provocative victim. Within-class pupil agreement was only significant for aggressor and provocative victim at 5 years (it was also significant for passive victim and defender at 8 years). Test-retest reliability (over an interval of one week) was moderately high for aggressor only, and provocative victim, in 5 year olds (it was high for all roles in 8 year olds). The 5 year olds tended to give similar nominations for aggressor and provocative victim. Peer and teacher ratings showed better agreement with each other than with self-nominations.

As this study illustrates, there has been no difficulty obtaining teacher (or parent) nominations for younger children. In addition, observational methods can be used. This is probably easier in nursery and kindergarten settings, and these have been used in some studies (see Monks & Smith, 2011). For example, in the

Figure 3.1 Cartoons to assess bullying-like behaviours in young children: physical, verbal, indirect, social exclusion (as used by Monks et al., 2003)

USA Ostrov and Keating (2004) found that observations of aggressive behaviour showed some agreement with teacher reports, and similar findings were reported by Ostrov (2008) for physical aggression and relational aggression as well as for prosocial behavior.

Ethical issues in assessment

General procedures for the ethical conduct of investigations have been set out by many professional bodies: for example, the British Psychological Society has a Code of Ethics and Conduct (www.bps.org.uk/what-we-do/ethics-standards/ethics-standards), and the American Psychological Association has a selection of publications on ethical issues (www.apa.org/). To approve a research study, an ethics committee will generally require reassurance that participants give fully informed consent to the procedure, and that no harm to the participants would normally be expected. Studies involving children and young people demand particular care, as they are not regarded as able to give their fully informed consent. The consent of parent(s), or teacher(s) if 'in loco parentis', should be sought; in addition the informed consent of the child or young person should still be obtained, even for young children as far as is possible.

Consent from parents may be 'active' (they must return a consent form) or 'passive' (they must receive information, and are assumed to consent unless they return a form saying they do not consent). Organisations and ethics committees vary in how much they require active rather than passive consent. Active consent requirements have a significant drawback in that they may result in low participation rates, thereby jeopardising the validity of the study. Shaw, Cross, Thomas and Zubrick (2014) have pointed out the importance of this issue and suggested a way forward. In a large sample of Western Australian schools, they first requested active consent; then, after two weeks, they contacted parents again requesting passive consent (enclosing a reply-paid envelope). They ended up with 7% active refusals, and of those taking part 35% had active consent and 65% passive consent. Comparing these latter two groups, bullying others (as well as other variables) was more prevalent among pupils in the passive consent group. The authors concluded that using active consent alone could lead to biased findings, and recommended the iterated active/passive consent procedure.

Finding out about bullying and victimisation is inevitably going to be a sensitive issue. Victims may feel insecure and vulnerable to further attack if they are known to be 'telling', while perpetrators may wonder if they will be sanctioned if they admit to bullying others. Yuile, Pepler, Craig and Connolly (2006) describe in detail a number of ethical issues around gathering data on bullying, including issues around privacy, payment for participation, and following up on serious issues. Anonymity (discussed earlier) is a common precaution to reassure participants, and is easiest to assure in the case of questionnaires. When using interviews or face-to-face peer nominations, it is normal for the researcher to say that anything said will be treated as confidential and not linked to the informant. But such anonymity might need to be qualified: for example, if a researcher finds that some of the bullying behaviour disclosed is serious, continuing, and unknown to adults or staff in the school, they should report this (consulting with the child concerned on how to do this, but not on whether to do this). Such a qualification to anonymity needs to be made clear to a child or young person at the start of an interview – many may already be familiar with such a procedure.

There are specific ethical concerns about some of the methods for obtaining data. One relates to peer nominations, where it has been suggested that the elicitation of peer-nominations of negative behaviours or victim traits may lead children to then behave differently towards peers nominated in this way. However, to date research has found little evidence to support this claim (Mayeux, Underwood & Risser, 2007). Another concern is about observations in the playground: do children need to be informed they are being observed, and might this change their behaviour as a consequence? These issues are discussed by Tapper and Boulton (2002) and Yuile et al. (2006). Legitimate ethical concerns need to be balanced with the knowledge that playground behaviour is in a sense 'public', and that there is a long-term benefit to gathering reliable and valid information on bullying behaviours. Tapper and Boulton (2002) obtained general parental consent for covert video recording in the playground, and the children were aware that their behaviour was sometimes being observed, but they were not told on which specific days this was happening.

A useful resource for ethical issues in working with young people, from the children's charity Barnado's (www.barnados.org.uk), is Alderson and Morrow's *Ethics, Social Research and Consulting with Children and Young People* (2004). This predates the growth of internet-based research, and a general guide to the ethics of research using the internet is available from the British Psychological Society (www.bps.org.uk) in *Conducting Research on the Internet: Guidelines for Ethical Practice in Psychological Research Online.*

Summary

Most studies on bullying have used self-reports. While convenient, this has its drawbacks, most seriously if other measures (for example, correlates of bullying) are also based on self-reports. Peer nominations are also widely used, with a recent development into network analysis. Teacher and parent reports are less widely used. Teacher reports may be more useful for younger children, and peer nominations for older children. It is widely advocated that studies should be multi-informant based, but this is relatively seldom achieved.

Again, most studies have used questionnaires. There are many issues around the use of questionnaires which are not always well attended to. Sometimes, it is not clear if bullying is really being measured rather than aggression generally. In their analysis of 44 cyberbullying questionnaires, Berne et al. (2013; see also

Frisén et al., 2013) found that this confusion between bullying and aggression was a particularly common issue in the cyber domain. Many did not take account of repetition, with a majority of instruments taking any occurrence, or just once or twice, as a cut-off. Only 13 out of 44 instruments mentioned imbalance of power. There was also great variation in the time reference period used. Finally, most instruments contained quite limited evidence on reliability and validity.

Questionnaires and nomination methods provide quantitative data. There are a variety of more qualitative methods available – interviews, focus groups, diaries – but these have been relatively little used and are arguably underexploited. Even quantitative questionnaire studies often do not exploit the potential of open-ended questions, which are relatively easy to add and content analyse. The paucity of observational data is more easy to understand, due to the difficulty of obtaining these and problems in going beyond physical bullying. The possibility of combining observations with participant interviews (used in studies of play, for example: see Boulton, 1992, or Smith, Smees & Pellegrini, 2004, for use of video playback and interview) has apparently not been used.

Studying bullying in children of preschool age, below around 6 years old, poses problems not only because they cannot be given the normal kind of questionnaires, but also because the concept of bullying may be less appropriate for them. Nevertheless, this is a vital age group to study for the origins of later bullying problems.

Finally, ethical issues need to be carefully considered, whatever measurement approaches are used.

FOUR

Basic knowledge about school bullying and cyberbullying

A lot of basic knowledge about school bullying has been acquired over the last twenty-five years, and cyberbullying over the last ten. This chapter discusses the prevalence of bullying, age and gender differences, various types of bullying, where it happens, how long it lasts, and attitudes towards bullying. As cyberbullying (or online bullying) has distinctive features, it is considered to be somewhat independent of what is often called traditional (or offline) bullying. Changes over time are also considered – both changes in individuals (individual stability in roles, school transitions, developmental trajectories) and secular trends (historical changes). Finally, there is a section on cultural differences.

Prevalence of bullying/victimisation

Meta-analyses and comparative studies

Chapter 3 described a range of methods for assessing bullying, and also a range of issues relevant to the figures actually obtained. The actual prevalence figures reported in a survey or research study can vary hugely, independent of the actual phenomenon. Even when solely considering questionnaires, prevalence figures will be influenced by what definition is used or behaviours given, what time span is being asked about, what frequency is regarded as bullying, and the time of giving a questionnaire in the school or calendar year. All these issues often make it difficult to make comparisons across different studies. They also mean that absolute prevalence figures are rather meaningless when taken in isolation.

In an attempt to generalise over many studies, Cook, Williams, Guerra and Kim (2010) examined quantitative studies of school bullying published from 1999 to 2006. A search revealed 82 studies that met the criteria for a meta-analysis. Sample sizes varied from 44 to 26,420! Of the 82 studies, 45 were in Europe, 21 in the United States and 16 in other locations. The majority, 61 studies, used self-report data, 13 peer report, and 8 teacher or parent report. About half (38) used a definition-based survey, and the other 44 a behaviour-based survey. Worryingly, the time referent period was not reported in 27 studies, but was the past year in 18, the past six months in 15, the past 30 days in 15, and the past week in 7.

Cook et al. provided both weighted (by sample size) and unweighted average prevalence rates. Broadly speaking, these were around 20% for bullies, 23% for victims and 8% for bully/victims. There was a high variability in figures across studies, but overall these are quite high figures. This may reflect a lack of consistency between studies as to how often bullying had to happen in order to be included. The time referent period was analysed as a variable, but the frequency within a time period was not; the authors seem to have taken an average of this, if more than one frequency criterion was reported in a study (2010: 350). This means that bullying that only happened 'once or twice' in a time referent period was probably included in a number of studies.

Cook and colleagues did, however, examine the influence of some factors on the prevalence figures obtained. First, *informant source*: peer nomination methods produced lower bully and victim rates than either self- or teacher/parent reports (but no difference for bully/victim rates). Second, *time referent period*: figures for all three roles naturally increased from 'past week' to 'past 30 days' and again to 'past six months', although 'past year' was no higher than 'past 30 days'. Third, *bullying measurement approach*: a definition-based approach gave higher prevalence rates for bullies, but a behaviour-based approach gave higher rates for victims and bully/victims. Fourth, *location of study*: bully rates were lower in the United States while victim and bully/victim rates were higher in other locations.

Two other large-scale sources of prevalence data come from the World Health Organisation (WHO) surveys on Health Behaviour in School-aged Children (HBSC) and the EU KidsOnline project. These have a substantial focus on differences between countries, which will be discussed later; here we shall look at the overall prevalence figures.

The HBSC surveys

The HBSC surveys collect data from 11, 13 and 15 years olds from nationally representative samples every four years, starting in 1993/1994: there is a minimum of 1,500 respondents per year group in each participating country. These are classroom-based, anonymous, self-report questionnaire surveys. The reports on bullying are based on a single victim item and a single bully item, adapted from the Olweus questionnaire (see Chapter 3), which asks about experiences over the past couple of months, with the five standard response options. Victim or bully rates are calculated from 'at least two or three times in the past couple of months' or more (thus ignoring 'it only happened once or twice'). A standard definition of bullying is given (mentioning repetition and imbalance of power).

Craig et al. (2009) provide findings from the 2005/2006 survey. This data set is from 40 countries, mostly European, but also including the United States, Canada, the Russian Federation and Ukraine. The rates for bullying others average out at 10.7%, and for being bullied (victims) at 12.6%, with 3.6% scoring as bully/victims. Currie et al. (2012) provide data from the 2009/2010 HBSC survey. This data set is from 38 countries, again mostly European, but also including the United States, Canada, the Russian Federation, Armenia and Ukraine. The rates for bullying others average out at 10.3%, and for being bullied (victims) at 11.3% (there was no separate category for bully/victims).

It can be seen that there is a slight decrease in figures between the two surveys, a trend discussed further in the latter section of this chapter. It is also noticeable that these figures are less than half the level from the Cook, Williams, Guerra and Kim (2010) review. Age and gender trends are also reported. For bullying others, there was some increase between ages 11 and 15 in many countries, and boys were more involved in almost all countries. For being bullied, there was some decline between ages 11 and 15 in most countries, and boys were more involved, but only significantly so in a minority of countries (Currie et al., 2012).

The EU Kids Online survey

Livingstone, Haddon, Görzig and Ólafsson (2011) reported findings on traditional bullying and cyberbullying from 25 European countries, from the EU Kids Online survey carried out in spring/summer 2010. The samples were based on random stratified sampling of some 1,000 children, 9–16 years old, in each country. Self-report survey questionnaires were given face-to-face in children's homes. The survey was on internet use, risks and safety. A section on bullying did not use the term 'bullying', but started with a statement:

> Sometimes children or teenagers say or do hurtful or nasty things to someone and this can often be quite a few times on different days over a period of time. For example, this can include: teasing someone in a way this person does not like; hitting, kicking or pushing someone around; leaving someone out of things.

The interviewer explained that these activities could be face-to-face, or via mobile phone calls or texts, or on the internet. A range of activities was therefore covered, as well as the repetition criterion, although the imbalance of power criterion was not explicitly mentioned. The child or young person was then asked whether someone had acted in this hurtful or nasty way to them in the past 12 months via these three types of activities. Following on from this they were asked if they themselves had acted in a hurtful or nasty way to others in the last year. Responses were scored as more than once a week, once or twice a month, less often than that, or never.

Across the entire sample of European countries, perpetrator or bullying rates averaged 12%. Only 2% said this had happened more than once a week, and another 3% once or twice a month, with 7% responding that it was less often. There was very little gender difference (with boys slightly higher at 3% in the more than once a week category), and bully rates increased somewhat with age.

Again across the whole sample, victim rates averaged 19%. Only 5% said this had happened more than once a week, and another 4% once or twice a month, with 10% responding that it was less often. Victim rates were slightly higher in girls, and increased slightly with age.

If one disregards experiences that were less frequent than once or twice a month, then bully prevalence is 5% and victim prevalence is 9%. These are lower than the HBSC findings with a corresponding frequency cut-off (and of course much lower than the figures from the Cook, Williams, Guerra and Kim meta-analysis). The HBSC figures are about 10% and 11% respectively, so the main discrepancy is the lower prevalence of bullying others in the EU Kids Online findings. This is unexplained, although one possible explanation could be a greater unwillingness to admit to bullying others in a face-to-face interview compared to an anonymous class-based questionnaire.

Examples of some studies in individual countries

As was obvious from the Cook et al. (2010) review mentioned above, there are many prevalence studies on bullying, and many more have been published since their cut-off inclusion date of 2006. Here, just a few surveys published after 2006 are reviewed: these are studies with reasonably large samples, and from a range of countries, to give an idea of the methodologies used and prevalence rates obtained. Some surveys, including oft-cited ones such as Nansel, Overpeck, Pilla, Ruan, Simons-Morton and Scheidt (2001) in the United States, used national data from the HBSC surveys; however, the studies reviewed next used different data sets.

United States

Carlyle and Steinman (2007) reported on data collected through a Primary Prevention Awareness Attitude and Use Survey, developed in Ohio, which assesses adolescent risk behaviours. The data reported were collected in 2003, from 188 schools in Colombus, Ohio. The survey was given to sixth to twelfth graders (about 11–17 years old), with a total of over 78,000 respondents. The sample was mainly White (63%) or African-American (21%).

The questionnaire was given out by trained teachers/school staff and was anonymous. Relevant to bullying were 13 items, asking about the frequency of direct and indirect bullying behaviours during the past year. This was therefore a behaviour-based questionnaire, with seven items on perpetration (for example, 'How often have you told lies or spread false rumours about someone?') and six on being victimised (for example, 'How often has someone physically attacked you?'). Responses were on a four-point scale (never, once, two–three times, four or more times), with only the last point (four or more times) being counted.

The results showed that the overall prevalence for bully was 18.8%, and for victim 20.1%. These figures included 7.4% who were bully/victims. The grade trends showed that bully rates increased up to eighth grade and then declined, being highest in grades 7 through 10: victim rates were highest in grades 6 through 8 and then declined. Males were involved more than females as both bullies and victims. African-American (and a smaller number of Native American) children showed higher prevalence rates for being bullies, and Native American for being victims.

These figures are not national, reflecting one urban area in one US state, but the sample is very large so the age, gender and ethnicity differences are representative of that area. The prevalence figures are quite high: although the authors chose a moderately high frequency criterion (four times or more in the past year), it is not clear that imbalance of power was assessed in this study. For example, an item like 'How often has someone physically attacked you?' measures an aggressive act, but might pick up fights between equals as well as bullying (see Chapter 2). None of the items assessed cyberbullying: awareness of cyberbullying mainly dates from a year or so after this survey was carried out, although some might have already been occurring.

England

Benton (2011) reports findings from a survey carried out by the National Foundation for Educational Research (NFER). These findings were based on 'almost 100 secondary schools' (2011: 6; further details are not given) from 35,311 young people in years 7–13 (so around 11–17 years old). They were asked about seven types of bullying they had experienced 'by people from their school' over the previous 12 months. This looks like a definition-based questionnaire, but details of whether a definition was provided and what response options were used are not given. Nevertheless, it appears that analyses are based on any experience of being bullied, so this is a very lenient frequency criterion. Overall, 44% of the young people said they had been bullied in at least one of the seven ways asked about.

This report contained a large sample of children, but unfortunately many procedural details are missing, including also the year that the data were obtained. The high prevalence figure certainly reflects the likelihood that even single instances of attacks were being picked up in the responses. In fact the author comments that the prevalence rate of 44% 'differs from some other published figures regarding the percentage of pupils who are bullied; for example results from the Tellus4 survey' (Benton, 2011: 7).

The Tellus4 survey (Tellus 4 National Report, 2010) was commissioned by the then Department for Children, Schools and Families. It was carried out in late 2009 with pupils in years 6, 8 and 10 (so around 10–14 years old), from 3,699 schools, and with a total of 253,755 children across England. It included a section on bullying, which started with a definition:

> We'd like to ask you about bulling. Bullying can mean lots of different things to different people. Bullying is when people hurt or pick on you on purpose, for example by teasing you, hitting or kicking you or saying that they will do this. It can involve people taking or breaking your things, making you do something you don't want to do, leaving you out or spreading hurtful and untrue rumours. Bullying can be face to face, by mobile phone or on the internet.

Table 4.1 Percentages of 10–14 year old pupils in England who reported being bullied in the Tellus4 survey of late 2009 (calculated from Figures 3.2 and 3.3 in the original report)

	When it happened			Frequency of bullying	
	In school	*Out of school*		*In school*	*Out of school*
Never	52	79	Never	52	79
More than one year ago	23	7	A few times this year	24	12
In the last year	12	6	Every month	4	2
In the last six months	4	3	Every week	3	1
In the last four weeks	9	5	Most days	11	3
			Every day	5	2

The young person was then asked if they had ever been bullied at school, and if so, whether it was more than one year ago/in the last year/in the last six months/in the last four weeks, and whether this had happened a few times this year/every month/every week/most days/every day. They were similarly asked about being bullied when not in school (including on the journey to school).

Altogether, 48% of young people said they had experienced bullying at some point in school, and 21% said they had experienced it out of school. The proportions responding to various options about when it happened, and how often, are shown in Table 4.1. Looking at the 'in school' figures, which are generally much higher than the 'out of school' figures, and if we take 'every week' as the frequency criterion, then the prevalence rate for victims in school is 19% – a fairly high figure. However, only 13% of pupils said they had been bullied in the previous six months (a common reference period), so some of the 19% must be referring to earlier times. It is also worth noting that the definition used, given above, although it covers a good range of behaviours, does not mention the imbalance of power criterion: thus depending on pupils' understanding of 'bullying', some behaviours not involving imbalance of power may also have been picked up.

The survey found no differences in victim experiences between boys and girls. Victim prevalence was higher in younger children, in children with disabilities, and in White rather than Asian or Black British pupils.

Wales

Bowen and Holcom (2010) carried out a survey on bullying for the Welsh Assembly Government, between April and June 2009, using the OBVQ. Findings were reported for year 6 (*n* = 1,500), year 7 (*n* = 2,275) and year 10 (*n* = 2,154) (so about 11, 12 and 15 years old), from 167 schools. Questions were asked about bullying over the previous two months. Some findings are shown in Table 4.2. The question about bullying others was split into a question on 'bullying others on my own' and a question on 'bullying others as part of a group'.

Table 4.2 Percentages of pupils bullying others and being bullied in Wales (data from Bowen and Holtom, 2010)

	Rarely or never	Once or twice a month	Two or three times a month	About once a week	Several times a week
		Bullying others on my own			
Y6	90	6	2	1	1
Y7	93	4	1	2	<1
Y10	94	3	<1	<1	2
		Bullying others as part of a group			
Y6	82	12	3	1	2
Y7	89	7	2	1	1
Y10	89	7	1	<1	1
		Being bullied			
Y6	69	12	7	6	6
Y7	71	11	7	6	5
Y10	87	7	2	2	2

If we take the 'two or three times a month' criterion as the cut-off, as is usual with the Olweus questionnaire, we get prevalence rates for bullying others of about 4% 'on my own' and also 4% in a group (it is not reported how these overlap), and about 14% as a victim. It is noticeable that the bully rates do not show much change with age, but victim prevalence shows a substantial decrease by year 10. Gender differences were reported as most noticeable in types of bullying rather than in the overall prevalence of being a bully or victim.

Northern Ireland and the Republic of Ireland

RSM McClure Watters (2011) gave the OBVQ to a representative sample of 904 primary and 1,297 post-primary pupils in Northern Ireland in March 2011, asking about experiences in the previous two months. The percentages who reported bullying others, and being bullied, at various frequencies, are shown in Table 4.3. Taking the 'Two or three times a month' frequency as a cut-off, at primary school 3.9% had bullied others and 17.2% had been bullied, and at post-primary 3.4% had bullied others and 11.1% had been bullied.

O'Moore and Minton (2009) gave a questionnaire (with similar wording for the main questions on bullying) to 2,974 post-primary students (aged 12–16 years) from eight schools in the Republic of Ireland. The corresponding figures in Table 4.3 indicate 5.2% of students bullying others and 8.5% being bullied – rather higher figures for bullies and lower figures for victims than in the Northern Ireland sample of equivalent age.

Table 4.3 Percentages of pupils bullying others and being bullied in Northern Ireland (data adapted from RSM McClure Watters, 2011) and from the Republic of Ireland (data from O'Moore and Minton, 2009)

	Only once or twice	Two or three times a month	About once a week	Several times a week
NORTHERN IRELAND				
Bullied others primary	17.6	2.2	1.1	0.6
Bullied others post-primary	17.8	1.6	1.1	0.7
Been bullied primary	22.1	7.7	4.6	4.9
Been bullied post-primary	18.4	4.3	3.3	3.5
REPUBLIC OF IRELAND				
Bullied others post-primary	19.7	2.6	1.6	1.0
Been bullied post-primary	21.7	3.5	2.5	2.5

Hong Kong

Wong, Lok, Lo and Ma (2008) surveyed 47 primary schools in Hong Kong. Although the publication date is 2008, the data were actually gathered in 2001. Altogether 7,025 children in grades 5 and 6 (range 10–14 years) returned questionnaires: 71% were born in Hong Kong while 29% had emigrated from mainland China. Focus groups were first held to construct an indigenous questionnaire. This included questions about bullying others and being bullied in relation to four types of bullying (physical, verbal, social exclusion, extortion) over the past six months. Some results are shown in Table 4.4.

Table 4.4 Percentages of pupils in Hong Kong aged 10–14 years bullying others and being bullied, for four types of bullying (data from Wong et al., 2008)

	Physical	Verbal	Exclusion	Extortion
Bullying others				
Never	75.8	47.9	75.6	90.5
1–5 times	19.4	39.3	19.2	6.7
6–10 times	1.7	5.5	2.3	1.0
11 or above	3.1	7.3	2.9	1.8
Being bullied				
Never	68.3	38.0	71.9	86.8
1–5 times	23.8	41.1	21.2	9.4
6–10 times	3.1	9.1	3.1	1.4
11 or above	4.8	11.7	3.8	2.4

Since the measurement period is six months, a frequency of 1–5 times is less than once a month. By the usual repetition criterion we might take the 6–10 plus 11 or above responses as representing bullying. The authors do not give composite figures over the four types of bullying, but clearly at least 13% of children report bullying others, and 21% report being bullied. Comparison of these figures with others is complicated by issues that often occur in cross-national comparisons (discussed later). We do not know what language the questionnaires were given in, or if in Chinese (Mandarin? Cantonese?) what word(s) were used for *bullying*. Nor do we know whether any definition of *bullying* was given.

Summary of prevalence rates

It is difficult to make any generalisation about prevalence rates, beyond saying that a substantial minority of children and young people are involved in bullying others or being bullied. But how large are those minorities?

Some studies seem to suggest figures of around 20–25% in each role (for example, Carlyle & Steinman, 2007; Cook, Williams, Guerra & Kim, 2010). This seems very alarming – are nearly half of children really involved in bullying (as bullies or as victims)? However, these figures are probably picking up some acts which are not bullying, by the definitional criteria of repetition and imbalance of power. It is apparent (for example in Tables 4.2, 4.3 and 4.4) that many pupils experience occasional aggressive acts. Every now and then a pupil might receive an insult or a shove, or feel left out. But this is not bullying unless it happens repeatedly (two or three times a month is a common cut-off), and unless there is some indication of an imbalance of power (either through the wording of items, or by giving a defined term of *bullying* or a term of similar meaning). Other studies (for example, HBSC, which included a standard definition) give figures of around 10–12% in each role. Yet others (for example, the EU Kids Online) give figures of around 5–9%. These are still substantial minorities, but seem more realistic.

Despite the difficulties associated with prevalence figures, such information is important for three main purposes. First, reports of prevalence can be crucial in awareness raising and associated publicity when concern about the topic of school bullying is lacking. Second, within a study meaningful comparisons can be made by age, gender, ethnicity and other risk characteristics (see Chapter 5). Third, prevalence figures are necessary for monitoring and evaluating the effects of school-based interventions (see Chapter 6).

Age differences in traditional bullying

The studies above have generally reported age changes. There is a shift with age away from physical bullying and toward indirect and relational bullying (Rivers & Smith, 1994), in line with general findings on aggression (Björkqvist et al., 1992). There are also changes in the prevalence of bullying roles. In a meta-analysis of 153 studies, Cook, Williams, Guerra, Kim and Sadek (2010) found a correlation of age with bully role of 0.09, but with bully/victim role of –0.01; and with victim role of –0.01; however, these are linear trends, and some trends are more complex.

Usually, self-report surveys suggest no decline or some increase with age in bullying others, during the mid-adolescent years (for example, from 11–15 in the HBSC study). Pepler et al. (2006), in a cross-sectional study in Canada of pupils from the sixth to eighth grade (elementary school) to the ninth to twelfth grade (high school), found that bullying others first increased, then declined, with a peak in the ninth grade (the beginning of high school). Bullying others was related to sexual harassment, which also peaked in the ninth grade, although this was followed by a slower age decline.

As far as being a victim is concerned, many reports find a decrease with age (the only exception above being the EU Kids Online survey). Smith, Madsen and Moody (1999) showed that most large self-report surveys showed a fairly steady downward trend in self-reports of being a victim through ages 8–16. They examined four hypotheses to explain this age-related decline: (1) younger children have more children older than them in school, who are in a position to bully them; (2) younger children have not yet been socialised into understanding that you should not bully others; (3) younger children have not yet acquired the social and assertiveness skills to deal effectively with bullying incidents and discourage further bullying; (4) younger children have a different definition of what bullying is, which changes as they get older. The authors suggested there was support for both (1) and (3), (2) appeared to have little impact before age 15, while (4) might explain high rates of report in children under 9 years old. However, peer nomination data do not give such clear age decreases in victim rates (Salmivalli, 2002).

Even if older pupils are less likely to experience being bullied, an exception to this may occur during the transition between primary and secondary school: here Pellegrini and Long (2002) highlighted an increase in being bullied experienced by pupils of both sexes, possibly due to disruptions in friendships and peer group affiliations brought about through a change in school environment.

Gender differences in traditional bullying

It is very commonly reported that boys are more likely to be involved in bullying others than are girls (for example, HBSC survey; Pepler et al., 2006). Gender differences are more variable in terms of being a victim: the usual finding is that boys again are more involved (for example, HBSC survey), but some studies find little difference, and the EU Kids Online survey found victim rates slightly higher in girls. In their meta-analysis of 153 studies, Cook, Williams, Guerra, Kim and Sadek (2010) found a correlation of gender (boys) with bully role of 0.18, with bully/victim role of .10, and with victim role of 0.06.

Gender differences vary according to type of bullying, however. Most studies find boys are more likely to be involved in physical forms of victimisation, while bullying among girls is more likely to be either relational or verbal (Besag, 2006; Crick & Grotpeter, 1995). For example, the study by Wong et al. (2008) in Hong Kong found boys more involved in both bullying others and being bullied by physical means, but no gender differences for verbal bullying or social exclusion.

Generally, this is explained in terms of how each gender can most effectively bully others of the same gender. Boys tend to be physically stronger than girls, and physical strength and prowess are more valued in boys' groups, therefore demonstrating greater physical strength is an effective strategy for the bully. In contrast, girls tend to be better in verbal skills, and value reputation in relationships: passing negative rumours about someone is a more effective strategy for the female bully (Besag, 2006).

Witnesses, bystanders and defenders

Many pupils witness bullying. For example, surveying 12–16 year old English students, Rivers et al. (2009) found that 63% reported having witnessed peers being bullied over the previous nine weeks. But what do witnesses of bullying do? In their Finnish sample, Salmivalli, Lagerspetz et al. (1996) found that, according to peer nominations, around 26% of pupils assisted or reinforced the bully, around 24% did nothing or were outsiders, and around 17% were defenders, helping the victim in some way.

O'Connell, Pepler and Craig (2001) and Hawkins, Pepler and Craig (2001) used their observational methodology (see Chapter 3) to videofilm peers' actions in playground bullying episodes seen among 6–12 year old Canadian children. They found peers to be present in most episodes (88% in Hawkins et al., 2001). O'Connell et al. (2001) found that for about 54% of the time, witnesses acted as passive bystanders (which they took as passively reinforcing the bullying); about 21% of the time, witnesses became reinforcers by actively encouraging the bullying; and about 25% of the time discouraged it. Hawkins et al. (2001) analysed a further 65 episodes where witnesses acted as defenders in this way (19% of all episodes, in this sample). For girls, this intervention was most often by verbal assertion, while boys used physical assertion as much as verbal assertion. These actions were most often directed at the bully. Boys were more likely to intervene when boys were involved, and girls when girls were involved, but there was no gender difference in the likelihood of intervening. Of these interventions, 57% were judged to be effective in stopping the bullying (26% were ineffective, and for 17% this could not be determined).

Most studies of defending, however, have used self-reports or peer nominations. These tend to show more reports of, or nominations for, defending in younger than older pupils, and for girls more than boys. These are similar to the age and gender differences found for attitudes to bullying (see later in this chapter) and for interest in peer support systems (see Chapter 6). For example, Rigby and Johnson (2006) showed a video depicting bullying in the presence of bystanders to late primary and early secondary school students in Australia: 43% indicated that they were likely to help the victim. Girls reported more defending behaviour than boys. Other significant predictors of defender behaviour included being in a younger age group (namely primary school), having rarely or never bullied others, having (reportedly) previously intervened, a positive attitude to victims, and believing that parents and friends (but not teachers) expected them to act to support victims.

Types of bullying

Usually some four or five main types of bullying behaviour have been distinguished (see Chapter 3), namely physical, verbal, social exclusion and rumour spreading, and more recently, cyberbullying. However, studies have varied; for example, Bouman et al. (2012) used a separate damaging property category, and Wong et al. (2008) did not include indirect relational in their Hong Kong study, but did include extortion, defined as 'asking for money or other's property' (see Table 4.4). Findings from some more detailed studies are considered below.

Del Barrio et al. (2008) reported data on 14 types of bullying from a survey of Spanish students. They gave questionnaires to a nationally representative sample of 3,000 pupils from 300 secondary schools in 2006 (a similar survey had been given in 1999 – see the later section on time trends). Regional languages were used (for example, Basque, Catalan, Galician) where appropriate. Victim rates were calculated for bullying being experienced 'often' or 'always': it is not clear whether a definition of bullying was given, or what the time referent period was, so the rather high victim figures obtained may reflect general experiences of being aggressed against.

From a victim perspective, types of bullying experienced were spreading negative rumours (31.6%), being insulted (27.1%), being called offensive names (26.7%), having belongings hidden (16.0%), being ignored (10.5%), not being allowed to participate (8.6%), being threatened/scared (6.4%), having belongings stolen (6.3%), being cyberbullied through a mobile phone or the internet (5.0%), being hit (3.9%), having belongings damaged (3.5%), being sexually harassed (0.9%), being blackmailed (0.6%), and being threatened with weapons (0.5%).

The study in England by Benton (2011) asked respondents about seven types of bullying: verbal, physical, being left out, property damaged/stolen, racism, sexual and cyber. The most common was verbal (both genders), and the next being left out (especially for girls); these were followed by physical (especially for boys) and property, cyber was less frequent, and sexual the least. There was a general decrease in victimisation with age for verbal, physical, being left out and property, but there was no clear decrease or increase with age in cyber and sexual. For a reason not explained in the report, such data on racist bullying were not explored.

The study by Bowen and Holcom (2010) in Wales also reported on seven types of bullying behaviours. Taking 'two or three times a month' as the cut-off, the relative rates in year 6 and year 10 are shown in Table 4.5. This also shows verbal bullying and rumour spreading to be most often reported, with a similar ranking for the two age groups.

A comprehensive national sample of data from Finland was analysed by Salmivalli and Pöyhönen (2012). Internet-based questionnaires were filled in at school by 17,627 students, aged 8–15 years, from 156 schools representing all five provinces of mainland Finland. Data were collected in May 2007 (grades 3, 4 and 5) and May 2008 (grades 7 and 8). The questionnaire gave the standard Olweus definition including repetition and power imbalance. For each of nine types of

Table 4.5 Percentages of pupils in Wales who reported different types of bullying experienced, from year 6 and year 10 (data from Bowen and Holcom, 2010)

Type of bullying	Year 6	Year 10
Called names or teased in a hurtful way	20	12
Lies or rumours spread about me	16	7
Left out of things on purpose, excluded or totally ignored	15	6
Mean names, comments or gestures that had a sexual meaning	10	5
Being hit, kicked or pushed	7	4
Threatened or forced to do things I didn't want to do	6	3
Money or other things taken away from me or damaged	4	2

bullying, students were asked how frequently they had been bullied during the previous few months: a cut-off criterion of at least two to three times a month was used. The rates reported were verbal (9.2%), sexual (7.1%), social exclusion (5.6%), spreading lies and nasty rumours (4.9%), physical (3.8%), racist (3.0%), cyber (2.0%), threatened/forced (1.6%), and taken or damaged property (1.3%). Notable here is the relatively high reporting of sexual bullying (mainly in the older students), which possibly represents a heightened awareness of the inappropriateness of such behaviour in Finland.

Perhaps surprising in these data sets from Spain, England, Wales and Finland is the comparatively low rate of physical bullying reported. The survey by Wong et al. (2008) in Hong Kong (see Table 4.4) showed verbal bullying to be most frequent (a very common finding), but with physical coming second, and then social exclusion and extortion.

In fact, physical forms of aggression (and bullying-like behaviours) are more frequent in nursery and primary age children, but decline by middle childhood. An example of data from a younger age group is provided by Monks, Smith and Sweltenham(2005). They used peer nominations, with four cartoon sketches of types of aggression or bullying, as more appropriate for a younger age group (see Chapter 3). Their sample was 104 children aged 4–6 years from reception classes and first grade classes in four primary schools in London. Some data on nominations for being a victim of four types of aggression/bullying, by gender, are shown in Table 4.6. At this age, physical is the most common, followed by verbal. Younger children are less likely to be identified as involved in social exclusion or rumour spreading. Some types of indirect and relational bullying probably require cognitive and verbal skills which are more available in older children.

Tremblay (2003) argues that younger children have not yet been socialised into learning that physical aggression is not normally acceptable. The majority of pre-schoolers are physically aggressive at times, but most learn how to control their aggression as they get older; thus he finds a peak in physical aggression at around 3 or 4 years old, which then decreases. Of course, in some older children those who bully others may not be too worried about what is socially acceptable, but even so, physical bullying may be more obvious and easy to detect by teachers in the school, so that other methods may come to be preferred.

Table 4.6 Mean number of peer nominations for each type of victimisation received by boys and girls aged 4–6 years (data from Monks et al., 2005)

	Physical	Verbal	Social exclusion	Rumour spreading
Male	1.58	1.09	0.78	0.71
Female	1.90	1.66	1.32	0.95

Overlap of types of bullying

Pupils may experience several types of bullying, and a systematic study of this aspect was carried out by Wang, Iannotti, Luk and Nansel (2010). They used data from the HBSC survey in the USA in 2005–2006, with students in sixth to tenth grade. Latent class analysis suggested that three models provided a good fit to explain the co-variation across the five different types of victimisation assessed. These were *all-types victims*, who scored highly on physical, verbal, social exclusion and rumour spreading, and moderately high on cyber as well; *verbal/relational victims*, who scored highly on verbal, social exclusion and rumour spreading; and *non-victims*, who were low on all types. Gender and ethnicity differences were not very marked for these three groups, but (consistent with general age trends) younger students were more likely to be verbal/relational victims, and older students to be non-victims.

Cyberbullying and its features

Cyberbullying refers to bullying carried out via electronic media – namely mobile phones and the internet. The rapid diffusion of mobile phones, and use of the internet, this century, were shown by Rideout, Foehr and Roberts (2010; see www.kff.org) in representative US samples of 8–18 year olds surveyed in 1999, 2004 and 2009. In 1999 there was no question on mobile phones at all, and in 2004 only one asking mobile *or* landline phones, but in 2009 time spent in a typical day with mobile phones was 1.33 hours texting and 0.33 hours talking. The average number of hours spent on a computer was 0.27 in 1999, 1.02 in 2004 and 1.29 in 2009.

Types and forms of cyberbullying

There are various methods of cyberbullying. Rivers and Noret (2010) started a survey in 2002, and at that time only assessed text message and e-mail bullying. Li (2007) distinguished between e-mail, chatroom and mobile phone bullying. Smith et al. (2008) used seven main media described by secondary school pupils: bullying by mobile phone calls, text messages, picture/video clip bullying, e-mails, chatroom, instant messaging and websites. Hinduja and Patchin (2010) used a nine-item cyber victimisation scale, covering similar media. Cyberbullying in internet game contexts is another form: one study found this to be especially common in South Korea (Tippett & Kwak, 2012).

Looking at the types of action, Willard (2006) described seven categories: flaming, online harassment, cyberstalking, denigration (put-downs), masquerade, outing and exclusion. These are to some extent independent of the media used. Rivers and Noret (2010) described the content of abusive text messages and e-mails. Their 10 main categories were: threat of physical violence, abusive or hate-related, name calling (including homophobia), death threats, ending of platonic relationship(s), sexual acts, demands/instructions, threats to damage existing relationships, threats to home/family, and menacing chain messages.

Pyzalski (2012) listed 20 categories of 'electronic aggression' in a study in Poland. He also looked at the recipients of cyber-aggression, in a sample of 2,143 pupils around 15 years old. Although many of these were other young people known to the perpetrator offline (often in school), many were also known only from the internet, or were just attacked randomly. Other prominent categories were former girlfriends/boyfriends, groups (for example, fans of a certain pop group or football team), celebrities, vulnerable people, and school staff or other known adults. Over the last year nearly two-thirds of the students had undertaken at least one cyber aggressive act against one of these recipients, although as Pyzalski is careful to point out, many of these would have been single acts with no obvious imbalance of power, so would not constitute cyberbullying.

As technology develops, new forms of cyberbullying emerge. The advent of smart phones that can access the internet made the earlier distinction between mobile phone and internet bullying less obvious. These bullying contexts are not restricted to young people, any more than is traditional bullying, and some forms have been mainly described in adults: for example, cyberbullying or 'griefing' in virtual worlds (Coyne, Chesney, Logan & Madden, 2009).

Distinctive features of cyberbullying

Although there are many similarities between traditional bullying and cyberbullying, the latter tends to have some particular characteristics. A number of commentators have discussed these (Dooley et al., 2009; Smith, 2012; Tokunaga, 2010; Vandebosch & van Cleemput, 2008). They include the following:

- It depends on some degree of technological expertise: although it is easy enough to send e-mails and text messages, more sophisticated attacks such as masquerading (pretending to be someone else posting denigrating material on a website) require more skill.
- It is primarily indirect rather than face-to-face. Thus there is a certain 'invisibility' to those doing the bullying. A perpetrator may try to withhold identification in text or internet postings to maintain anonymity. Smith et al. (2008) reported that about one in five victims did not know who it was that had

cyberbullied them, and Vandebosch and van Cleemput (2008) found that half of victims did not know who the cyberbully was.

- Relatedly, the perpetrator does not usually see the victim's reaction, at least in the short term. On the one hand, this can enhance moral disengagement from the victim's plight and thus might make cyberbullying easier; without such direct feedback there may be fewer opportunities for empathy or remorse (see Chapter 5). On the other hand, many perpetrators enjoy the feedback of seeing the suffering of the victim, and would not get this satisfaction so readily by cyberbullying.
- The variety of bystander roles in cyberbullying is more complex than in most traditional bullying. There can be three main bystander roles rather than one: the bystander is with the perpetrator when an act is sent or posted; the bystander is with the victim when it is received; or the bystander is with neither, but receives the message or visits the relevant internet site.
- Relatedly, one motive for bullying is thought to be the status gained by showing (abusive) power over others in front of witnesses. The perpetrator will often lack this in cyberbullying, unless steps are taken to tell others what has happened or to publicly share the material.
- The breadth of the potential audience is increased. Over time, cyberbullying can reach particularly large audiences in a peer group compared with the small groups that are the usual audience in traditional bullying. For example, when nasty comments are posted on a website, the audience that may see these comments is potentially very large.
- It is difficult to escape from cyberbullying as there is 'no place to hide'. Unlike traditional forms of bullying, where once the victim gets home they are away from the bullying until the next day, cyberbullying is more difficult to escape from: the victim may continue to receive text messages or e-mails, or view nasty postings on a website, wherever they are.

These are important distinctions that may impact particularly on both the motives for (cyber)bullying and the impact such acts have on the (cyber)victim (see Chapter 5). However, they should not be overstated: some forms of traditional bullying (such as rumour spreading) are not face-to-face, for example. A case can also be made that these distinctive features are differences in degree rather than differences in kind (Pyzalski, 2011).

Prevalence of cyberbullying

Given the diversity in definition and measurement, it is not surprising that the reported prevalence of cyberbullying varies just as widely as for traditional bullying. In addition, the date of a study is especially important (even though this is often not given!).

The EU Kids Online survey (Livingstone et al., 2011), carried out in 2010, found that across European countries, bullying others was reported by 3% on the internet (this was mostly on a social networking site or by instant messaging), and by 2% using a mobile phone. This compared with 10% who reported face-to-face or offline bullying. For experiences of being a victim, this was reported by 6% on the internet (again mostly on a social networking site or by instant messaging), and by 3% using a mobile phone. This compared with 13% who reported being bullied face-to-face or offline.

Genta et al. (2012) reported findings from a cross-national study of 12–15 year olds in Italy, Spain and England, carried out in 2008. They compared mobile and internet cyberbullying over the previous two months, using an Olweus-type definition. Percentages for severe (two or three times a month or more) mobile bullying ranged across the three countries from 0.9–2.7%, and internet bullying from 1.0–1.6%: for mobile victim from 0.5–2.2%, and internet victim from 1.3–2.6%. Olweus (2012a) reported similarly low figures from large surveys carried out in the USA and Norway from 2007–2010. In the USA, rates of being cyberbullied were around 4.1%–5.0%, and of cyberbullying others 2.5%–3.2%. In Norway, rates for being cyberbullied were around 3.2%–4.2%.

Some other researchers find these low figures difficult to believe, and report much higher figures. For example, in a commentary on Olweus (2012a), Hinduja and Patchin (2012a) stated that 'Olweus' findings that 4.1–5.0% of youth have been cyberbullied and 2.5–3.2% of youth have cyberbullied others are simply out of line with the weight of the available evidence' (2012a: 541). They cite their own work as an example, with about 20% of 11–18 year olds having been victims of cyberbullying (Hinduja & Patchin, 2012b). In a review of 35 published articles, they found on average 24% of pupils had been cyberbullied and 17% had cyberbullied others. As another example of high percentages, we can take a study in Turkey by Arslan, Savaser, Hallett and Balci (2012). They sampled 372 children aged 8–11 years, from three primary schools (the date of the study is not given). Using a definition-based questionnaire, they reported that 17.5% of the children had cyberbullied others, and 27.4% had been cyberbullied.

In a response to Hinduja and Patchin's (2012a) criticism, Olweus (2012b) pointed out the importance of the time reference period and frequency criterion. The figures cited by Hinduja and Patchin cover whether someone has ever been involved in cyberbullying (similarly, Arslan et al., 2012, asked 'Have you ever been cyberbullied by other people?'). On the other hand, the studies producing smaller figures generally ask about the last month or term (or year, in EU Kids Online).

Similarly, the frequency criterion is crucial. As another example, O'Moore and Minton (2009) reported separate data on cyberbullying frequencies, shown in Table 4.7 (this is a subset of the data on general bullying shown in Table 4.3). The date of the survey was not given but appears to be around 2008; the questions referred to experiences in the previous few months. Taking the standard 'two or three times a month' criterion, frequencies of cyberbullying others and being cyberbullied are 1.6% and 2.8% respectively. However, the authors prefer to highlight the figures of 8.7% and 14.2% obtained by including those for whom it only happened once or twice, and this obviously gives substantially higher figures.

Table 4.7 Percentages of 12–16 year old pupils in the Republic of Ireland, cyberbullying others and being cyberbullied (data from O'Moore and Minton, 2009)

	Only once or twice	Two or three times a month	About once a week	Several times a a week
Cyberbullied others	7.1	0.6	0.5	0.5
Been cyberbullied	11.4	1.1	0.8	0.9

Both the frequency criterion and the time reference period are crucial to the kinds of prevalence rates obtained; but other factors are also likely to contribute to the very wide range of prevalence figures reported. One is the definition of cyberbullying or cyber-aggression used – does it include repetition, and/or imbalance of power? Rates of cyber-aggression can be expected to exceed cyberbullying, more strictly defined. The nature of the sample is obviously important, and this may vary by country or culture, age and gender, as well as other demographic characteristics. Also, what behaviours are sampled? Earlier surveys, such as Rivers and Noret's (2010), only assessed text message and e-mail bullying; later surveys have used a much broader range. The date of a survey is very important in such a fast developing and changing area. Bullying through websites, and specifically through social networking sites, has recently become a common form as social networking escalates in popularity in the adolescent years (Patchin & Hinduja, 2010; Tippett & Smith, submitted).

Age differences in cyberbullying

We know little about when children start cyberbullying, and most studies have focused on the middle or secondary/high school age ranges. There have been some variations in reports, but the review by Tokunaga (2010) argued that there is a curvilinear relationship, with the greatest prevalence in the seventh and eighth grades (around 13–15 years old). This appears to be consistent with much of the literature, and suggests a slightly later age peak than is found for traditional bullying. Ševčíková and Šmahel (2009) reported on being an aggressor or target amongst persons from a wide age range (12–88 years old) in the Czech Republic. They found the 12–15 year age group most involved as aggressors, and the 16–19 and 20–26 year old age groups most often involved as targets, although both roles were present throughout older age groups including 50 plus.

Gender differences in cyberbullying

The area of gender differences in cyberbullying has been accurately described as 'fraught with inconsistent findings' (Tokunaga, 2010: 280). Examples can be found of boys being more involved than girls (for example, Calvete et al., 2010), few or no significant differences (for example, Smith et al., 2008), and girls being more involved than boys (for example, Rivers & Noret, 2010). Overall, there may be relatively greater involvement of girls in cyberbullying, just as there is in relational bullying, when compared to traditional physical (mainly boys) or verbal bullying, which is consistent with seeing cyberbullying as more similar to relational bullying.

Both age and gender differences may vary by the different media for cyberbullying, cultural background and historical time; for example, in recent years girls in some countries, including the UK, are particularly involved in social networking sites such as Facebook, and thus more at risk of cyberbullying involvement in that medium (National Family Week Survey, 2010).

Bias, prejudice or identity-based bullying

Identity-based characteristics such as race, religion or belief, disability, sexual orientation, gender or gender identity can be used as a pretext for bullying behaviours, and also be manifested in the kinds of behaviour (such as insulting words) based on these characteristics. Often based on stereotyped views of particular social groups, these are also referred to as bias bullying or prejudice-related bullying. They are not only targeted at an individual, but also reflect negative attitudes towards a wider sub-community or group whom that individual identifies with (or is believed to identify with).

Racist bullying

Bullying which is related to a child's race or ethnicity is commonly referred to as racist bullying. Although racist attitudes can be widespread and can affect children's behaviour, it is not necessarily the case that children from ethnic minority groups are more likely to experience bullying than ethnic majority children. In England, early studies by Moran et al. (1993) and Boulton and Smith (1992) studied Asian and White school pupils in England: both Asian and White pupils had comparable numbers of friends, enjoyed school to an equal degree, and reported the same level of being bullied or bullying others. The only significant difference reported in these studies was that Asian children who had experienced bullying were more likely to have been victimised through racist name calling, which was experienced as hurtful and damaging. Eslea and Mukhtar (2000) surveyed Hindu, Indian Muslim and Pakistani children: about half reported some experience of victimisation, with little variation in involvement by ethnic background. While all three Asian groups were equally likely to be bullied by white children, victims indicated that in most cases the bullies were other Asian children from a differing ethnic group, with the bullying often related to the child's religious or cultural differences.

More recently, Smith, Thompson and Bhatti (2013) investigated the effects of ethnicity on both bullying and cyberbullying in a sample of 11–16 year old pupils in 14 English secondary schools. The data were gathered in 2008. Comparing White, Asian, Mixed and Black ethnic groups, no consistent ethnic differences were found for either traditional (direct, indirect) or cyber (mobile, internet) bully or victim rates.

Tippett, Wolke and Platt (2013) examined ethnicity and bullying involvement in a sample of 10–15 year olds, drawn from the UK Household Longitudinal Study. The survey was conducted between 2009 and 2011, and included questions on physical and relational bullying and victim experiences. White children were not any more involved than other ethnic groups, even when controlling for age, gender, parental qualifications and economic situation. African children were the least likely to be victims, and Caribbean and Pakistani children were most often involved in bullying others – these differences being significant for girls, but not for boys. This study did not cover cyberbullying.

Sawyer et al. (2008) examined racial and ethnic differences in children's reports of being bullied in a US sample. Minority group pupils were less likely than white children to report being the victim of frequent bullying when using a single-item definition based measure; however, using a multi-item behaviour-based measure, minority youth were more likely to report at least one form of being bullied. This suggests there may be cultural differences in the way experiences of bullying are perceived or defined.

Monks, Ortega-Ruiz and Rodríguez-Hildago (2008) examined racist bullying in multi-cultural schools in Spain and the UK. No difference in personal victimisation was found between majority or minority pupils; however, those from minority groups were more likely to experience cultural name calling and social exclusion.

In summary, racist kinds of bullying clearly occur. However, it is not clear whether there are major differences in experiences of bullying among racial groups, although there may be methodological issues around how racist bullying is defined and interpreted by children. Faith-based bullying is a related although under-explored issue: Eslea and Mukhtar (2000) reported some bullying among Hindu, Indian Muslim and Pakistani children that was related to the places in which they worshipped.

Bullying based around gender and gender identity

Some bullying is specifically targeted at an individual's gender and based on sexist attitudes or gender stereotypes. This is commonly referred to as sexist bullying (based on sexist attitudes) or sexual bullying (based on bullying behaviour that has a specific sexual dimension).

Some qualitative studies in England and Wales have reflected on sexual bullying in primary and secondary schools. Sexual harassment of girls by boys mainly took the form of sexually abusive and aggressive language which predominantly centres on a girl's sexual status, for example using terms such as 'bitch', 'slag' etc. (Duncan, 1999; Renold, 2002, 2006).

Research by Besag (2006) and others (see also a review by Jennifer, 2013) shows that girls also engage in sexual bullying of other girls, for example spreading nasty gossip about a girl's sexual reputation, or ridiculing their breast development. A study of Welsh adolescents (Ringrose, 2008a,b) found instances where sexually aggressive terms were used by girls in relation to other girls, in order to regulate their own and others' behaviours in the context of heterosexual competition. Williams (2013) found that girls' use of social networking sites now provides a frequent forum for (mainly) girl-to-girl bullying of this kind. Although less commonly reported than verbal or indirect forms of bullying, physical forms of sexual harassment are also experienced by some girls (Duncan, 2002).

Girls thus may suffer sexual harassment from both other girls and boys, often about appearance and reputation. Boys too can experience these kinds of harassment, but some of this is more likely to reflect comments on sexual orientation. Wolfe, Crooks, Chiodo and Jaffe (2009) suggested that, particularly in early adolescence, gender-role expectations play a central role in young people's peer acceptance. These gender-roles can be enforced through abusive tactics such as gender-based harassment and homophobic bullying, which emerge in the context of other socialisation agents, such as the media.

Bullying based on sexual orientation: homophobic bullying

Homophobic bullying is bullying directed at lesbian, gay or bisexual (LGB) people, or those perceived to be LGB, because of their (real or perceived) sexual orientation. Some studies include transgendered individuals, with prevalence reported for LGBT individuals combined.

A particular issue to consider in measuring homophobic bullying is that some young LGB people may not feel ready to disclose their sexual orientation (Carragher & Rivers, 2002). Several retrospective studies have been conducted with LGB identified adults, asking them about bullying experiences when they were younger. In these reports verbal bullying is usually found to be the most common type of bullying behaviour associated with homophobic bullying (Carragher & Rivers, 2002; ChildLine, 2006; Ellis & High, 2004). This is consistent with general bullying trends. Another similar finding is the gender differences in the types of bullying behaviour experienced by young lesbian girls and gay young men (King et al., 2003). Physical bullying is more commonly experienced by males, whilst indirect or relational bullying appears to be more commonly reported by females.

Surveys of young people who identify themselves as LGB show high rates of victim experiences. One conducted in the UK by Stonewall (Hunt & Jensen, 2007), with 1,145 secondary students who identified themselves as LGB, found that 65% had experienced direct bullying; this figure was even higher in faith schools, at 75%. Even if LGB youths did not directly experience bullying, they reported being in an environment where homophobic language was commonplace. By asking 377 adolescents to list abusive terms they commonly heard at school, Thurlow (2001) found 10% of all abusive language used by 14–15 year olds in Welsh and English schools to be of homophobic origin. Homophobic items were much less common than sexist terms, but were used significantly more than racist pejoratives as a means of insulting fellow pupils. Thurlow (2001) also found that homophobic terms were rated by young people to be less taboo and offensive than racially abusive terms.

Toomey and Russell (2013) identified 18 studies where school-based victimisation was directly compared for sexual minority (LGBT) and heterosexual pupils, and carried out a meta-analysis. The risk of victimisation was significantly higher for LGBT pupils, with an effect size of d = 0.33 (small/moderate). Age was not a moderator in this, but gender was: the effect size was higher for boys than girls. Depressingly, effect sizes were larger for more recent studies (in the 2000s) than older studies (in the 1990s).

The gender difference was confirmed in a longitudinal study in England reported by Robinson, Espelage and Rivers (2013). Their findings were based on a sample of 4,135 young people 13–14 years old in 2004, followed up until 2010 (by which time they had left school). Of the sample 4.5% identified themselves as LGB, and they experienced significantly more victimisation than their heterosexual peers. Over the study's six years there was a fairly steady decrease in victimisation with age in the total sample (in line with the general age trends mentioned earlier). However, the relative risk for LGB young people increased, but for males only. Their odds ratio for increased risk of victimisation increased from 1.78 at the start of the study to 3.95 at the end. For females the odds ratio started at 1.95, but by the end had decreased to 1.18 (not significant). Thus while victimisation experiences were higher for LGB young people, generally they declined with age, whereas the relative risk compared to heterosexual peers got worse for males but better for females.

Robinson et al. (2013) also assessed emotional distress, such as feeling unhappy or depressed. This was higher in LGB young people. Using structural equation modelling, it appeared that about 50% of this greater emotional distress experienced, compared to heterosexual peers, could be attributed to prior victimisation experiences.

In summary, LGB young people are generally at substantially higher risk of being a victim of bullying; this is especially so for males.

Bullying based on disability

Disablist bullying can affect any child who is classed as having a disability: this can be physical or sensory, or refer to learning difficulties. Many studies show high rates of bullying in children with disabilities, but these are most informative when there is a well-matched comparison group. In an early study, Whitney, Smith and Thompson (1994) compared the experiences of 93 special needs children, drawn from eight schools in Sheffield, England, with those of 93 mainstream children, matched for age and year group, school, gender and ethnicity. They found that the special needs children were two to three times more likely to experience being bullied compared to the mainstream children; they were also nearly twice as likely to be involved in bullying others. For example, one girl with a physical disability told the interviewer:

Because of my disability I can't balance and with a heavy tray with my dinner on it I can't balance ... In class they say 'Look Elisabeth's here' and they call me names all the time or they stand up and do impressions of me walking up and down the classroom. (Whitney et al., 1994: 223–224)

This study also compared bullying prevalence among types of special needs. Interestingly, blind or visually impaired children were not at greater risk, but those with moderate learning difficulties and physical disabilities were, and those with a hearing impairment were at the highest risk (although the sample sizes were small in some of these sub-categories).

In Northern Ireland, the survey by RSM McClure Watters (2011) reported on the relationship between involvement in bully/victim problems and disability. Using a lenient criterion (see Table 4.3), the prevalence of being bullied for children with a disability, compared to those without, was higher both in primary school (44.3% vs. 38.6%) and in post-primary school (44.9% vs. 28.2%). The prevalence of bullying others was also higher in primary school (27.8% vs. 20.8%) and post-primary school (29.1% vs. 20.5%) for those with a disability.

A study in Canada by Hamiwka and colleagues (2009) compared the prevalence of bullying in three groups: children with epilepsy, children with chronic kidney disease (CKD) and healthy controls. The children were aged around 12 years and the two medical groups were recruited via clinics and hospitals. Self-report data was gathered via the OBVQ. Victim rates on the 'two or three times per month' criterion were 42% for children with epilepsy compared to 18% for CKD and 21% for healthy controls, while the bully rates were 15%, 10% and 5%, and the bully/victim rates 9%, 5% and 0%, respectively. Children with epilepsy were clearly more at risk of involvement as bullies or victims, compared not only to healthy controls but also to children with CKD – another chronic disease but without the obvious physical symptoms of epilepsy.

A study in the USA by Christensen et al. (2012) compared the experiences of 13 year olds classed as having typical cognitive development (TD) or intellectual disability (ID). They were drawn from a variety of schools, as part of a larger longitudinal study. According to self-report, 62% of ID adolescents reported having been bullied (presumably, ever) compared to 41% of TD adolescents.

In Sweden, Holmberg and Hjern (2008) used the HBSC questionnaire with fourth graders in a municipality in Stockholm. They compared children diagnosed with varying degrees of ADHD with controls. The rates for being bullied were around eight times higher in children with ADHD, and rates for bullying others were around three times higher.

In England, Knox and Conti-Ramsden (2003) examined the risk of bullying among 11 year old pupils with specific language impairments. They found that 36% considered themselves at risk of bullying, compared to 12% of pupils with no language difficulties.

Children with various disabilities are clearly at greater risk of bullying involvement, so why should this be so? There may be three main reasons for this, varying, of course, with the individual and the type of disability. First, for children with disabilities who are in mainstream schools, there are often problems in social acceptance, specifically having few friends and lower quality friendships, negative peer perceptions and social rejection (Mishna, 2003). Nabuzoka and Smith (1993), using peer nominations, found children with learning disabilities were significantly more likely to be nominated as a victim than children without learning disabilities; they also had fewer friends and were more sociometrically rejected in the peer group.

Second, some children with disabilities may lack some social skills that would help in avoiding or coping with bullying. Christensen et al. (2012) found that the greater risk of victimisation for ID adolescents correlated to greater social problems and social withdrawal. The psychosocial characteristics of children with autism and Asperger's syndrome – such as a lack of social skills, and difficulties expressing non-verbal forms of communication – can increase their vulnerability to bullying by peers. Van Roekel, Scholte and Didden (2010) studied Dutch children with autistic spectrum disorder, attending a special school, and found high rates of involvement in bullying; they also found that those involved in bullying were more likely to misinterpret short video clips of peer interaction: those who were victims tended to classify non-bullying situations as bullying, whereas those who were bullies tended to classify bullying situations as non-bullying.

Third, some characteristics of a disability, such as clumsiness or a stammer or poor hearing, may make someone an easy target for those who enjoy bullying others. Children or young people who stutter or stammer can easily be made fun of, as was shown in a study by Hugh-Jones and Smith (1999). They carried out a retrospective study with adult respondents from the British Stammering Association. A majority (83%) had experienced bullying at school, especially those with a more severe stammer.

Children with sensory disabilities may be at greater risk of being bullied, but Whitney et al. (1994) found that this was not the case for visually impaired children. Perhaps visual impairment is something easy to empathise with, as we all know what it is like to be blindfolded or to stumble in the dark, so they might present less of a target for bullies, or bullies might not gain social rewards from bullying visually impaired children if they do not get bystander support. Unfortunately, this understanding does not seem to extend to hearing impaired children, who were at the highest risk in the Whitney et al. (1994) study.

In a qualitative study, Dixon, Smith and Jenks (2004; see also Dixon, 2011) found that deaf children were likely to be considered 'second class citizens' by non-deaf children, and 'put down'. As one mainstream pupil observed:

> ... some of them, like, just put the deaf children down. When the deaf children want to explain something, talk about something, some of the people probably, like, talk over them – enough to say they're nothing. (Dixon et al., 2004: 52–53)

Here some of the explanation for the greater victimisation of deaf children lies with the peer group. However, deaf children may also be more at risk even when they are educated separately from normally hearing children. Bauman (2012) investigated traditional and cyberbullying in 12–19 year old deaf and hearing pupils. She compared two schools in the USA, one a School for the Deaf, using

American Sign Language for instruction, and the other a school sharing the same campus, but for hearing children. She selected 30 children from each, matched for grade, gender and ethnicity. The rates for traditional bullying (both victim and bully) were considerably higher in the deaf children, as was the rate for being a victim of cyberbullying (the rates for being a cyberbully were too small to analyse).

The location and duration of bullying

Location of bullying

The playground is a common location for bullying in school, especially in primary schools. For example, the survey in Wales by Bowen and Holcom (2010) found that in year 4 pupils (around 9 years old), 55% of bullying was reported in the school yard, 24% in the classroom, 14% in the corridors, 13% in the toilets and 12% in the canteen. Areas that are generally less well supervised are where bullying (especially overt bullying) is most likely to happen.

Cyberbullying presents a somewhat different picture, as it is often initiated or received outside school. Smith, Mahdavi et al. (2008) asked secondary school pupils in England if they had ever experienced traditional or cyber bullying inside school, outside school, or both. The figures for traditional bullying were 37.0% for only inside, 4.7% for only outside and 12.4% for both, but for cyberbullying 3.4% for only inside, 11.1% for only outside and 2.6% for both. Many schools place restrictions on mobile phone and internet use within the school premises. But even though cyberbullying may escape school boundaries, it will often be pupils at that school who are involved in the bullying. Smith et al. found that when victims knew who the cyberbully was, for 58% of them the perpetrators were from the same school.

Duration of bullying

Some bullying can last just a few days, while some can go on for years. Questionnaires such as the OBVQ often contain a question about how long a victim has experienced bullying. Sharp, Thompson and Arora (2000) reported some analysis of this, based on data gathered from secondary schools in England. They found that 30.5% of pupils reported being a victim in the previous school term (this was presumably on a lenient criterion including 'just once or twice'): this comprised 15.0% (so nearly half the victims) who said it had lasted less than a week, 7.1% who said it had happened just this half term, 2.2% this term, 1.9% all year and 4.3% more than one year. Longer duration bullying tended to also occur more frequently, and was experienced as more stressful. The short-term bullying was more often social exclusion, while the longer-term bullying was more often being called names, threatened, and having nasty rumours spread.

Smith, Mahdavi et al. (2008) found that for those who were victims of cyber-bullying, most said it had lasted one or two weeks (56.5% of victims), followed by about a month (18.8%), about six months (5.8%), about a year (8.7%) and several years (10.1%).

A consistent pattern here is that about half of all bullying reported appears to be quite short term – perhaps constituting some social exclusion or relatively mild bullying that works itself out after a week or so. However, a substantial amount of bullying goes on for some months. Finally, a small but significant percentage of pupils experience bullying for a year or several years, perhaps for much of their schooling.

Using a Retrospective Bullying Questionnaire (see Chapter 3), Schäfer et al. (2004) asked adults from three countries (Germany, Spain and the UK) for their recollections of being bullied in primary and secondary school. While 72% had no recollections of being bullied at school, 11% remembered being bullied but only in primary school, 9% only in secondary school, and 8% had memories of being bullied in both primary and secondary school. This study did not measure duration in detail, but – consistent with the findings above – about half of those who recollected being victims said that it had lasted for just a few days, while about half said that it had lasted for weeks or months, or even longer.

Attitudes towards bullying

Some questionnaires ask about attitudes towards bullying, in contrast to experiences, and some findings are unexpected. Although most pupils say they do not like bullying, a significant minority do say they could join in bullying. Perhaps surprisingly, these 'pro-bullying' or 'anti-victim' attitudes increase with age up to 14–15 years old (after which they start to decline). This was first shown by Rigby and Slee (1991) in a study of Australian school children, and confirmed in a report by Rigby (1997) based on a survey of primary and secondary school pupils from South Australia. They used an Attitude to Victim Scale, made up of 20 items such as 'I like it when somebody stands up for kids who are bullied', or (negatively scored) 'Nobody likes a wimp'. Thus, high scores mean sympathetic attitudes to victims. They found that attitudes were slightly more sympathetic for girls than boys, but for both boys and girls these sympathetic scores declined steadily from 9–10 years old through to 13–14 (girls) or 15–16 (boys) before rising again slightly at 17–18 years. These findings have been broadly confirmed in Italy and England by Menesini et al. (1997).

Some findings from Olweus and Endresen (1998), on Norwegian students 13–16 years old, suggest that attitudes may vary by gender dyad – specifically, for boys to boys. They did not measure attitudes to bullying as such, but gave empathy scales with items such as 'seeing a [boy][girl] who is sad makes me want to comfort [him][her]'. Girls were more empathic than boys, and their empathy scores increased with age. Boys' scores did not increase with age, specifically when asked about empathic feelings for other boys in distress, but did increase when asked about girls in distress.

In summary, although sympathetic attitudes to victims predominate, they decrease from middle childhood to early or mid-adolescence. Unsympathetic attitudes may be especially marked among boys.

Stability of bully and victim roles

Do children tend to stay in the same roles over time – or, how easy is it to 'exit' a role? There are various ways of looking at the stability of roles such as bully or victim. Given two or more time points in a longitudinal study, one can calculate correlations (for example, in percentage of peer nominations), look at the proportions for those who change role (for example, 'escaped' versus 'continuing' victims), or look at the relative risk of staying in a role (for example, risk of being a victim at time 2, compared to being or not being a victim at time 1). Whichever measure is used, there is consistently found to be some stability in bully and victim roles, but with some variability by age, gender and type of bullying, as well as measurement technique.

Stability tends to be relatively low among young children of nursery or kindergarten age, but increases through the elementary school years. This is especially true of victim status. For example, Kochenderfer-Ladd (2003) gathered self-report data on victimisation from US children in kindergarten, first grade, second grade and third grade. Some stability correlations obtained are shown in Table 4.8. All correlations are statistically significant (the sample size was around 380 children), but from kindergarten to first grade it is only a modest value of 0.26 (in other words, about 7% of the variance is explained in terms of continuity). The stability increases such that between grade 2 and grade 3 it is 0.41 (that is, about 17% of the variance).

Table 4.8 Stability for peer victimisation, and aggression, between kindergarten and first three grades of elementary school in a US sample (data from Kochenderfer-Ladd, 2003)

Correlations from:	to Grade 1	to Grade 2	to Grade 3
Peer victimisation			
Kindergarten	.26	.27	.16
Grade 1		.35	.27
Grade 2			.41
Aggression			
Kindergarten	.59	.52	.58
Grade 1		.56	.56
Grade 2			.67

Other studies at kindergarten age, whether based on peer reports, self-reports or observational data, find low stability of victim role over time: different children are victimised over the period of the study. For example, Monks et al. (2003) found that in children moving from reception class to first grade in two English schools, the correlation between peer nominations received was only 0.19: only about 13% of victims in reception class remained victims in first grade.

Stability for aggressors is relatively high in the early years, however (bearing in mind that the 'bullying' label may be less applicable, precisely because victim stability is low). As seen in the US data in Table 4.8, the inter-grade correlations are around 0.5–0.6: a qualification here, however, is that a different assessment method was used for these aggression ratings which came from teachers. Monks et al. (2003) used the same peer nomination procedure for all roles, and found a high correlation of 0.78 for aggressor between reception and first grade (as well as a relatively high correlation for defender at 0.38). Thus some 60% of children nominated as aggressors in reception class were again so nominated in first grade.

The low stability of the victim role (but not the aggressor role) during these early years suggests that although some children may experience some repeated attacks from aggressive peers, for many of them this is not likely to last for long. Monks et al. (2003), following Perry, Perry and Boldizar (1990), suggested that aggressive children may direct attacks towards a large number of children initially before they get to know which children would prove the most rewarding targets for them (namely those who do not cope well; see Chapter 6). Furthermore, the social structure of young children's peer relationships is less stable in general than those found among older peer groups. Schäfer, Korn, Brodbeck, Wolke and Schulz (2005) suggested that young children are less likely to occupy a particular 'role' within their peer group as yet, making it easier for those who are victimised to avoid being labelled as such and thus also avoid further victimisation.

Stability of the victim role increases by middle childhood and adolescence. A study of 8–9 year olds in English middle schools by Boulton and Smith (1994) found appreciable stability in both victim and bully roles, but some variation by gender. They gathered peer nominations at four time points – October, March and June in one school year, and October soon after the start of the next school year. For victim status, the correlations across time points varied from 0.57–0.80 for boys, but from 0.15–0.78 for girls – for five of the six correlations calculated, the value was lower for girls than boys (and equal in one case). For bully status, the correlations across time points varied from 0.63–0.89 for boys, and from 0.46–0.91 for girls – again, the value was lower for girls in five of the six correlations, although the difference was much less than for victim status. Overall, stability was high, especially for bully status, and lowest for girl victims.

Wolke, Woods and Samara (2009) followed up English primary school children from ages 6–9, up to ages 10–11. They found that victims of direct bullying at the first time point, compared to non-victims, were twice as likely to be victims at the second time point, but that this was more the case for girls. This is unlike the finding of Boulton and Smith, above, who did not distinguish types of bullying. Wolke et al. found stability was not significant for victims of relational bullying, which would more commonly involve girls. Sapouna et al. (2012) followed up samples of 8–9 year old English and German children over a short nine-week period. Over this shorter time period stability was naturally higher, with victims at the first time point, compared to non-victims, being six times more likely to become victims over the follow-up period.

In secondary schools, although the overall incidence of being a victim falls, stability of roles can be high. Smith, Talamelli, Cowie, Naylor and Chauhan (2004) followed up 413 pupils from 35 secondary schools in England, from when they were 11–14 years old to when they were 13–16 years old. Of 204 pupils victimised at the first time point, 58 were still (continuing) victims and 146 were not (escaped victims). The continuing victims reported fewer friends at school (but no fewer outside school), and liked other pupils and breaktimes less than did escaped victims or non-bullied pupils. Of 209 comparison pupils (matched for school, year group, gender and ethnicity), 175 had never been bullied over the intervening two years, seven had experienced some bullying but not continuing, and 27 could now be classed as new victims.

Rueger, Malecki and Demaray (2011) followed up seventh and eighth graders (aged 12–13 years) in a US middle school over a 10-month period. The correlations for victim scores (on a self-report measure) were .50 for boys and .53 for girls. Altogether, about half of the victims were stable over the period, and about half changed status.

In summary, stability of the victim role is low in primary school but increases with age; stability of bully (or at least 'aggressor') is higher from early on. While there is a tendency for many children to stay in the same role over a number of years, there are also appreciable changes over time, possibly influenced by gender and type of bullying, as well as age.

School transitions and longer-term studies

The above studies on stability were carried out within classes and schools. But what happens when a pupil changes class or moves up to a higher level of schooling?

Salmivalli, Lappalainen and Lagerspetz (1998) followed up children from sixth to eighth grade (around 12–13 to 14–15 years old) in 17 school classes in Finland. Children changed schools at seventh grade; the researchers identified 29 children who were in a new class with no or at most one prior classmate from sixth grade (class changers), and 35 children who were still with a great majority of the same classmates as in sixth grade (class stay-ons). The stability of participant roles in bullying tended to be higher in the class stay-ons, but this was not the case for victims: children who were victimised and moved peer groups (that is, classes) were often repeat targets for victimisation in their new peer group.

Pellegrini and Bartini (2000b) followed pupils from fifth grade in US elementary school, to fall (entry) and spring in sixth grade in middle school. Overall rates for bullying others increased at entry to sixth grade in the new school, then decreased by spring – a finding that the authors attribute to children sorting out dominance positions in a new peer group setting, and some children using bullying tactics for these ends. However, both individual bully and victim scores showed some stability over the time period.

In another US study, Paul and Cillessen (2003) followed up children moving from fourth grade in elementary schools to seventh grade in middle schools. They measured victimisation each year (but not bullying). Victimisation was stable from year to year (correlations of .68, .70) and also stable across the transition (correlation of .62). Over the total three years, the correlation was .44, meaning that about one-third of victims in fourth grade were still victims in seventh grade.

In a study in Germany, Schäfer et al. (2005) examined the stability of victim and bully roles from second and third grade in primary school up to seventh and eighth grade in secondary school. Over this relatively long six-year period they found no significant stability of being a victim or bully-victim, although there was some stability for being a bully. However, the stability of being a victim was influenced by a measure of peer hierarchical structuring (in their case, measured by the standard deviation of social impact scores: a high hierarchical structuring meant that there was a high degree of variability in who was liked and disliked in a class). The researchers hypothesised that if a strong peer hierarchy was already established in primary school, then there were more likely to be clearly labelled victims who would be low in the hierarchy, and this would carry through to secondary school. Conversely, if there was not yet a strong peer hierarchy, this would be a situation more similar to that in infant schools, with some stability in aggression/bullying but not in who is a victim. Their analyses tended to confirm this idea, as victim stability was significant for pupils coming from primary school classes with a strong peer hierarchy, but not significant for those coming from a weak peer hierarchy.

An even longer eight-year longitudinal study was reported by Sourander, Helstelä, Helenius and Piha (2000) in Finland, with data from 580 children at around age 8 and age 16. Rates for bully and victim were much less at 16 years, so there were many 'drop-outs', but those who were involved were also quite likely to have been involved at 8 years, especially for victim role and for boys. Altogether about half of boy bullies and almost all boy victims at age 16 had been in the same role at age 8, and similarly for about a quarter of girl bullies and a half of girl victims.

In summary, although findings are varied, there can be considerable stability of roles even over a transition to a new class or school.

Developmental trajectories

Longitudinal studies also provide an opportunity to classify pupils according to their developmental trajectories and relate this to other factors. Goldbaum, Craig, Pepler and Connolly (2003) used a modified OBVQ to assess pupils in fifth to seventh grade from seven Canadian schools, at three time points over the span of a year. They distinguished four trajectories as regards victim scores: non-victims, late-onset victims, desisters and stable victims. These are perhaps rather obvious trajectories to obtain, but meaningful relationships were gained with, for example, internalising problems (highest in stable victims: high levels of anxiety preceded increases in victimisation) and friendship variables (lowest trust and affection in stable victims), with desisters showing improving scores.

So what about trajectories for bullying others? In a study in Scotland, using data from the Edinburgh Study of Youth Transitions and Crime, Barker, Arsenault, Brendgen, Fontaine and Maughan (2008) obtained self-reports on bully and victim roles from adolescents for each year between ages 12 and 16. Overall, both bully and victim rates declined with age in this sample. However, for bully scores, while 84% of students followed a low and decreasing trajectory, 16% (more boys) followed a high and increasing trajectory. For victim scores, 85% followed a low trajectory, 10% followed a high but decreasing trajectory, and 5% followed a high but increasing trajectory. These researchers also examined delinquency and self-harm. Pupils who were in the high/increasing bully trajectory and also high/increasing victim trajectory (so bully/victims) were most at risk, although for boys this was primarily for delinquency, and girls primarily for self-harm.

Trends over time – is bullying increasing or decreasing?

The media often portray bullying as a problem that is on the increase. Whether this is so was investigated by Rigby and Smith (2011), drawing upon empirical studies undertaken in a wide range of countries in which findings had been published describing its prevalence at different points in time between 1990 and 2009.

Relatively few studies have involved collecting data in one place from equivalent samples across time. One referred to earlier is the regular HBSC survey, where there was a slight decrease in bully and victim rates between 2005/2006 and 2009/2010. Molcho et al. (2009) analysed data preceding this, collected from students aged 11–15 years at four-year intervals between 1993/1994 and 2005/2006. They presented trends over time for 27 countries, for occasional and frequent victim and bully rates, by gender. For all these indices, decreases were observed in the majority of the 27 countries for which there were data over all the time points. The most striking findings were for frequent bullying of others, where the country average fell from 19.3% in 1993/1994, to 16.1% in 1997/1998, 11.1% in 2001/2002 and 10.6% in 2005/2006. On a larger set of countries, this figure fell further from 10.7% in 2005/2006 to 10.1% in 2009/2010. This is a very substantial reduction, even though it has been levelling off more recently.

This evidence of a decline in bullying involvement is supported by other studies that have been independent of the HBSC surveys. Rigby and Smith (2011) reviewed supportive findings from England (including the Tellus surveys), Wales, Finland and Australia.

In Spain, Del Barrio et al. (2008) compared the prevalence of bullying between 1999 and 2007. There were significant reductions in the percentage of students who had been involved (as bullies, or victims) in several types of bullying, notably 'being called names, 'being insulted', 'being ignored', 'having belongings hidden', 'being threatened' and 'being sexually harassed'. Similar reductions were indicated from responses about bullying others. The authors concluded that 'the most important finding of the resulting longitudinal study is the evidence of a decrease in prevalence of several forms of bullying in secondary schools all over Spain along the last seven years' (2008: 611).

In the USA, changes in abusive behaviour involving children have been reported by Finkelhor et al. (2009). They examined data from two similar national surveys conducted five years apart, in 2003 and 2008. Both surveys provided information through randomised telephone interviews relating to abusive behaviour experienced by children between the ages of 2 and 17 years. Caregivers answered questions about children under the age of 11 years, while older children were interviewed directly. For the 2003 survey, data were obtained for 2,030 children; for the 2008 survey from 4,046 children. Overall, there was a reduction in abusive behaviour experienced by children between 2003 and 2008. This included a large drop in having been physically attacked by a peer or sibling, from 21.7% to 14.8%. The authors comment that 'The decline apparent in this analysis parallels evidence from other sources, including police data, child welfare data, and the National Crime Victimization Survey, suggesting reductions in various types of childhood victimization in recent years' (2009: 238).

A more complex pattern has come from comparisons in Norway, reported by Roland, Bru, Midthassel and Vaaland (2010) and Roland (2011). Surveys of a nationally representative sample of schools, with around 1,200–5,000 pupils in grades 5, 6, 7 and 9, were conducted in spring 2001, spring 2004 and spring 2008. In 2001 the proportion of victims was 6.3%, while in 2004 this had decreased to 4.9%; however, in 2008 this had risen again to 6.2%. Similarly, for bullying others in 2001 the proportion was 2.3%, and in 2004 this had fallen to 1.9%, but in 2008 it had risen again to 3.7%. Roland (2011) attributes the decrease between 2001 and 2004 to the success of the first Norwegian Manifesto (Manifesto-I) against School Bullying (2002–2004), and the subsequent increase to the failure to follow this up so effectively with a second Manifesto (Manifesto-II) launched in 2006 (discussed further in Chapter 6). Olweus (2012a) also reports separate data from 41 Norwegian schools, from 2006 to 2010. There are slight peaks in both victim and bully rates in 2008, with a slight decrease in 2009 and 2010.

While not universal then, there is good evidence that in most countries and for many indices bullying involvement has fallen in the last decade or so. Given that we know that anti-bullying interventions generally have some success (see Chapter 6), it is likely that increased awareness and the implementation of anti-bullying interventions have helped produce this decline. However, as of yet the evidence mainly concerns traditional bullying. There is scant evidence for a decline in cyberbullying.

There is no doubt that cyberbullying increased as the relevant technology has become more and more accessible in the early years of this century, but has this rise continued? In England, Rivers and Noret (2010) surveyed some 2,500 students aged 11–13 years old from 13 schools for each year between 2002 until 2006. Students were asked *'Have you ever received any nasty or threatening text messages or emails?'*. The percentages who had experienced this at all over each of the five years were 13.0, 12.5, 16.4, 16.3 and 15.5; taking a stricter criterion of 'sometimes this term' or more, the percentages were 2.6, 2.2, 3.2, 2.9 and 2.4. On either criterion there is some suggestion of an increase, but levelling off or slightly decreasing later. The slight decreases in 2005 and 2006 are suspect in that the survey only covered text message and email bullying, and by these dates cyberbullying was already diversifying into other forms.

Wolak, Mitchell and Finkelhor (2006) reported data from the First and Second Youth Internet Safety Surveys (conducted in 1999–2000 and 2005 respectively), and Jones, Mitchell and Finkelhor (2012) have updated these with data from the Third Youth Internet Safety Survey conducted in 2010. Each used telephone interviews with a nationally representative sample of 1,500 US internet users, aged 10–17 years old, covering internet use, safety and unpleasant experiences. A measure of unwanted sexual solicitations showed a steady decline over the three time points. However, the data closest to cyberbullying are those on internet harassment, defined as 'feeling worried or threatened because someone was bothering or harassing you online', or 'someone ever using the internet to threaten or embarrass you by posting or sending messages about you for other people to see'. The three surveys showed an increase in internet harassment from 6% to 9% and then 11%, with this being more marked for girls. This increase might in part be related to increased internet use: the same surveys showed that a composite measure of amount of internet use increased from .24 to .41 and then .49 over the three time points.

Ybarra, Mitchell and Korchmaros (2011) reported data from the Growing Up with Media survey in the USA. This collected data in three waves (2006, 2007 and 2008) from the same households (*N*s were 1588, 1206 and 1159 respectively). In each household, a young person aged 10–15 years filled in an online survey. They found that 'most rates of youth violent experiences online were stable over the 36-month observation period' (2011: 1379), although there was some increase in the perpetration of harassment online. Using an Olweus-type definition of bullying, Ybarra et al. specifically measured 'bullying victimization' (being a victim of bullying) on the internet and via text messaging, at 2007 and 2008 only; the changes in both measures were small and not significant.

Olweus (2012a) reported data from a very large US sample (about 440,000 pupils) from 2007 to 2010. No systematic time trends were found, although if anything the trend is slightly upwards. He also analysed data from 41 Norwegian schools, and again found little in the way of a systematic trend, although if anything the direction is slightly downwards.

In England, Tippett and Smith (submitted) surveyed the same four secondary schools in 2008 and 2011. Taking a lenient 'once or twice' criterion, there were decreases for being a direct victim (17.3–16.9%), indirect victim (21.4–16.1%), direct bully (10.1–6.8%) and indirect bully (10.8–7.5%); these were all statistically significant, and some reductions were present using the 'often' criterion as well.

Thus traditional bullying involvement decreased on all four indicators. However, there was little change for mobile victims (4.5–4.5%), internet victims (7.5–7.7%), mobile bullies (2.4–2.6%) or internet bullies (3.6–2.7%). These changes were non-significant, although there was a trend for the cyberbullying involvement to become less frequent by the 'often' criterion. Although there was little change in the overall incidence of cyberbullying, by 2011 much more of it was on social networking sites (for 69% of victims, compared to 42% in 2008).

In summary, there is good evidence from many studies that, in many countries, rates of involvement in traditional bullying have shown some decline over the last ten or twenty years. There is much less evidence about cyberbullying involvement, but it clearly increased in the early years of this century, and has since proliferated into different forms. Nevertheless, as the proportion of students in most communities having access to mobile phones and the internet approaches saturation, the indications are that rates of cyberbullying are not rising substantially over the last few years, but neither are they declining so clearly as is the case for traditional bullying.

Cultural differences

Comparative surveys suggest considerable variations in the incidence of bullying problems across countries. The HBSC surveys show great variations in bully and victim rates in European and North American countries. Country differences often outweigh age and gender differences. Craig et al. (2009) reported victim rates varying between 8.6% and 45.2% among boys, and 4.8% and 35.8% among girls; high rates of bullying were reported in the Baltic countries (Lithuania and Latvia scoring the highest), and low rates in northern European countries (with Sweden scoring the lowest). Livingstone et al. (2011) also reported large variations from the EU Kids Online survey across 25 European countries. Experiences of being bullied (at all, online or offline) varied from 9% to 43%, with Estonia the highest and Portugal the lowest.

Unfortunately, for the many countries overlapping in these two large cross-national datasets, there is rather little correspondence! For example, Lithuania comes out as average in the EU Kids Online survey, although highest in the HBSC. Sweden comes out as fourth highest in the EU Kids Online, although lowest in the HBSC. These discrepancies are worrying. Besides some methodological differences between the two surveys (described in more detail in Chapter 3), these might reflect issues about how representative the samples are for each country.

Besides variations in prevalence across countries, there are also variations in some structural aspects of bullying. These are not so strong amongst the western countries themselves, but do appear significant when looking at the Pacific Rim countries of Japan and South Korea, especially.

In Japan, Kanetsuna and colleagues (Kanetsuna & Smith, 2002; Kanetsuna, Smith & Morita, 2006) examined the kinds of situation in which high school pupils say that *ijime* (in Japan) or *bullying* (in England) occurs, using corresponding questionnaires and interviews in the two countries. Consistently, they found that in Japan pupils reported *ijime* as most likely to come from pupils that they knew well, of a similar age, and often within the classroom; in England, pupils reported bullying as often coming from pupils they did not know well, often older, and often in the playground. The greater incidence of bullying in the classroom, in Japan, is partly based on a greater emphasis on social exclusion, and is reflected in a greater ratio of bullies to victims compared to studies in England or western countries (Morita et al., 1999).

A somewhat similar pattern comes from studies of *wang-ta* in South Korea, by Koo, Kwak and Smith (2008). *Wang-ta* also seems to occur between pupils who know each other (for example, former friends), and the ratio of bullies to victims is even higher than in Japan. A milder form is *eun-ta*, in which some short-term social exclusion of a victim by a small group of former friends occurs – not so different from what is found in western countries (for example, Besag, 2006). But *wang-ta* is more severe, and within a classroom context this can mean the whole class shunning one pupil. An even more severe form of social exclusion is *jun-ta*: this refers to the whole school labelling the victim and shunning that person. Not surprisingly, many such victims of *jun-ta* show psychiatric symptoms and may have to receive special schooling (Koo, 2004). This emphasis on social exclusion is found throughout childhood and into the workplace context (Lee, Smith & Monks, 2011), but is not static; these terms were unfamiliar a generation ago, & new terms are being introduced – some pupils have created a new word, *jjin-ta* (not in any current dictionary) to replace *wang-ta* to indicate a bullied/socially isolated person (Lee, Smith & Monks, 2012).

Linguistic issues

The apparent differences in prevalence and structural characteristic across countries might reflect real behavioural differences – the obvious interpretation – but equally, they may reflect differences in interpreting the term 'bullied' or related concepts primarily used in that country. For example, in Italy the term *prepotenze* has been widely used as the appropriate term for *bullying* in Italian questionnaire studies. However, *prepotenze* has a broader meaning profile than *bullying*, as shown by the cartoon test (see Chapter 2 and Table 2.4), as it includes physical aggression as well as physical bullying. Italian researchers have found that the use of different terms to translate *bullying* significantly affects the incidence rates obtained (Fonzi et al., 1999).

What is considered unjustified?

As noted in Chapter 2, bullying is generally considered unjust aggression, but what is actually considered unjust varies by culture. For example, the expanded cartoon set (see Chapter 2) has one cartoon where the rest of the team won't let a pupil take part in a competition, even though s/he is one of the best players, because s/he is from a lower year group; 81% of 14 year old English pupils say this is *bullying*, but only 29% of 14 year old Japanese pupils say this is *ijime*. What this example shows is that some (ab)use of power by older pupils might happen in Japan, as in England, but not be reported as *ijime*: the same behaviour may be thought of as abusive or unjust in one culture, and reported as such, but not in another culture.

Explanations for cultural differences in bullying

Whether cultural differences are behavioural, linguistic or rooted in normative beliefs, they need explaining. One obvious approach is how cultures vary in their characteristics in ways that can affect interpersonal relationships. Hofstede (2001) proposed five dimensions, of which two – power distance and individualism/collectivism – may be the most relevant in considering differences in bullying. Power distance may be relevant in understanding the acceptance or not of hierarchically imposed behaviours: Japan and South Korea may be considered more hierarchical, with a greater respect for older persons, including older pupils, such that (ab)use of power by older persons will be more likely to be seen as legitimate and not unjust. The individualism/collectivism dimension contrasts individualistic cultures, in which the social ties between individuals are loose and cultural values emphasise self-reliance, autonomy and personal achievement, and collectivistic cultures, in which people are in strong and cohesive in-groups and group goals take priority over individual goals when there is conflict between them. Thus, in harming someone else, individual attacks may be seen as most effective in individualistic societies (western Europe, North America, Australia), but social exclusion is more likely to be adopted in collectivist societies (Japan, South Korea).

Other factors to consider here are how different societies view violence generally (in the mass media, the home, other contexts), and specifically in schools – are anti-bullying policies required, for example? The organisation of schools can be important – for example, how playground breaks are supervised and the extent of homeroom class teaching. And for cyberbullying, clearly the availability and penetration of mobile phones (and especially smart phones) and the internet will be a key factor.

Summary

Many factors affect prevalence rates, which vary widely across different studies. Particularly important are the definition, time reference period and frequency criterion. High prevalence figures generally mean a relaxation in one of these factors.

Age trends are different for bullies (not declining in the school years) and victims (general downward trend with age), but with a general shift from more physical to more relational and indirect types. There are well-established gender differences in the frequency and types of bullying, although for defenders a gender disparity in verbal reports has not been confirmed by observation. Gender differences are more uncertain and possibly changing rapidly in the case of cyberbullying.

Cyberbullying has a number of distinctive features contrasting it to some extent with traditional bullying, nevertheless there is considerable overlap with traditional forms of bullying. It now forms a significant minority of victimisation experiences. Prejudice-based bullying exists in a variety of forms. Young people of a minority sexual orientation, as well as those with many kinds of disability, are clearly more at risk of victimisation.

Bullying tends to take place in poorly supervised locations. Much bullying is short term, but for a minority it can last for months or years. There is some stability in roles in bullying, and this is greater in older children, most clearly for victims. Pupil attitudes to bullying, while mainly against it, tend to get less provictim with age, at least up to mid-adolescence.

A number of studies suggest that – over recent decades – bully and victim rates have not increased, and in many countries have decreased; any such decrease is not yet obvious for cyberbullying, however.

Cultures vary widely in bully and victim rates, but consistent findings are not yet available. In Japan and South Korea, bullying appears to be more based on group processes and social exclusion. However, these may be actual differences in behaviour – perhaps due to dimensions such as individualism-collectivism, or power distance, or more prosaically, to differences in schooling arrangements. There are also differences in conceptions of unjust (ab)use of power, and differences in the words available to describe these. In addition, all of these factors can and do change through historical time.

FIVE

Who is at risk and what are the effects?

Aggressive behaviour and inequalities of power are commonplace in human groups, including peer groups in school, so bullying can be a temptation. But why do some children become victims, or take part in bullying others, and why do some become defenders, or manage to stay non-involved? A range of factors have been investigated:

- Individual level: genetics, temperament and personality.
- Family level: nature of parent–child and sibling relationships.
- Peer group level: nature and quality of friendships; sociometric status.
- Class level: class norms, ingroup/outgroup attitudes; scapegoating.
- School level: school climate and quality of teacher and pupil relationships.
- Community level: neighbourhood levels of violence and safety; socioeconomic conditions.
- Society level: portrayals of violence, bullying and abuse of power in the mass media; economic inequality.

This chapter also looks at the effects or consequences of being a victim or bully. This is often difficult to separate clearly from causes, as the majority of studies are correlational in nature. As a result we are not certain of cause and effect. For example, does timidity lead to increased risk of being bullied, or does being bullied lead to increased timidity, or does the pathway go both ways? Regression analyses can attempt to take account of other confounding factors in associations, but do not really help with deciding causal direction.

In some areas one direction of effect is much more plausible. Violence in the home is a plausible predictor of a child bullying at school, but it is less likely (though not impossible) that a child bullying at school leads to violence in the home. Committing suicide is certainly a possible outcome of severe victimisation, but cannot be a cause: even suicidal ideation seems much more likely as an outcome than a cause.

Longitudinal studies are the best way to help decide what is most likely to be a cause, or a consequence. For example, does being a victim at time 1 predict changes in timidity at time 2, or does level of timidity at time 1 predict changes in victimisation at time 2? Or are both true, indicating a reciprocal or transactional model? Ideally, several time points should be used. The chapter looks at likely outcomes of victim or bully involvement, bearing these issues in mind.

Predictors of involvement in bully or victim roles

Cook, Williams, Guerra, Kim and Sadek (2010b) carried out a meta-analysis of studies from 1970 to mid-2006, which reported predictors (correlates) of bully, victim or bully/victim status. Altogether they obtained 153 independent sample studies (37 from the USA, 76 from Europe, 40 from other countries). Most (61%) were from the 2001–2006 period, illustrating the rapid growth in studies by then, and most (78%) used self-report data: 120 studies reported on bullies, 121 on victims, but only 31 on bully/victims. They analysed seven individual-level predictors (plus age and gender; findings relevant to these were mentioned in Chapter 4) and five contextual-level predictors that go beyond the individual level.

Their main findings are summarised in Table 5.1. On conventional guidelines, effect sizes (here, correlation coefficients) can be taken as small if they reach .10, medium at .30 and large at .50. None of the effect sizes are large, but the medium ones are highlighted in bold.

For bullying others, it is not surprising that externalising (aggressive and defiant behaviour) is a strong predictor, given that bullying is anyway a subset of aggression. A lack of empathy, and negative peer influence, are also medium predictors. For victims, a lack of social skills and peer rejection stand out as medium predictors. For bully/victims, there are a number of medium-level predictors, picking up most of those for bullies and victims separately, but also including low

Table 5.1 Effect sizes (weighted) of predictors of bully, victim and bully/victim status, from Cook et al. (2010). Medium effect size ($r > .30$) in bold; non-significant effects sizes in brackets

	Bully	Victim	Bully/victim
Externalising (defiant, aggressive, disruptive)	**.34**	.12	**.33**
Internalising (withdrawn, anxious, depressive)	.12	.25	.22
Social competence (interactive social skills)	−.12	**−.30**	**−.36**
Self-related cognitions (self-esteem, self-efficacy)	−.07	−.16	**−.40**
Other related cognitions (empathy, perspective taking)	**−.34**	(.03)	−.20
Social problem solving	−.17	−.13	−.18
Academic performance	−.21	(−.04)	**−.32**
Family/home environment	−.17	−.10	−.20
School climate	−.18	−.16	**−.32**
Community factors	−.22	−.15	no studies
Peer status (rejection, popularity, likeability)	−.10	**−.35**	**−.36**
Peer influence (deviant or prosocial group affiliations)	**−.34**	(.01)	**−.44**

self-esteem, low academic performance and poor school climate. However, there were fewer studies on bully/victims – the figure for academic performance relied on only one study.

Cook, Williams, Guerra, Kim and Sadek (2010) also looked at whether age was a moderating factor in any of the bully or victim group analyses. For bullies, peer status had an effect size of –.16 in the primary years, falling to –.01 in the secondary years: this means that bullies were generally not liked in primary school, but this was no longer true in secondary school. Bullies also showed a lesser association with externalising factors but a greater association with internalising factors at secondary school. For victims, the only finding was an even greater association with internalising factors at secondary school (.38) than at primary school (.23).

Individual level

Genetics

Behaviour genetic research has revealed interesting findings. The main studies have used the classic twin method, comparing concordance for monozygotic (genetically identical) and dizygotic (non-identical) twins. The variance between individuals in a measured trait (such as bully or victim role) can then be allocated to genetic factors, a shared environment (common to the twins) or a non-shared environment (experienced differently by the twins). Two important such studies are the Quebec Newborn Twin Study, a population of 648 twin pairs born in the greater Montreal area of Canada between 1995 and 1998, and the Environmental Risk (E-Risk) Longitudinal Twin Study of 1,116 families with same-sex twins born in England and Wales during 1994–1995.

Brendgren et al. (2008) reported data from the Quebec study on peer victimisation at 6 years old, as assessed by peer nomination. Their calculations suggested no genetic influence on being victimised by peers. Their best fit model ascribed 29% of the variance to shared environment and 71% to non-shared environment.

A quite different finding was reported by Ball et al. (2008) from the E-Risk study, however. Being victimised by peers was assessed at 9–10 years by mothers' report. Their best fit model suggested that 73% of the variance was genetic and 27% non-shared environment (zero for shared environment). They also assessed bullying others, from a combination of mother and teacher reports: 61% of the variance was genetic and 39% non-shared environment (zero for shared environment). In this study the children were three or four years older, and a different assessment method was used.

Brendgren et al. (2011) subsequently reported on a sub-sample of the Quebec data at 7 years old, and found 25.5% of the variance in peer-nominated victimisation was genetic and 74.5% non-shared environment (zero for shared environment). Reporting on a fuller sample, Boivin et al. (2012) reported on peer victimisation using peer, teacher and self-report data, at kindergarten, grade 1 and grade 4 (about 6, 7 and 10 years old). As is usual (Chapter 3), the levels of agreement between peer, teacher and self were only moderate (mostly around .2 and .3) but did increase with age. The estimates of genetic and environmental variance also varied considerably by informant. However, for peer nominations there was a clear increase with age in the proportion of genetic variance: 21% at 6 years old, 29% at 7 years old and 66% at 10 years old.

There are limitations to these twin studies, one being how readily one can generalise from a twin population to the majority non-twin population. Also, the proportions of variance do depend on the models used, and in Boivin et al. (2012) do vary greatly by informant. Nevertheless, it seems to be reasonably well established that there are genetic factors involved in being a victim or bully. Also, it seems that the genetic contribution to being a victim increases through the primary school years: this may reflect the more transient nature of peer victimisation in the 4–6 year old period (see Chapter 4) and its more stable nature by middle childhood.

Any genetic factors must operate through various mechanisms – it is clearly much too facile to say that there is a gene for being in a bully or victim role. Ball et al. (2008) suggest a number of such mechanisms: for being a victim, they mention introverted personality, social cognitive deficits and emotional regulation and displays; for bullying, they mention impulsivity and sensation seeking, biases in social cognitions, and low emotionality and poor emotional regulation. These are considered further in the sections below.

Ball et al. (2008) assessed both being a victim and bullying others, and found only a limited correlation between the two characteristics, of $r = 0.25$: however, they suggested that this modest linkage was largely genetic, and that it might be due to a common factor of emotional dysregulation (also found to be highly heritable).

Temperament and personality

Early research had indicated that bullying others was associated with having a hot-tempered personality (Olweus, 1993), readily attributing hostile motives to others, and having defensive egotism – namely reacting angrily to minor threats to self-esteem (Salmivalli, Kaukiainen, Kaistaniemi & Lagerspetz, 1999).

A promising dimension of personality to examine has been Machiavellianism, generally defined as thinking that other people are untrustworthy, and can be manipulated in interpersonal situations. In a Scottish sample of 9–12 year olds, Sutton and Keogh (2000) found that bullies held more Machiavellian attitudes than non-involved children. Andreou (2004) explored four components of Machiavellianism (a lack of faith in human nature, manipulation, dishonesty and distrust) in a Greek sample of 9–12 year olds. She found that a lack of faith in human nature correlated with both bully and victim roles for boys, while manipulation correlated with bully role for girls (perhaps reflecting the more relational forms of bullying common in girls). Distrust characterised both boy and girl victims. Bully/victim children were particularly characterised by a lack of faith in human nature, as well as overall Machiavellianism.

Another important personality factor in terms of bullying others may be impulsivity. Jolliffe and Farrington (2011) found impulsivity to be the most important predictor from a range of factors examined in English adolescents (see below).

Tani, Greenman, Schneider and Fregoso (2003) related bullying roles in 8–10 year old Italian children to the Big Five personality factors: friendliness, emotional instability, intellectual openness, energy and conscientiousness. They used an adaptation of the Participant Role scale, with pro-bully (bully, assistant, reinforcer), defender, outsider and victim. Both pro-bully and victim children showed high levels of emotional instability and low levels of friendliness. Victims were also low on conscientiousness. Defenders scored highest on friendliness, and low on emotional instability.

Empathy

Empathy is typically viewed as having two dimensions. Cognitive empathy refers to the ability to recognise the emotions of others, while affective empathy refers to sharing the feelings of others. As Table 5.1 indicates, empathy tends to be negatively related to bullying and also to being a bully/victim, but not to being a victim (only). The findings regarding bullying tend to be stronger for affective empathy. For example, Endresen and Olweus (2001) found bullying behaviour was related to low affective empathy for both boys and girls in Norwegian adolescents.

Jolliffe and Farrington (2006, 2011) examined cognitive and affective empathy of English 13–17 year olds in relation to bully and victim self-reports. In their first (2006) report, female bullies scored lower on affective empathy, but not for cognitive empathy; male bullies did not significantly differ from non-bullies on either. However, a later re-analysis (2011) took account of other factors (SES, non-intact family, parental supervision, verbal fluency, impulsivity) using regression analysis. This moderated the findings, such that now, boys who bullied had lower affective empathy, but not lower cognitive empathy, and the findings for girls became non-significant. However, the empathy relationships were considerably less strong than those found for impulsivity (see above).

Finding low affective empathy in bullies is hardly surprising, but according to Muñoz, Qualter and Padgett (2011) callous-unemotional (CU) traits, and particularly the uncaring subscale of this, may be more important than empathic scores per se. In a sample of English 11–12 year olds, they found that an association between CU traits and bullying remained, even when taking empathy deficits into account. They suggested that being an uncaring child is more important in predicting bullying than recognising or even feeling other people's emotions.

Some research has also been carried out on defenders. Nickerson, Mele and Princiotta (2008) showed that in a US middle school sample, those nominated as defenders scored higher on empathic concern (similar to affective empathy) than outsiders. However, empathic concern is probably not enough in itself to strongly predict the defender role. Caravita, Di Blasio and Salmivalli (2009) found that in Italian 9 and 12 year olds, high affective empathy predicted defending behaviour in boys, but especially for those with high social preference scores – that is, those who were liked a lot by classmates. Gini, Albiero, Benelli and Altoè (2008) showed that in Italian 12–14 year olds, it was a combination of high empathic concern plus high levels of social self-efficacy that best predicted defending.

Relationships with empathy might be different for cyberbullying because of the 'online disinhibition effect', namely that the cyber bully cannot see the victim or his/her reactions, at least in the short term; thus, low affective empathy might not be such an important predictor. However, the research does not support this. Ang and Goh (2010) worked with adolescents from one middle school and one high school in Singapore, and examined the association between affective empathy, cognitive empathy and gender on cyberbullying among adolescents. As main effects, both low cognitive empathy and low affective empathy predicted cyberbullying, and this was clearly so for boys with no interaction between the two kinds of empathy. However, for girls, the level of cognitive empathy had no effect if they had high affective empathy.

Renati, Berrone and Zanetti (2012) reported findings on cognitive and affective empathy with Italian adolescents aged around 16 years. Empathy measures were compared for those involved as cyberbullies, cyber victims, both (cyber bully/victims) or neither (not involved). Although cyberbullies scored lowest on cognitive empathy, the differences were not significant. However, on affective empathy cyberbullies scored significantly lower than cyber victims or not involved students (with cyberbully/victims intermediate).

In sum, it appears that empathy deficits – and particularly affective empathy deficits – are characteristic of children who bully frequently, whether this is traditional or cyberbullying. Defenders are likely to be high on empathic concern, but actual defending behaviour will be influenced by other factors such as self-efficacy and social status in the class.

Moral disengagement

Related to the concept of empathy is that of moral disengagement – a process by which someone can bypass the normal kinds of reasoning which would hold us back from severely hurting or even killing another person. Bandura (2002) described a number of ways in which this can occur. Taking examples commonly found when interviewing children who bully others (for example, Cowie, Smith, Boulton & Laver, 1994), these ways can involve cognitive restructuring (seeing the attack as justified – 'he deserved it'), minimising one's agentive role ('I didn't start it'), disregarding or distorting the consequences ('it was just for fun') or blaming the victim ('he started it'). A full list of such examples can be found in Hymel, Schonert-Reichl, Bonnano, Vaillancourt and Henderson (2010).

Based on Bandura's work, self-report scales of moral disengagement (MD) have been developed, and a number of studies have used this to see if children identified as bullies score higher on MD. Gini, Pozzoli and Hymel (2014) reported a meta-analysis of such studies. Some studies they examined were on general aggression, but 11 were on bullying and 4 on cyberbullying. The countries contributing in these areas were Australia, Denmark, Italy, Japan, Portugal (mistakenly labelled as 'Spain' in the article), Switzerland, the UK and the USA. The effect size relating MD to bullying was $r = 0.25$, and for cyberbullying, $r = 0.31$ (for aggression generally, it was $r = 0.27$). These associations were similar for boys and girls, but were significantly stronger for adolescents compared to younger children. The association was higher when there was shared method variance (self-reports of both MD and bullying) but still significant when shared method variance was absent.

In a later study outside the Gini et al. (2014) review, Renati et al. (2012) reported findings from MD on their sample of Italian adolescents (see earlier). Again, cyberbullies, and also cyberbully/victims, scored significantly higher on MD than either cyber victims or non-involved students.

Clearly moral disengagement is associated with bullying others, as with aggression more generally. The slightly higher association for cyberbullying in the meta-analysis is only based on four studies and not statistically significant. In fact the authors had supposed that MD might be less associated with cyberbullying, because of the 'online disinhibition effect' (see earlier). But we also know that there is a substantial overlap in the perpetration of cyberbullying and traditional bullying, which would suggest that we would not find very different associations with MD – as borne out by this meta-analysis, but with the strong proviso that more studies are needed in the cyberbullying domain.

Self-concept/self-esteem

As Table 5.1 suggests, in many studies low self-concept or self-esteem is related to victim status, and even more with being a bully/victim. There is a lesser negative association with bullying others. Before the Cook, Williams, Guerra, Kim and Sadek (2010) meta-analysis, an earlier meta-analysis by Hawker and Boulton (2000) had found that victimisation was moderately associated with lower social and global self-esteem.

Many studies have been cross-sectional, but self-esteem is one area where both directions of causality seem plausible, namely a transactional model. Egan and Perry (1998) did find a longitudinal reciprocal relationship between victimisation and self-concept for social competence in US third to seventh grade children; however, this relationship was not found for the more composite measure of global self-worth. Salmivalli and Isaacs (2005), in a longitudinal study of 11–13 year old Finnish pupils over one year, also found some support for a transactional model. Negative self-perceptions predicted being a victim, and being a victim in turn predicted more negative perceptions of how peers thought about them, although not more negative self-perceptions. Boulton, Smith and Cowie (2010) reported longitudinal data from an English middle school sample over a five-month period. Earlier victimisation significantly predicted negative changes in global self-worth, social acceptance and – for girls only – physical appearance scores, and earlier social acceptance scores significantly predicted changes in victimisation.

In summary, there is fairly good evidence for a transactional model between being a victim and low self-concept. Data for children who bully are more inconsistent. Many studies do not find bullies lower in self-esteem (for example, Boulton & Smith, 1994; Olweus, 1993), but some studies do (for example, O'Moore, 2000). These discrepancies may be partly explicable in terms of which types of self-esteem are considered: bullies do usually recognise that their behaviour is not approved of by adults, thus scoring lower on the behavioural component of self-esteem. How bullies are identified is a consideration; Cole et al. (2006) found that although self-reported bullies had lower self-concept, this was not the case for peer-nominated bullies. Another issue is whether bullies and bully/victims are considered separately, as there is no doubt that bully/victims score low on self-esteem (see Table 5.1).

Social cognitive skills

The meta-analysis in Table 5.1 suggests modest negative associations of social problem-solving skills for bullies, victims and bully/victims. However, this covers a range of measures. If we consider social cognitive skills, one that has generated some discussion is theory of mind – the ability to understand what someone else is thinking and feeling (in fact, not dissimilar to cognitive empathy, but with a broader focus on what someone else is thinking or wanting or knows, as well as just their emotional state). Related aspects are social or emotional intelligence, and moral reasoning.

A conventional view has been that bullies, and aggressive children generally, lack social skills. This was challenged by Sutton, Smith and Swettenham (1999a), although defended by Crick and Dodge (1999). Sutton, Smith and Swettenham (1999b) assessed theory of mind in 7–10 year old English children. Using the Salmivalli PRS, they found that children nominated by peers as ringleader bullies scored highest on theory of mind – higher than reinforcers or assistants. They suggested that the ability to recognise another person's mental state might help ringleader bullies plan and engage in more hurtful bullying behaviour and in recruiting other children to bully: they can be 'skilled manipulators'.

Indirect or relational aggression may require more consideration of others' thoughts, beliefs and desires than physical or verbal forms. In a Finnish sample, Kaukiainen et al. (1999) found a positive correlation between indirect aggression and peer-rated social intelligence.

Gini (2006) examined theory of mind in relation to the PRS in 8–11 year old Italian children. He did not replicate the superior theory of mind ability in bullies found by Sutton et al. (1999b), but neither did bullies show any deficits. On the cognitive stories used in the theory of mind tasks, victims scored the lowest and defenders the highest; bully/victims were not analysed separately. In another Italian sample of 9–13 year olds, Gini, Pozzoli and Hauser (2011) found that bullies as well as defenders were better than victims on moral reasoning (specifically, judging attempts to harm someone as morally wrong). However in both these studies, bullies did show significantly higher moral disengagement (see earlier).

In the longitudinal E-risk study in England and Wales, Shakoor, Jafee, Bowes et al. (2011) followed children from 5 through to 12 years old. Poorer theory of mind scores at age 5 predicted victim, bully and bully/victim roles at age 12. However, when other factors (SES, maltreatment) were taken account of, the association for bullying became non-significant, whereas the associations for victim and bully/victim remained significant, suggesting that for these latter groups poorer theory of mind did constitute an additional risk factor.

Peeters, Cillessen and Scholte (2010), in a Dutch sample of 13 year olds, found a possible explanation for the discrepant results concerning theory of mind in bullies. A cluster analysis suggested three kinds of pupils who were peer nominated as bullies: one group was popular and socially intelligent; a second group was relatively popular and with average social intelligence scores; a third group, the smallest numerically, was unpopular and had lower than average scores on social intelligence.

In summary, findings regarding theory of mind and other social cognitive skills are varied, but it seems that some bullies are not deficient in such skills, at least when other factors are taken account of, whereas victims do score lower.

Some risk factors in cyberbullying

Who gets involved in being a cyberbully or cyber victim? One well-established predictor is involvement in traditional bullying. Many studies have found a substantial overlap between involvement in traditional bullying and cyberbullying, and similarly for being a victim (see Smith, 2012). A predictor for being a cyberbully is involvement in other antisocial behaviours. Ybarra and Mitchell (2004, 2007) reported that young people with problem behaviours were almost four times more likely to say they were an internet aggressor/target versus those who reported victimisation only.

Another predictor of cyberbullying involvement is time spent with ICT and relevant internet skills. Both Hinduja and Patchin (2008b) and Smith, Mahdavi et al. (2008) found that more time spent on the internet was a correlate of being a cyber victim. Vandebosch and van Cleemput (2008) found that pupils with more advanced internet skills were more likely to have experience with deviant internet and mobile phone activities.

Internalising problems: anxiety and depression, psychosomatic symptoms

Internalising problems cover a range of measures, including anxiety, depression, withdrawal, loneliness, and psychosomatic symptoms – negative outcomes directed into oneself rather than out to other people. In an early meta-analysis, Hawker and Boulton (2000) found that victimisation was strongly related to depression, and less strongly associated with anxiety. The Cook, Williams, Guerra,

Kim and Sadak (2010) meta-analysis in Table 5.1 shows that internalising problems are associated with victims and bully/victims most, followed by bullies.

Gini and Pozzoli (2009) did a meta-analysis of studies specifically examining psychosomatic symptoms. For example, their earliest study was by Williams, Chambers, Logan and Robinson (1996), who interviewed nearly 3,000 children in East London aged 7–10 years. Bullied children were significantly more likely to report not sleeping well, bed wetting, feeling sad, and experiencing more than occasional headaches and stomach aches. Gini and Pozzoli found 11 such studies on victims, with an average odds ratio of 2.0 for victims compared to uninvolved peers (meaning that victims were twice as much at risk for having such symptoms). They also found six studies on bullies and these yielded an average odds ratio of 1.65. Finally, there were five studies that included bully/victims, and here the average odds ratio was 2.22. Overall, between 7 and 16 years old, bully/victims, victims and then bullies all had a significantly higher risk of psychosomatic problems compared to uninvolved peers. In a follow-up four years later, Gini and Pozzoli (2013) identified 30 relevant studies, of which 24 were cross-sectional and 6 were longitudinal. Their analysis here was just on victims, and they found that the odds ratio for increased psychosomatic symptoms was 2.39 in the longitudinal studies and 2.17 in the cross-sectional studies.

Such findings are mostly from Europe, North America or Australia. However, they are consistently found in other countries. For example, Fleming and Jacobsen (2009) reported findings from 8,000 middle school students in Chile. Being victimised predicted depression, with an odds ratio of 1.72, and there was a 'dosage effect', such that those bullied more often in the past month had higher scores on depression. As another example, Penning, Bhagwanjee and Govender (2010) surveyed 486 male students aged 12–17 years in a South African school: the sample was 83% black. Measures of trauma (such as anxiety and depression) were highest in victims of bullying, followed by bully/victims, bullies and bystanders (who had observed bullying), compared to non-involved pupils. Again there was a dosage effect, as more frequently bullied children experienced more signs of trauma.

These two studies, however, and indeed most of the studies reviewed in the meta-analyses above, were cross-sectional. Reijntjes, Kamphuis, Prinzie and Telch (2010) managed to identify 18 longitudinal studies, between 1995 and 2006, that examined being a victim of peer bullying, and some measure of internalising problems. For 15 of these studies, they were able to examine whether victimisation at baseline predicted changes in internalising problems: they did, with a mean effect size (correlation) of .18. For 11 of the studies, they were able to examine whether internalising problems at baseline predicted changes in victimisation: they did, with a mean effect size (correlation) of .08. It looks like the pathway from victimisation to internalising problems is stronger than the other way, but in fact the difference between the two correlations was not statistically significant, so the authors concluded (2010: 244) that 'Internalizing problems function as both antecedents and consequences of peer victimization.

These reciprocal influences suggest a vicious cycle that contributes to the high stability of peer victimization'.

A later longitudinal study, by Zwierzynska, Wolke and Lereya (2013), used data from the Avon Longitudinal Study of Parents and Children (ALSPAC) based around the Bristol area of England. Children were assessed for being a victim (of both direct and indirect bullying) at 8 and 10 years old (from mother, teacher and self-report), and for internalising problems (depression, emotional problems, well-being) between 11 and 14 years old. In line with previous studies, victimisation predicted later internalising symptoms, but this study also showed that the odds ratios were especially high for severe depression, and also that the risks were increased if the victimisation involved multiple forms (direct and indirect) and was stable from 8 to 10 years old. The authors also advance reasons for why victimisation leads to depression: one is an alteration in the physiological response to stress (to which some children may be more genetically susceptible); another, that the victim develops cognitive biases, such as self-defeating ideation and rehearsal in memory of negative experiences, that are characteristic of depression.

A study by Perren, Ettekal and Ladd (2013) points to two different developmental pathways. They followed Swiss children from grade 5 to grade 7. They found that being victimised by peers was associated with both internalising and externalising problems later on. However, which way this went seemed to depend on the child's cognitions: those who engaged in hostile attributions developed more externalising problems, while those who engaged in self-blame developed more internalising problems.

The impact of cyberbullying

Although some of the distinctive features of cyberbullying (such as breadth of audience and difficulty of escape) might suggest a greater negative impact, this needs to be counterbalanced by the fact that it is, ultimately, a virtual world. Smith, Mahdavi et al. (2008) investigated whether pupils in general perceived cyberbullying to have less, equal or more of a negative impact compared to traditional bullying. This varied across media, with picture/video clip bullying especially perceived as having a greater negative impact than traditional bullying, but generally there was a range of opinions, with some pupils replying that cyberbullying had the same effect on the victim ('I think they are equally as bad'; 'they both can hurt'), could be worse ('loads of people can see it if it's on the internet'; 'it's constant all the time, really hard to escape') or could be less harmful ('you can be more damaged by face-to-face bullying than cyber bullying, that's just words'; 'a text is easier to ignore than something that happened in a specific place').

These were what children thought generally: a cross-national study in Spain, Italy and England by Ortega, Elipe et al. (2012) examined the kinds of emotion that victims actually experienced. The most common emotion reported was anger: 44% for experiencing traditional bullying, 34% for experiencing cyberbullying. Upset was reported by 23% and 20% respectively, stressed by 18% and 11% respectively, and worried by 16% (both kinds). Not bothered was the response chosen by 25% of traditional victims, but 36% of cyber victims. This study seems to confirm that being cyberbullied is indeed hurtful for many victims, but not more so (perhaps on average less) than for traditional victims. Similar findings were reported by Campbell, Spears, Slee, Butler and Kift (2012) in an Australian adolescent sample.

So how about relative outcomes for internalising symptoms? Some cross-sectional studies allow such comparisons and give varied results. In a study of Austrian adolescents aged 14–19 years old, Gradinger, Strohmeier and Spiel (2009) found that being a cyber victim was significantly associated with both depressive and somatic symptoms, but the association was about the same strength as for traditional victims. Combined victims (both traditional and cyber) were especially at risk. Bully/victims were more at risk than only victims.

Beckman, Hagquist and Hellstrom (2012) assessed psychosomatic problems in 15–16 year old Swedish students. Both traditional and cyber victims scored worse than not involved children. Although cyber victims had a higher score on psycho-somatic problems than traditional victims, this was not statistically significant. However, again those who were both traditional and cyber victims had the worst scores.

In their Australian study with 9–19 year old pupils, Campbell et al. (2012) assessed scores on the Strengths and Difficulties Questionnaire (SDQ), as well as depression, anxiety and stress. Although cyber victims had expressed less negative emotions (for example 30% said they felt nothing, compared to 14% traditional victims), on all the outcomes measures cyber victims scored worse than traditional victims (although both groups were worse than non-involved children). Consistent with the previous studies, those involved as both traditional and cyber victims had the worst scores.

A few studies have assessed longitudinal relationships in this area. For example, Gámez-Guadix, Orue, Smith and Calvete (2013) analysed the temporal and reciprocal relationships between being a cyber victim and depressive symptoms, substance use and problematic internet use, in a 15 year old Spanish sample followed over a six-month period. Being a cyber victim predicted later depressive symptoms and problematic internet use, and earlier depressive symptoms and substance use predicted more cyber victimisation. This supported a reciprocal relationship between depressive symptoms and being a cyber victim. Bully/victims had higher levels than only victims on all three problem variables, at both time points.

This study did not compare cyber victimisation with traditional victimisation, or look at bullying perpetration. Lester, Cross and Shaw (2012) examined both traditional and cyber bully and victim involvement at age 12 and problem behaviours at age 14, in an Australian sample. Their measure of problem behaviours was mainly externalising behaviours such as stealing or fighting. Here, being a traditional bully was the strongest predictor. Being a traditional victim, or a cyber bully or victim, was also associated less strongly; however, after taking account of the effects of traditional bullying, cyberbullying involvement was not a significant independent predictor.

Summary of problem behaviours

In summary, there is good evidence that victimisation is not only associated with a range of internalising problems, but also that it has a causative role. More chronic victimisation, and experiencing more types of victimisation, make matters worse. If further proof were needed, Arseneault et al. (2008) reported further twin data from the E-risk study in England in Wales, comparing monozygotic twins where one had been bullied and the other had not. The bullied twin had significantly greater internalising problems: this was true at 10 years old, even when controlling for pre-existing internalising problems at 7 years old. The authors concluded (2008: 145) that 'Being bullied at a young age is an environmentally mediated contributing factor to children's internalizing problems'.

It is not surprising that being bullied at school has such negative effects, but research is also starting to pinpoint some causative factors. Engström, Hallquist, Möller and Laflamme (2005), in a study of 10–15 year old Swedish children, showed that shortly after a child was victimised at school, there was an increase in risk of that child experiencing an unintentional injury. They suggested that this might be due to 'disturbed concentration and attention processes'. Interestingly, the effect was more significant among those seldom victimised than among those regularly victimised.

Repeated victimisation probably results in some changes in responses to stress. In more data from the E-risk study, Ouellet-Morin et al. (2011) – again comparing bullied and non-bullied monozygotic twins – found a blunted cortisol response to a psychosocial stress test. In other words, the bullied children were responding in a more muted way to stress. This might be adaptive in the immediate sense that continued high cortisol activation could be damaging, but in the longer term, low cortisol secretion can lead to poorer responsiveness and physical and mental health.

Those involved in bullying also score higher on externalising problems, especially bullies and bully/victims (see Table 5.1). This is hardly surprising, as bullying others is a kind of externalising behaviour. Here, the research on empathy and moral disengagement points to why some children do not feel inhibited in hurting others, in the way that most children usually do.

Suicidal ideation, suicide attempts and suicide

Suicide can be the extreme outcome in cases of being bullied – a most tragic outcome, although in some cases it has led to practical initiatives to reduce bullying (see Chapter 6). In 1982, three 10–14 year old boys in northern Norway committed suicide, in large part due to bullying. This aroused much public concern, and Olweus (1999b) credits this with the genesis of the first Norwegian nationwide campaign against bullying. In England, the suicide of an adolescent girl due to bullying in 1992 was featured on a BBC programme and led to an advice pack being circulated in all schools (Smith, 1999). In Japan, the death of a 13 year old boy in 1994 by hanging himself attracted much media attention: besides being physically bullied, he had given large sums of money to his tormentors, and his suicide note made clear this was the reason for his suicide (Morita et al., 1999). Unfortunately such cases continue, now including cases of suicides related to being cyberbullied (or 'cyberbullicide'; see http://cyberbullying.us/cyberbullicide-the-relationship-between-cyberbullying-and-suicide-among-youth/).

As part of a Special Issue of the *Journal of Adolescent Health* on bullying and suicide, Karch, Logan, Daniel, Floyd and Vagi (2013) described the circumstances leading to suicide generally, among young people aged 10–17 years in 16 states of the USA. At this age, suicide is the third leading cause of death (after unintentional injury and homicide). Causes of suicide did not vary greatly by gender. Leading causes (as established by legal and medical reports) were relationship problems with a non-intimate partner (friends, parents; 51%), intimate partner problem (boy/girl friend, father/mother in teen pregnancy; 27%) and school problems (26%). In addition, a life stress or crisis in the past or impending two weeks was present in 42%. Of the school problems, about one in eight were ascribed to school bullying: this would then be about 3% of total suicides, although it seems likely that relationship problems with friends might also be implicated in bullying. However, victimisation experiences appear to often interact with other factors in producing suicidal ideation or suicide.

While completed suicides are thankfully rare, much larger numbers of younger people sometimes think of suicide, or self-harm in some way. A number of studies, mostly cross-sectional, have shown an increased risk of these measures for victims of bullying.

A study in the Netherlands by Herba et al. (2008) followed children from 11–13 years old. The results showed that simply being a victim of school bullying did not significantly increase risk of suicidal ideation (odds ratio 1.04), but that rejection at home (hostile, derogating parenting) was a strong predictor (odds ratio 6.42). Being a victim and rejection at home interacted: compared to uninvolved children who experienced parental rejection, victims who experienced parental rejection had an odds ratio of 5.50 for suicidal ideation, while bully/victims had an odds ratio of 2.03.

The lesser risk found in this study for bully/victims (compared to victims) is unusual. In a study in South Korea of middle school children, Kim, Koh and Leventhal (2005) found victims to be more at risk of suicidal ideation over the previous six months (odds ratio 1.29, adjusted for confounding factors), although this was not statistically significant; however, 'victim-perpetrators' were significantly more at risk (odds ratio 1.90). Perpetrators only had the least (and non-significant) enhanced risk (odds ratio 1.11). In a further prospective study, from 13–14 years of age, Kim, Leventhal, Koh and Boyce (2009) found that being bullied increased the risk of suicidal ideation over time, for both victims and victim-perpetrators, the risk being highest for victim-perpetrators. This association was independent of a number of other risk factors. These findings contrast with those of Herba et al. (2008), although the studies used a similar methodology of peer nominations for victim status. However, the studies are consistent in finding that females were more at risk generally for the link between victim experience and suicidal ideation.

Klomek et al. (2009) carried out a longitudinal study in Finland, from 8 years old to early adulthood. Frequent bullying and victimisation were associated with later suicide attempts by boys, but this was not significant after controlling for conduct and depression at age 8: for girls, frequent victimisation was associated with suicide attempts, even after these controls. This greater effect on girls is explained by the researchers in terms of girls experiencing more relational victimisation and consequent problems of loneliness and depression.

The important additional role of depression (but not the gender difference) was also found in a longitudinal study with US high school students, from the ninth to the twelfth grade, by Klomek et al. (2011). Involvement in bullying at 8 years old (as a victim or bully) did not in itself increase the risk of later psychiatric problems or suicidal ideation, but it did increase the risk for those 8 year olds who already had some depression or psychiatric problems. Victimisation only acted as a risk factor when combined with these predisposing conditions.

Fisher et al. (2012) reported data from the E-risk study in England and Wales. Exposure to frequent bullying in 12 year old children predicted higher rates of self-harm, even after taking account of prior emotional problems: the odds ratios were 1.92 for mother report, 2.44 for self-report of victimisation. Other strongly contributing factors to self-harm were a family history of attempted or completed suicide, and maltreatment by an adult. The family situation again emerges as significant here, but using the twin data available in this study, victimised twins were more likely to self-harm than their non-victimised co-twin (though sample numbers here were small), supporting some direct causal link between peer victimisation and self-harm.

Cyber victimisation has also been linked to suicidal outcomes. Hinduja and Patchin (2010) surveyed US middle school students about experiences of offline and online harassment over the previous 30 days. They found that being a victim of cyberbullying was significantly associated with suicidal thoughts, but at a comparable level to the association with traditional bullying. Similarly, in a sample of 15 year old US students, Hay and Meldrum (2010) found that being victimised by either traditional or cyber forms of bullying linked to suicidal ideation and self-harm at about equal strength. They also examined the moderating effects of this link: these were weaker if the young person experienced authoritative (supportive) parenting at home, and also if they had good control of their emotions.

Bauman, Toomey and Walker (2013) found similar links, but with some complex gender associations: there was a stronger association between traditional victimisation and suicide attempts for females, but a stronger link between cyberbullying of others and suicide attempts for males. Depression emerged as a significant mediating factor between victimisation and suicide attempts, especially for females.

In summary, there are clear associations between being bullied and suicidal ideation and self-harm. These are usually stronger for females, but with a possible reversal for cyber victims. Three longitudinal studies cited confirm the link, but for two studies with the proviso that predisposing conditions such as depression are present. A common theme is that other factors are important, including family factors. Thus victim experiences at school appear to contribute to cases of suicidal ideation, and in a small number of cases to actual suicide, but it is very likely that pre-existing depression and/or family difficulties will be present as well. This makes it difficult to say that a suicide is 'caused' by bullying, although in some cases it may appear to have a leading role.

Academic achievement

Would victims of school bullying be expected to be poorer in academic achievement? Here the issue is complicated. On the one hand, there is evidence that being smart at school and getting good grades can be a reason for being bullied. Peterson and Ray (2006) found that smart students in a range of US high schools were often called derogatory names such as geek or nerd, although they had no comparison group so they could not say whether this was higher than average. On the other hand, the kinds of internalising symptoms often experienced by victims could be expected to adversely effect school performance. Also, children with learning difficulties are more likely to be victimised (see Chapter 4). In South African schools, Townsend, Flisher, Chikobvu, Lombard and King (2008) found that bully/victims, but not pure victims, were more likely to drop out of high school early.

The Cook, Williams, Guerra, Kim and Sadek (2010) meta-analysis (see Table 5.1) suggests negative effects on academic performance for bully/victims and bullies but not for victims. A meta-analysis specifically on this latter topic, by Nakamoto and Schwartz (2010), identified 33 relevant studies between 1978 and 2007. The mean effect size (correlation) of victimisation with academic achievement measures was around –.10, so there was a modest but significant effect of victims having lower academic achievement. However, there was very great variance between studies with effect sizes varying from –.40 to +.14.

These were mostly cross-sectional studies. One longitudinal study was reported by Schwartz, Gorman, Nakamoto and Toblin (2005). They gathered data in two US elementary schools, following pupils from 9–10 years of age. They found evidence that victimisation at baseline predicted a decrement in academic achievement one year later, and also increases in depression: there was some evidence that depression mediated the effects of victimisation on academic achievement. There was no evidence that academic achievement at baseline predicted any change in victimisation one year later, so they suggested that the link from victimisation to lower academic achievement was unidirectional rather than transactional.

In a study later than the Nakamoto and Schwartz review period, Rothon, Head, Klineberg and Stansfeld (2010) reported cross-sectional data from England on

11–14 year olds. Victimisation was found to be associated with lower academic achievement, but the link was ameliorated if pupils reported high social support from friends, and also if they reported moderate (not high) levels of family support (high levels of family support might imply over-protection; see later).

The issue of support by friends is not clear-cut, however. Ma, Phelps, Lerner and Lerner (2009) reported on a longitudinal study of 11 year olds in US schools, followed up over two years. For children who bullied others, there was a steady decrement of academic achievement, and the authors describe a 'vicious cycle' (or transactional model) as applying well to them. For victims, the link to academic achievement was also negative, but much less strong than for those who bullied (about one-third as strong); also, it did not get worse over time. In this study peer support did not help victims – it did not lessen the link to academic achievement. This discrepancy with Rothon et al. (2010) does not seem to be methodological: both studies used self-report items for peer support such as 'I trust my friends' (Rothon et al., 2010) or 'I can count on my friends when things go wrong' (Ma et al., 2009). Both studies had large multi-school samples as well as a similar age range. One possibility might be a cultural difference in friendship patterns in US and UK schools.

In summary, many studies suggest poorer academic performance in bully/victims and bullies. The link, if any, for victims seems more complex and varied, but two longitudinal studies do suggest a link, with some uncertainty as to how cumulative this is and what role social support might have in mediating it.

A cross-national study of psychosocial adjustment

Using HBSC data from 1997–1998, Nansel, Craig, Overpeck, Saluja and Ruan (2004) reported correlates of bullying involvement for 11–15 year olds in 25 countries (mostly European, but including the USA, Canada and Israel). Despite large country variations in incidence (see Chapter 4), the correlates of roles (as bully, victim or bully/victim) were generally very consistent across countries. Based on five measures of psychosocial adjustment, the main findings were that not-involved children scored best on all measures; for example, better than all the other roles as regards health problems. Bullies and bully/victims scored lowest on school adjustment, and highest on alcohol use – an externalising symptom. Victims and bully/victims scored lowest on relationships with classmates and emotional adjustment – an internalising symptom. These findings were found for most, and often all, of the 25 countries contributing data.

Family level

Family factors showed up as modest predictors of bullying involvement in the Cook, Williams, Guerra, Kim and Sadak (2010) meta-analysis (see Table 5.1), though more so for bully/victims and bullies than for victims. Family factors have also emerged as quite important moderating factors in some of the studies on internalising problems above, and there has been a considerable amount of research directly on the topic.

In a qualitative study, Bibou-Nakou, Tsiantis, Assimopoulos and Chatzilambou (2012) used focus groups with 13–15 year old pupils in Thessaloniki, Greece, to explore issues around bullying and relationships in school. They extracted material relating to family factors, and reported that three main themes emerged – a difficult home environment, issues around protection and control, and abuse.

The first theme was a difficult home environment, with many conflicts between the spouses or between the parents and the adolescent. For example, a student called Anna was quoted as saying '... there were a lot of fights, they would shout at each other most of the times ... I believe this is a reason why I started doing it [behaving as a bully]' (2012: 60).

The second theme covered parental overprotection, a lack of supervision, or excessive control. Eleni commented on overprotection: 'I believe that sometimes parents are too protective ... These children can't cope successfully; they don't believe in themselves, they feel inferior. . . . in this way they can easily become the victims of students who are looking for trouble and fights. You see, when overprotected, you can't stand up for yourself when you are left on your own' (2012: 62).

Xenia commented on possible effects of excessive control: 'I remember a classmate – she had a lot of problems with her family. They would control her excessively; they did not trust her at all ... then at school, she would behave like that, she would make fun of others, she got herself into trouble most of the time, she was a real bully' (2012: 62).

The third theme of domestic abuse and its effects is graphically illustrated by a quote from Elli: 'I don't really mind if they swear at me or if they insult me [referring to her classmates]. I am used to it. All these years that's the way my father treated me. And now, I don't really care if they behave towards me like this [referring to the other students]. I get them back the same way, sometimes ... To tell you the truth, I don't feel anything. It is like they [referring to her parents] have made me feel like trash' (2012: 63).

On the positive side, Kostas commented: 'It has a lot to do with the parents, the family. If your family is good, if they talk with you, they give you advice, if they trust you, I believe that you don't get involved [in bullying]' (2012: 61).

These themes coming from the young people themselves are echoed by many research findings – for example, the kind of abusive family situation that is associated with aggressive victim or bully/victim behaviour at school, such as Elli describes, the conflicts and lack of warm supportive relationships in families of bullying children, and over-protecive families for some victims.

Another way of obtaining such information from children and young people is the Family System Test (FAST: see Gehring, Debry & Smith, 2001). This is a figure placement task: the child or young person places figures representing their family on a 9 × 9 checkered board, and the distance between the figures, as well as the use of blocks to make some figures taller, show cohesion (closeness) and power relationships as perceived in the family.

Bowers and colleagues (1992) gave the FAST individually to 80 pupils aged 8–11 years, in Sheffield, England. There were 20 each of non-involved controls, victims, bullies and bully/victims, as identified by peer nominations. There were significant differences in the kinds of family configurations coming from each group. Typical plots from one of each group are shown in Figure 5.1.

Figure (a), from a non-involved child, shows a close but not over-cohesive grouping of figures, away from sides and corners. Figure (b), from a victim, shows a highly cohesive grouping (with no gaps between figures), also away from sides and corners. Figure (c), from a bully/victim, shows a non-cohesive grouping with figures on two sides and corners. Figure (d), from a bully, shows a very wide spread of figures, with two sides and one corner occupied. Statistically, bullies had the lowest cohesion scores. By contrast, victims had the highest cohesion scores, with the lack of any separation in the figures (found in 15/20 victims) perhaps indicative of over-protection.

The more usual approach to family factors has been to use questionnaires. Lereya, Samara and Wolke (2013) reported a meta-analysis of 70 such studies, published between 1970 and 2012, that provided quantitative data on parenting

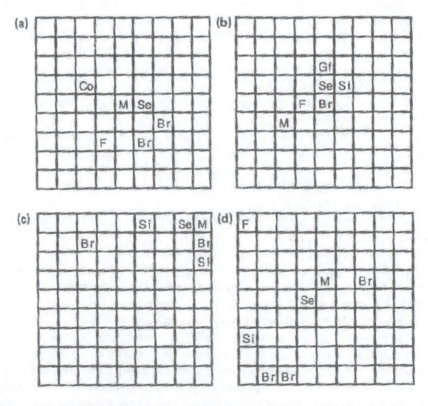

Figure 5.1 Examples of four FAST test figure placements, for (a) a non-involved child, (b) a victim, (c) a bully/victim and (d) a bully. Se = self; F = father; M = mother; Br = brother; Si = sister; Gf = grandfather; Co = cousin (from Bowers et al., 1992)

Table 5.2 Effect sizes for link between parenting practices and being a victim or bully/victim (data from Lereya et al., 2013)

Parenting measure/effect sizes	Victims	Bully/victims
Authoritative	−0.19	−0.39
Warmth and affection	−0.19	−0.33
Involvement and support	−0.22	−0.30
Communication	−0.12	−0.17
Supervision	−0.16	−0.34
Overprotection	0.26	0.13
Maladaptive parenting	0.27	0.49
Abuse and neglect	0.31	0.68

and peer victimisation: they separated out effects on victims and bully/victims, and used a statistic called Hedges' g for effect size, which can be considered as small (around 0.2), medium (around 0.5) or large (around 0.8). Their findings are summarised in Table 5.2. There are five measures of positive parenting, then three measures of negative parenting.

As expected, positive parenting protects against being a victim, while negative parenting is associated with greater risk. Overall the effect sizes are small; however, they are statistically significant (with the one exception of overprotective parenting for bully/victims). This is in line with the broad-sweep meta-analysis by Cook, Williams, Guerra, Kim and Sadek (2010) shown in Table 5.1. However, the links in Table 5.2 are noticeably larger for bully/victims for all measures except overprotection. Parental abuse and neglect stands out as having the strongest link, and indeed the 0.68 effect size for bully/victims is between 'moderate' and 'strong'; together with the 0.49 effect size for maladaptive parenting (taken as authoritarian, coercive, punitive), this suggests an important aspect in explaining why some children are bully/victims (as in Eleni, earlier). However, as the authors point out, most studies were cross-sectional, so they cannot confirm cause and effect.

Positive parenting as protective

The positive aspects of parenting indicated in Table 5.2 can be protective against involvement as a victim, but also as a bully. In work with 14–18 year old British adolescents, Flouri and Buchanan (2002, 2003) documented positive associations with aspects of parental involvement, such as spending time with their child and taking an interest in their school work. Flouri and Buchanan (2002) showed that for boys, father involvement was a protective factor against being bullied, and they later (2003) found that both mother and father involvement was protective against being involved in bullying others. High involvement by one parent could compensate for low involvement by the other, while low involvement by both parents was associated with bullying. The effects were similar for both boys and girls.

Spriggs, Ianotti, Nansel and Haynie (2007) obtained data from US adolescents in sixth to tenth grade regarding predictors of bullying involvement. The strongest family predictor was ease of communication with parents. If this was difficult, it predicted both bully and victim status. Low school involvement of parents (such as helping with homework) predicted both bully and victim status in White and Black, but not Hispanic, pupils. Also, not living with both biological parents predicted both bully and victim status for White pupils only.

In a study not included in the Lereya et al. (2013) review, Bowes, Maughan, Caspi, Moffitt and Arsenault (2010) reported findings from the E-risk study in England and Wales. Children were assessed at 10 and 12 years old. In terms of emotional and behavioural adjustment, children's resilience to victimisation was increased by maternal warmth, sibling warmth and a positive atmosphere at home. These longitudinal data give more confidence in cause and effect, and in addition these researchers used the twin data to compare monozygotic twins who were both bullied on maternal warmth – the twin who received the most warmth had fewer behavioural problems, pinpointing a causal environmental effect.

Positive parenting may go beyond helping children avoid bully or victim involvement and predict defending others. Nickerson et al. (2008), in their US middle school sample, found that secure attachment to mother predicted defender status.

Negative aspects of parenting

Turning to the negative aspects of parenting in Table 5.2, having an overprotective mother appears to be a risk factor for victimisation, and especially for boys. On the other hand, coercive, hostile or authoritarian parenting can affect both sexes, but in some circumstances girls more severely.

In the USA, Ladd and Kochenderfer-Ladd (1998) made home observations of mothers and their 5 year old children engaging in a series of semi-structured tasks. Boys who had an unusually emotionally intense relationship (sitting close together, and lots of positive touching, cuddling, smiling) were more likely to be victims in kindergarten. This relationship between emotionally close behaviours (similar to overprotection) and victimisation was not significant for girls. However, both girls and boys were affected by high intrusive demandingness by parents – this refers to how much a parent interrupts a child or overrides a child's initiatives. When combined with low responsiveness, they found that this predicted being a victim, and especially for girls. Ladd and Kochenderfer-Ladd argued that intrusive-demanding parenting socialises children to be compliant and dependent rather than independent and assertive.

Different gender pathways in middle childhood were suggested from work by Finnegan, Hodges and Perry (1998), again in the USA. They assessed victim status in 9–12 year olds by peer nomination, and children provided verbal reports about their mothers' and their own behaviour at home during conflict and control episodes. For boys, maternal over-protectiveness was associated with being a victim, but only for those boys who reported that they felt afraid and compelled to submit to their mothers during conflicts. For girls, being a victim was associated with maternal hostility, especially for girls seen by peers as lacking in physical strength. Finnegan et al. suggested that where maternal behaviour hinders a child's progress towards relevant social and developmental goals for their gender, then peer victimisation may be more likely to occur. For boys, a mother's over-protectiveness can hinder their search for independence and autonomy, while for girls, mothers' hostility may lead to anxiety or depression, affecting the quality of their relationships with others.

In a now classic study of Swedish boys aged 13–16 years, Olweus (1973/1978) found that mothers of victimised boys often treated their sons as younger than they actually were and were overcontrolling of the boys' spare time. A child's weak temperament (such as being shy and unassertive) predicted over-protectiveness in mothers, which in turn predicted victim status. A separate pathway was from father's negativism, which predicted a lack of identification with the father, which in turn predicted victim status. Either pathway could lead to a boy who had difficulty in asserting himself with other boys of his own age. Thus, according to Olweus, a boy who is most likely to become a victim is a shy sensitive boy who has a close overprotected relationship with his mother, or who has a critical and distant father who does not provide a good male role model. If combined with physical weakness, this could make victimisation especially likely.

Abuse and aggressive victims

Abusive behaviour between parents, or of children, is the strongest association in Table 5.2. It appears to be a particularly strong predictor of being an aggressive victim or bully/victim.

In the USA, Schwartz, Dodge, Pettit and Bates (1997) observed 4–5 year old children in the home and interviewed the mothers, rating the child's exposure to violence, aggression, marital conflict, stressful events and physical harm. Preschool exposure to violence and marital conflict significantly predicted child bullying in school at ages 8–9 years. Aggressive or bully/victims were three times more likely than others to have experienced physical abuse from family member(s). In a later study, Schwartz, Dodge, Pettit and Bates (2000) showed that early harsh, punitive parenting is associated with later victim outcomes, especially if the child has few friends at school: having good relationships with friends at school might be a protective factor mitigating the effects of abusive relationships at home. Schwartz et al. also hypothesised that violent and aggressive family role models can cause children to learn goal-oriented aggressive behaviours, and that harsh discipline and physically abusive experiences may lead them to develop a view of the world as a hostile dangerous place and to develop hostile attributional biases. This results in high rates of angry reactive aggression, rejection by peers and becoming an aggressive victim.

Shame management theory/reintegrative shaming theory

A different angle on how parents communicate with children and deal with conflicts and discipline comes from shame management theory. This especially concerns how parents manage misbehaviour by the child: Do they just stigmatise the child, or do they give space for them to acknowledge wrong but also be forgiven? Is the child able to acknowledge shame (that what they did was wrong), or do they suppress such feelings or displace hostile feelings elsewhere? This theoretical perspective is linked to the idea of restorative justice (see Chapter 6), with its emphasis on acceptance of responsibility for wrongdoing, but moving to restore good relations rather than to punish.

Ahmed (2001) and Ahmed and Braithwaite (2004a) proposed that shame acknowledgement plays a central role in maintaining adaptive personal relationships, through effective acknowledgement, making amends, and discharge of shame. By contrast, shame displacement is seen as maladaptive: debilitating feelings of persistent shame may lead to externalised hostility and scapegoating, and unidentified shame can lead to distancing from others and other-directed anger. These ideas can be applied to parent–child relationships in the family, and to the consequences for peer relationships.

Some evidence for this came from an Australian study of 9–12 year olds by Ahmed and Braithwaite (2004b). If a parent used non-stigmatising shaming, and the child showed shame acknowledgement, the child was less likely to be involved in bullying others. Conversely, if the parent used stigmatising shaming, and the child showed shame displacement, then the child was more likely to be involved in bullying. They also found that shame acknowledgement mediated some individual and school risk factors predicting bullying. Ttofi and Farrington (2008) tested a version of this approach, which they called Reintegrative Shaming Theory (RST). They assessed bullying of siblings in families, and of peers in schools, in 11–12 year old children in Cyprus. They also assessed bonding to the mother and father, reintegrative or disintegrative shaming by parents, and shame acknowledgement or shame displacement by pupils. They found that mother (but not father) bonding related to reintregrative shaming and shame acknowledgement, and thus to less sibling bullying, in partial support of RST, but with some significant gender effects. Disintegrative shaming of children who bully (shaming that leads to stigmatisation) had a negative effect on those children's emotional regulation.

Siblings

The role of siblings in the family may be important, but is rather under-researched. In a US study, Duncan (1999) used self-report data on sibling relationships and peer relationships among 13 year olds, and found significant links between them. Taking a lenient criterion of involvement, she found that 32% of non-involved children (at school) were involved in bullying a sibling, but this increased to 38%

for victims at school, 56% for bullies and 77% for bully/victims. Similarly, 24% of non-involved children (at school) were bullied by a sibling, but this increased to 36% for victims at school, 29% for bullies and 60% for bully/victims. Bullying a sibling significantly predicted bullying peers at school, and both bullying and/or being bullied by a sibling predicted bully/victim status at school, although there is a shared method issue as all the data come from self-report. A study in Israel, by Wolke and Samara (2004), also found links between sibling and school bullying. Of children bullied by a sibling, 51% were bullied at school, but if they were not bullied by a sibling, this fell to 12%. Consistent with Duncan (1999), being bullied by a sibling also predicted being a bully/victim at school, but not for being a bully (only).

Parent factors in cyberbullying

Studies of parenting in relation to cyberbullying suggest similar factors are at work as for traditional bullying. For example, Ybarra and Mitchell (2007) related internet harassment to greater caregiver–child conflict, and Wang et al. (2009) found that lower parental support of adolescents predicted greater involvement in all kinds of bullying, including cyber. There may be specific issues around parental control and supervision of mobile phone and computer use, however. Law, Shapka and Olson (2010) linked adolescent online aggression to a lack of communication with parents, although it was unrelated to attempts to limit time on the internet or sites visited.

Summary of parenting factors

Positive parenting – such as being authoritative, showing warmth but not too intense emotional closeness, having secure attachment relationships to children, and being involved with them and providing appropriate but not intrusive supervision – appears to act as protection against being involved in bully or victim relationships at school. This seems generally true for both sexes. Most of the evidence is correlational, but the E-risk study by Bowes et al. (2010), for example, suggests a causal relationship. Positive parenting provides a good role model for behaviour in relationships, and is likely to make children feel more secure and confident generally.

Overprotection is associated with increased risks of being a victim, perhaps especially maternal overprotection and for boys. Overprotection may hinder the development and practice of assertive strategies. Hostility from parents or harsh discipline is another well-established risk factor, and possibly more so for girls. When such parenting moves into the domain of abuse and neglect, then there is a strong link to children being bully/victims at school.

While cyberbullying raises particular issues, probably the general quality of the parent–child relationship, and communication about safety issues, matter more than particular supervisory practices.

Peer group

Friendships and sociometric status

Whether a pupil – perhaps one who is shy or vulnerable in some way (individual factors) – actually gets bullied will depend a lot on the peer group as well as the class and school situation. Well-identified factors in the peer group are friendship and sociometric status.

Pellegrini, Bartini and Brooks (1999) looked at these issues in 12 year old students in the USA. They found that sociometric popularity (being liked by peers) was associated with less victimisation, and so – to a lesser extent – was number of friends. However, a qualification here was that having friends who were also victims was not protective, while having friends who were not victims was protective.

Hodges, Malone and Perry (1997) examined individual and peer group predictors of being a victim in 8–13 year old students in the USA. Victimisation was predicted by internalising and externalising problems, and physical weakness; however, this link was strongest when a student had few friends, or friends who were not able to protect them (unpopular or weak), or if they were disliked generally by peers (sociometric rejection). In a longitudinal follow-up, Hodges and Perry (1999) confirmed a transactional link between internalising problems and peer rejection, and victimisation, over time. If a child was, or became, more sociometrically rejected, this increased the chances of being a victim. In this longitudinal study, number of friends did not serve as a protective factor over time. However, this conclusion about friendships is partly moderated by findings from another longitudinal study – of Canadian 10 year olds – by Hodges, Boivin, Vitaro and Bukowski (1999). Here, having one reciprocated best friend was protective, especially if that friend was perceived as someone who could help them effectively.

In a longitudinal study of 9–11 year old English children, Fox and Boulton (2006) found that children who lacked good social skills were at greater risk of increasing victimisation over time. However, this relationship was weaker if the child had many friends, or if he or she had one best friend who was popular in the peer group. Of course, it will not always be easy for a victim, especially one who has a reputation as such, to have many friends or a popular high-status friend. Boulton (2013), using hypothetical vignettes with English 11–13 year olds, found that pupils said they would be less likely to befriend a new pupil (or think that other pupils would do so) if they were told that this new pupil had been the victim of bullying in previous schools. Boulton argued that this is probably because pupils would see this as risky for their own status in the peer group, and their own chances of being victimised.

The dominance hypothesis for bullies

Bullying children tend to be peer rejected in infant/junior school but less so in secondary school. Towards adolescence, some aggressive and bullying children can have quite a high status in peer groups. This does not necessarily mean they are well-liked, however. Caravita et al. (2009) found that children who bullied others did not score particularly highly on social preference scores (not so many pupils actually liked them a lot), but they did score high on perceived popularity (many pupils thought that they were popular, or at least of high status in the peer group).

Pellegrini and Bartini (2001) and Pellegrini and Long (2002) argued that a number of strategies, both prosocial and aggressive, can be used to gain and maintain status or dominance with peers. Some children may use bullying tactics to do so, and this may be particularly prominent at school transitions (see Chapter 4) as pupils jockey for status positions in new social groupings. It is also more important in adolescence, especially in terms of appearing attractive to young people of the opposite sex (Pellegrini & Long, 2002).

Salmivalli (2010) has reviewed the general evidence for what might be called a dominance hypothesis, namely that some children who bully are driven by a desire for dominant status in the peer group. Ringleader bullies especially may be rewarded if followers and reinforcers support their bullying actions, and if many bystanders remain passive (as is often the case; see for example Pepler et al., 1998). If this is so, we would predict that the likelihood of a child taking part in bullying another will be influenced by such factors as peer group norms and expectations about bullying and defending (see below), as well as what support the victim might have (for example, high quality friendships) – predictions which are born out by research. Correspondingly, children with high popularity or peer group status can be the most effective defenders (Caravita et al., 2009; Nickerson et al., 2008).

Faris and Felmlee (2011) looked at the influence of social status, and what they labelled as 'network centrality', on aggression, in over 4,000 high school students in the USA. Their measure of aggression ('picked on or were mean to') was similar to bullying. Their findings suggested that aggression was an intrinsic part of status and to being recognised in peer group social networks; for some adolescents at least, picking on others was a way to increase their status in the peer network. The least aggressive individuals were those at the bottom of the social hierarchy (who had little power to be aggressive) and also those at the top (who did not need to). The authors concluded that 'aggression is not primarily a maladjusted reaction from socially marginal or psychologically troubled adolescents. Rather, aggression is intrinsic to status but in a nonlinear fashion. Individuals at the bottom of the status hierarchy do not have as much capacity for aggression, while those at the very top do not have as much cause to use it' (2011: 67).

Summary of peer factors

For pupils at risk of being bullied (perhaps for individual-level reasons such as shyness or depression), the peer group can be important in moderating this risk. If a child is generally liked, or has one or more best friends who can be trusted or who are not themselves of low status, then the chances of being bullied are reduced. These peer group factors also influence the likelihood that children who are prone to bully others (for individual-level reasons) will actually do so, and this is especially the case for those whose motivation for bullying is to gain or maintain peer group status themselves.

School class

Class norms

The school class provides a social unit, within which many friendships are formed, and also within which bully–victim relationships can occur. The importance of the class may vary culturally (for example, it may be even more important in Japan and South Korea; see Chapter 4) and with age (in some countries, such as the UK, there is less emphasis on a homeroom class in secondary schools, with pupils mixing by ability and subject choice for different lessons). Multilevel modelling enables statistical comparisons to be made (with large enough samples) of individual, class and school contributions to outcomes such as bully and victim rates.

Besides individual attitudes, within the classroom context there can be injunctive and descriptive norms (Pozzoli, Gini & Vieno, 2012). Injunctive norms are defined in terms of what behaviour is commonly expected by other people within the class. Descriptive norms are defined in terms of the perception of what most people in the class do. Various methods have been used to assess these kinds of classroom norms as regards bullying.

The importance of these group norms within a class was signalled by Salmivalli and Voeten (2004), in a study of 9–12 year olds in Finland: 48 school classes were examined, with class sizes of around 25 students. Besides the Participant Role Scale, they measured attitudes towards bullying and classroom norms. Attitudes were assessed by asking students about their own opinions, but classroom norms were assessed by giving students five hypothetical situations (such as someone laughing at a victim in their class, or someone making friends with the victim) and asking how others in the class would react to this (namely, descriptive norms).

Both anti-bullying attitudes and anti-bullying norms decreased with age (consistent with other findings; see Chapter 4). However, particular interest was paid to whether these predicted participant role behaviour. At the individual level, attitudes correlated with participant roles, but only modestly. At the class level, anti-bullying norms did contribute significantly to explaining variations in participant roles (the strength of this varying somewhat by age, gender and specific role).

In subsequent research, Kärnä, Voeten, Poskiparta and Salmivalli (2010) reported data on 9–11 year olds from 378 classrooms in 77 schools. In this study, they used the proportion of reinforcer and defender roles in a class as a measure of classroom descriptive norms. They analysed the impact of these on the association between social anxiety, peer rejection and victimisation. They found that at the individual level, both peer rejection (strongly) and social anxiety (less strongly) predicted victimisation, as expected from previous research. But these predictive effects were significantly affected by what classmates were perceived as doing in bullying situations. In classes where there were more reinforcers the link was stronger, while for classes where there were more defenders the link was weaker. Calculating intra-class correlations (ICCs), some 13% of the variation in victimisation was due to classroom (including school) effects (the remainder being due to individual effects).

The effect of more reinforcers in the class is consistent with the dominance hypothesis, such that bullies are encouraged if their attempts to gain status by bullying are more often reinforced by others. The effect of more defenders in the class was also present but substantially smaller in magnitude. Perhaps the defender effect depends on the status of the defenders (Caravita et al., 2009), or perhaps a critical number or proportion of defenders is needed to act as a realistic deterrent to bullying.

Pozzoli et al. (2012) examined individual attitudes to bullying, self-reported behaviours in bullying situations, and perceived peer and teacher pressure (what peers and teachers would expect of individuals) in Italian pupils aged 10 and 13 years from 54 classes, with an average class size of 18 pupils. Class attitudes were calculated by aggregating individual attitude scores within a class, class injunctive norms by aggregating individual peer and teacher pressure scores, and class descriptive norms by aggregating peer nominations for defending as compared to passive bystanding. The findings indicated that both individual measures and class characteristics predicted levels of defending and passive bystanding behaviour. At the individual level, in addition to the usual age and gender findings, they found that pro-victim attitudes and perceived peer pressure for intervention predicted defending behaviour. The effect of peer pressure was stronger in middle than primary school, and the effect of teacher pressure was not significant. At the classroom level, class pro-victim attitudes, peer injunctive norms and peer descriptive norms all predicted defending behaviour.

Saarento, Kärnä, Hodges and Salmivalli (2013) used data from the Finnish KiVa project (see Chapter 6) to study individual, classroom and school effects in 358 classrooms in 74 schools. Besides individual measures, including antibullying attitudes, they assessed what a pupil thought would be likely to happen to them if they defended a victim (an injunctive norms measure), and also what their homeroom teacher thought about bullying. The main dependent variable assessed was being a victim. Victimisation was assessed by both self- and peer reports: for peer report data, 22% of the variance in victimisation was due to classroom differences, and an additional 3% just by school differences, while for self-reports these figures were 6% and 2% respectively.

So what explained the classroom differences in victimisation? Both the extent of antibullying attitudes in the class and the injunctive norms for defending measure had significant effects. In addition, the general perception of a homeroom teacher's attitude to bullying was a significant predictor of classroom differences, and also contributed significantly to school differences.

Homeroom teacher

The importance of the class or homeroom teacher was also indicated by Troop-Gordon and Quenelle (2010), who worked with 10–12 years old pupils in the USA. Pupils were asked how their teacher would respond to a child being victimised. This did affect the impact of peer victimisation, particularly when teachers were perceived as not directly helping (by involving parents, or punishing the aggressors), but rather as asking the pupil to cope on their own (by standing up for themselves, or working it out, or ignoring or avoiding the situation). Perceptions of the teacher asking pupils to cope on their own increased the link between victimisation and internalising problems for boys. As with Saarento et al. (2013), this suggests that what teachers do in the classroom (or at least, are perceived to do) is an important consideration.

In-group and out-group attitudes

A somewhat different approach to looking at group dynamics in classrooms has come from social psychology, and in particular from social identity development theory (SIDT). This supposes that as children get older, social group awareness and categorisations increase, and some in-group preference develops. This in turn may lead to out-group hostility, depending on factors such as beliefs concerning and attitudes to the out-group or its members.

A number of studies have used this kind of perspective to study bullying. As one example, Nesdale, Durkin, Maass, Kiesner and Griffiths (2008) worked with 7 and 9 year old Australian children. Children were assigned to groups that they were told had a norm of either out-group dislike ('kids in your team really don't like kids in the other teams …'), or out-group liking ('kids in your team really like kids in the other teams …'). They were then given vignettes concerning team events and possible behaviours towards a child in another team or out-group, including possible direct or indirect bullying behaviours, and asked to choose a response. Children's bullying intentions were greater when the group they were in had a norm of out-group dislike: the tendency was to choose more direct bullying in younger children and more indirect bullying in older children.

This kind of approach has limitations, as it uses an artificial manipulation to produce groups with different kinds of out-group liking. In real classroom situations, there could be various and overlapping 'out-groups' (based on gender, race, status, disability, etc.) in contrast to the straightforward team situations usually used in the vignettes. However, it does provide a slightly different perspective on group dynamics from that coming from the developmental psychology stream of research. Another approach from group dynamics is that of scapegoating.

The scapegoating theory of victimisation

The concept of scapegoating is that hostility is redirected to an innocent victim. Fraczek (1996: 81–82) argued that 'the term "scapegoat" is used mainly as a name for a person and/or outgroup to whom is ascribed, without sufficiently rational reason, guilt for the failure and unrealized expectations of a social group … The same phenomenon is observed in a classroom or school where some child is, temporarily or permanently, and without sufficient rational reason, blamed for various ingroup failures'.

Does scapegoating occur widely in school classrooms in western societies, in the sense that one pupil is selected as the 'victim', labelled as such, and becomes a focus for any hostility such that other vulnerable pupils in the class do not become victims? This was suggested by Schuster (1999), who gathered peer nominations of victims in German schools, with pupils aged 10, 12 and 16 years. She found that in 29 of the 34 classes studied, only one or two victims were identified. In conclusion she posed the question, '… does every class have its whipping boy or "scapegoat"?' (1999: 178).

If each class needs a victim or scapegoat as a near-inevitable consequence of group processes, then focusing on risk factors or indeed any general programme of school-based intervention might seem unproductive; indeed, Schuster (1999: 187) surmised that perhaps it is 'not realistic to attempt to entirely eliminate bullying in schools'.

Two separate studies, however, failed to confirm Schuster's hypothesis about number of victims. Mahdavi and Smith (2007) analysed data from 67 classes of 8–13 year olds in England. There were one or two victims in only 27 of them, and calculations indicated that this was what would be expected by a chance model of individual risk factors. In quite a number of classes there were no victims. In a study in Austrian schools, Atria, Strohmeier and Spiel (2007) analysed data from 86 different classes (in grades 4 to 9). Again, there was wide variability in the number of victims in each class: some had no victims, some had many. This was true using a variety of measurement criteria. These studies were commented on (with a reply by Schuster) in a special (2007) issue of the *European Journal of Developmental Psychology*, 4 (3).

Disproving the particular scapegoat hypothesis that Schuster proposed is not an argument against considering group processes in classrooms. It is also possible that something like scapegoating occurs in other cultures, such as classrooms in South Korea (Koo, 2004; see also Chapter 4). However, the existence of many classrooms with no victims is encouraging, and the variability at class level points to the importance of the school class as a social unit for intervention efforts.

School factors

School factors may operate via the school climate, and the use of effective school policies and anti-bullying strategies. The school climate can embrace aspects such as perceptions of safety in school, liking of school, and teacher–pupil as well as peer–peer relationships.

The Saarento et al. (2013) study (above) found significant but small percentages of variance in victimisation due to schools. This is a somewhat common finding when multilevel analyses are done on individual, school and classroom factors. A partial explanation for this apparently small effect of schools may be that classroom variance absorbs much of the non-individual variance: even though classrooms are within schools, the school variance is what is finally left over. Nevertheless, the impact of school-level anti-bullying strategies (see Chapter 6), as well as some other findings, suggest that the school level is important. For example, the E-Risk study in England and Wales found that school factors were associated with victim risk (Bowes et al., 2009). Pozzoli et al. (2012) did not find teacher expectations to be a significant predictor of defending in Italian schools, but Saarento et al. (2013) did find that the school-level measure of perceived teacher attitudes to bullying was a significant school level predictor of victimisation in Finnish schools.

A study in Israel by Khoury-Kassabri, Benbenishty, Astor and Zeira (2004), with students in grades 7–11 at 162 schools, found that the variance between schools accounted for between 9% and 15% of the variance in pupil victim rates. Of this, much was accounted for by school climate – here, a composite measure of students' perceptions of school rules and policies on reducing violence, teacher support and student participation. By contrast, school size was unimportant.

The significance of school policy and school climate was also indicated by Birkett, Espelage and Koenig (2009), looking specifically at homophobic bullying. Working with 27 middle schools in the USA, they found that although LGB students tended to feel more depressed and have more suicidal thoughts, this was less so when pupils generally perceived a positive school climate (such as the adults caring for them, and getting a good education).

Gendron, Williams and Guerra (2011), in a longitudinal study of 78 elementary, middle and high schools in the USA, found that bullying rates were predicted by (poor) school climate, as well as by normative beliefs about bullying. They also found an interesting interaction effect: when pupils perceived a poor school climate, pupil high self-esteem predicted higher levels of bullying, but when pupils perceived a good school climate, high self-esteem predicted low levels of bullying.

Summary of class and school-level factors

Aggregate measures of attitudes to bullying, and of injunctive and descriptive norms – expectations of what others should do, and would do – are predictive of levels of bullying at the class level. So also is the number of pupils seen as being reinforcers (on the one hand) or defenders (on the other hand). Although not all studies are consistent on the role of teachers, there is some evidence for the importance of perceived teacher attitudes, at both the class and school levels. Classes vary in all these aspects. There is little support for a scapegoating theory, namely that all classes will have one or two victims as a focus for hostility or frustration. School-level variations (beyond classroom-level variations) come out as relatively small, but significant in various aspects and some studies, as would also be indicated by the success of some school-level interventions (discussed in Chapter 6).

Community level

It might be expected that levels of violence and antisocial behaviour in the neighbourhood or community would impact on school bullying levels. Some evidence for this came from a study in the USA by Schwartz and Proctor (2000). Children who had witnessed community violence were more likely to be aggressive to classmates; this link was mediated by social cognitions supporting aggression. They also found that those who had been victims of community violence were more likely to be victims at school as well; here, emotional regulation was a mediating factor. Thus neighbourhood violence may change normative beliefs about aggression (facilitating bullying in some children), and may particularly upset those who are victims in both school and community settings, thereby increasing their vulnerability.

A study in Colombia by Chaux, Molano and Podlesky (2009) provided an analysis of a wide range of variables. They obtained data from over 53,000 children in the fifth and ninth grades (average ages 11 and 15 years old), from 1,000 schools in 308 municipalities across the country. The data on bullying were fairly basic – three yes/no items on bully, witness or victim, which were added to make up one measure of bullying involvement. This, and other measures (of empathy, anger management, hostile attribution bias, beliefs supporting aggreession, trust, family democratic/peaceful practices, family socioeconomic conditions and neighbourhood violence) were assessed by individual self-report, but the analyses were carried out at the school level and not the individual level. In addition, data on poverty, inequality, population density, homicide rate and armed conflict were gathered from institutional records, and analyses were carried out at the municipality level.

The analyses at the school level showed that at both the fifth and ninth grades, there were strong and significant relations to bullying involvement for all of the measures, except for family socioeconomic conditions. This included the neigbourhood violence measure, which remained significant in multilevel analyses. The municipality level analyses did not yield significant findings for poverty, population density or homicide rate, but there were significant associations for armed conflict in the fifth grade, and economic inequality in the ninth grade.

Society level

Media

The mass media, and especially violence in the media, have often been cited as an influence on aggression, although the extent of this remains the subject of debate. For example, a meta-analysis by Anderson et al. (2010) on 136 studies on violent video game playing and aggression found an effect size of 0.189 linking exposure to violent video games to aggressive behaviour. Ferguson and Kilburn (2010) argued that such an effect size was quite small compared to many other factors affecting aggression. They also pointed out that the rapid growth of violent video games in the last fifteen years has coincided with a steady reduction in violent crime rates in the USA, UK, Japan and many other industrialised countries over the same period. The overall conclusion appears to be that there can be harmful effects of video game violence, but that it is (for most children at least) not a major factor in understanding violent behaviour.

Nevertheless, some recent studies have established links between violent media exposure and involvement in bullying or cyberbullying. For example, Lee and Kim (2004) found that exposure to violent media was associated with face-to-face bullying, amplified by feelings of anger and by contact with delinquent friends, in South Korean pupils. Calvete and colleagues (2010), in a study in Spain, and Fanti, Demetriou and Hawa (2012), in a study in Cyprus, both found links from violent media exposure (on television, the internet, movies, video games) to cyberbullying and cyber victimisation.

Hamer, Konijn and Keijer (2013) built on these findings, carrying out a study in the Netherlands on young people aged 13 years. Although based on cross-sectional data only, their findings supported a possible 'Cyclic Process' model. This supposes that in addition to direct links from victimisation, and anger, to cyberbullying behaviour, there may be an important indirect link via exposure to violent media, specifically that adolescent victims of (mainly traditional) bullying feel anger and frustration. They may then tend to use violent media more, as a way of coping with or finding outlets for their anger feelings, and this exposure in itself may lead to cyberbullying behaviors (through mechanisms such as desensitisation, imitation, and the modelling of action scripts). Structural equation modelling of their data supported such links. They called the model 'cyclic' because the cyberbullying might then increase the chances of becoming a victim once again (although this final link was not ascertained in their study).

Societal variations in risks online

The EU Kids Online study (Livingstone et al., 2011; see also Chapter 4) compared European countries in terms of internet/mobile use, opportunities, risks and parenting. In an analysis, Helsper, Kalmus, Hasebrink, Sagvari and De Haan (2013) arrived at a four-fold classification of countries: 'supported risky explorers' (Denmark, Finland, the Netherlands, Norway, Sweden); 'semi-supported risky gamers' (Bulgaria, Cyprus, Czech Republic, Estonia, Poland, Romania); 'unprotected networkers' (Austria, Hungary, Lithuania, Slovenia); and those 'protected by restrictions' (Belgium, France, Germany, Greece, Ireland, Italy, Portugal, Spain, Turkey, the UK). Levels of socioeconomic stratification, regulatory framework, technological infrastructure and educational system were suggested as possible explanatory factors for these country differences.

Economic inequality

The HBSC surveys (see Chapters 3 and 4) provide cross-national data on bully and victim rates, which invite comparisons in terms of societal characteristics. Limitations of the HBSC data need to be born in mind, including issues of translation across languages/countries (see Chapter 3).

While overall country wealth might be one factor to examine, generally the research within countries has not thrown up much significance in terms of socioeconomic status (for example, Chaux et al., 2009). Attention in cross-national research has focused particularly on income inequality as a measure of power differentials between those who have access to resources and those who do not. Income inequality has been associated with crime rates and homicides. Due et al. (2009) and Elgar, Craig, Boyce, Morgan and Vella-Zarb (2009) used HBSC data from the 2005/2006 surveys to examine variations in victim and bully rates, respectively, in relation to income inequality.

Due et al. (2009) analysed data for victim rates in 11, 13 and 15 year olds from 35 countries. At the family level, lower wealth was a predictor of victim rates, but wealth was not a predictor at the school or country level. However, after taking account of family wealth differences, both socioeconomic disparity at the school level and income inequality at the country level predicted higher victim rates. Elgar et al. (2009) found strong relations of income inequality to bullying rates (a correlation of around 0.6). Country wealth was a negative predictor of bullying rates, but income inequality was independently a strong contributor. Another (negative) predictor of bullying rates was school support (essentially a measure of school climate), which was more significant than measures of family or peer support.

Elgar et al. (2009: 357, 358) suggested that 'feelings of shame, humiliation and distrust intensify with greater income inequality and create a harsh social environment where violent acts such as school bullying may be condoned or ignored', and argued that 'it is possible that redistributing wealth and creating more egalitarian societies would do more for reducing bullying than school-level policies or individual-level intervention'. This is a challenging statement, certainly for politicians; nevertheless, school-level interventions are more feasible and have some success (see Chapter 6). Interestingly, Great Britain was one of the outliers in the Elgar et al. analysis, being high (8/37) in income inequality but low (31/37) in the index of bullying others used. This arguably indicates the impact of sustained anti-bullying work in the UK over the last twenty years. (Another country with sustained school-level intervention prior to 2006, Norway, is low on both bully rates and income inequality, as are the Scandinavian countries generally.)

Summary of community and society factors

Neighbourhood violence is associated with bullying involvement at school, although no causal relationship has been established. Exposure to violent media content has been suggested as a factor in bullying, with a specific model proposed for cyberbullying involvement. Countries vary considerably in their attitudes to managing internet/mobile risks and opportunities in young people. Finally, variations in economic inequality are associated with variations in bully and (to a lesser extent) victim rates across many countries.

Summary

Perhaps not surprisingly, a wide range of factors is associated with bully, victim and also defender roles. The findings in Table 5.1 provide a useful summary; however, different factors often interact and there are variations by age and gender. Genetic factors seem well established and presumably operate through other individual-level factors such as temperament, personality or social cognitive skills.

By and large, victims are likely to be temperamentally shy or unassertive, have low self-esteem and poor social skills; thus, they are not as able to cope with attempts to bully them as many other children might be. If they have been over-protected at home, or conversely if they have been bullied by siblings, this makes things more difficult for them. If they are nevertheless well-liked at school, or if they have good friends or even one best friend with some status in the peer group, this will be protective. However, long-term victims may gain a reputation as such, which means that protective friendships might be more difficult to obtain. In some cases their school work and academic achievement will be badly affected. Victims of prolonged or multiple types of bullying from peers, from which they lack protection, are especially likely to develop internalising symptoms such as psychosomatic disorders, depression and perhaps suicidal ideation, although actual suicide attempts are generally caused by a range of factors of which the victimisation is likely to be only one.

Children with a propensity to bully others are likely to be temperamentally hot-tempered, easy to take offence, and to have low affective empathy or be uncaring of others. They are also likely to be morally disengaged from the suffering of victims. Such characteristics may to some extent be caused or exacerbated by hostile parenting, or stigmatising shaming by the parents(s), or generally abusive relationships in the home perhaps also involving siblings. This does not mean that such children lack cognitive skills – some will have learnt to be skilful manipulators of others, with Machiavellian traits. Their self-esteem may not be low, although they may feel it is easily threatened (defensive egotism); they are likely to recognise that their behaviours are not approved of by adults, and their affiliation to school and academic achievement is likely to be low. Especially by secondary school, such children may capitalise on the possibilities of gaining or maintaining status or respect from peers by their bullying actions. Although not especially liked, they may be seen as influential and powerful by classmates.

Bully/victims are relatively small in number, if proper (that is, not too lenient) criteria are used in defining the bully and victim categories. They are likely to exhibit many of the characteristics of both bullies and victims. They will probably be particularly low on academic achievement, and to come from particularly troubled or abusive family backgrounds.

The problems that victims have, and the abusive opportunities that bullies have, will be influenced by peer group, class and school factors. In particular, injunctive and descriptive norms within the class or school may (or may not) encourage the 'silent majority' – who generally do not like bullying – to act as defenders, and thus provide less rewards for those tempted to bully. Many children get classified as outsiders (who keep away from any bullying) rather than defenders; according to Pronk, Goossens, Olthof, De Mey and Willemen (2013), who gathered peer nomination data from 10–14 year old Dutch children, many outsiders feel they might help victims indirectly, but they lack the competence or self-efficacy that defenders have, to intervene directly.

The extent of power that teachers and the school have here is still not entirely clear, but some studies suggest that perceptions of teacher attitudes to bullying, and how they respond to bullying, plus the general climate of the school, will be of considerable importance. This is borne out by the reasonable success of many whole-school anti-bullying programmes discussed in Chapter 6. Such programmes need to build on the knowledge of risk and protective factors which is being accumulated by research.

Finally, it should be noted that bullying goes beyond individuals, families, the peer group and the school. There is considerable evidence for some influence from further factors such as community violence, violence in the media, and also economic inequality in society.

SIX

Coping with bullying and the success of interventions

Bullying in schools is clearly prevalent (see Chapter 4) and has negative consequences for all involved, but especially victims (see Chapter 5). So what can be done about it? This chapter first examines what victims of bullying often do (or say they would do) – their coping strategies – and how successful these may be. Parents also have a role and this is considered. Then a range of interventions by adults in school is reviewed – proactive and reactive, as well as the potential for organising peer support. Finally, there is a discussion of comprehensive anti-bullying programmes introduced in schools, and reviews of their effectiveness.

Individual actions against bullying – victim coping strategies

Every pupil is going to experience some provocations, and attempts to take advantage of them, at some point. How they react is going to be one factor in whether this is likely to continue. Do they try to deal with it themselves – perhaps by internalising strategies (such as feeling upset, crying), distancing (ignoring it, pretending nothing has happened) or externalising strategies (such as fighting back)? Do they problem solve (change behaviour, keep away from the bullies)? Or do they seek help or support? The general advice from adults has been to tell an adult, such as a teacher or parents, and indeed the title of the first anti-bullying pack in England, *Don't Suffer in Silence* (DfE, 1994), symbolises this viewpoint.

When pupils are asked what they would do, or did, if bullied, it is clear that they adopt a variety of such coping strategies. In a survey in England, Smith, Shu, and Madsen (2001) investigated coping strategies used by 10–14 year old victims. The most common coping strategies used were 'ignored the bullies', followed by 'told them to stop', 'asked an adult for help' and 'fought back'; the least used coping strategies were 'ran away', 'asked friends for help' and 'cried'. The younger children more often reported crying or running away, while the older children more often reported ignoring the bullies; girls more often reported crying or asking friends or adults for help, whereas boys more often reported fighting back. In another survey in England, Oliver and Candappa (2003) found that telling teachers was commonly reported, but often seen as risky: telling parents and friends, ignoring the bullying, and talking back (by younger pupils) or hitting back (by older pupils) were also frequently used. A consistent finding is that rates for telling a teacher are less in older pupils and boys (Hunter & Boyle, 2004; Naylor, Cowie & del Rey, 2001).

Some studies have looked at how coping strategies vary by status types: victim, bully, bully/victim and not involved. Using data from 10 to 12 year olds in Åland, Finland, Olafsen and Viemerö (2000) found, not surprisingly, that bully/victims reported using more 'aggressive' strategies compared with victims and not-involved children, as well as more 'self-destructive' strategies relative to all other children. In a study with 9–13 year olds in Flanders, Belgium, Bijttebier and Vertommen (1998) also divided victims into those who were victims of direct bullying, and those who were victims of social isolation. They found that male victims of both types scored higher on internalising coping strategies, compared with not-involved male peers: in contrast, male bullies and bully/victims scored higher on externalising coping strategies, relative to not-involved male peers. The findings for females were less clear, with internalising strategies being high in female victims of direct bullying but not in female victims of social isolation.

Kristensen and Smith (2003) investigated the coping strategies that Danish children aged 10–15 years said they would employ, in response to five different types of bullying: physical, verbal, indirect (rumour spreading), social exclusion and attacks on property. Five coping strategies were distinguished, and in order of preference by the pupils, these were self-reliance/problem-solving, distancing, seeking social support, internalising and, lastly, externalising. Consistent with the previous findings, they found that externalising was used significantly more by bully/victims compared with victims and not-involved children. Seeking social support and internalising were more frequent in girls, while externalising was more frequent with boys. They also found that distancing, seeking social support and internalising were more frequent in younger children. Looking at coping strategies in response to different types of bullying, the main effects were for attacks on property; compared to other types of bullying, pupils would use seeking social support significantly more, and distancing significantly less. Attacks on property are perhaps often more serious and easier to evidence, and ignoring such attacks is a less feasible option.

Coping strategies in England and Japan compared

Kanetsuna and Smith (2002) and Kanetsuna and colleagues (2006) compared the kinds of coping strategies that pupils would use or recommend, for various types of *bullying* in England, and *ijime* in Japan (using the same methodologies in both countries).

For direct physical and verbal bullying/*ijime*, and rumour spreading, most pupils in England suggested that the victim should seek help from others (teachers, parents and friends), while fewer Japanese pupils suggested this. However, more pupils in Japan than in England said that the victim should take direct action against the bullies (fighting back, arguing back, telling the bullies to stop or asking the bullies why they were doing it). For being ignored and social exclusion most English pupils recommended making new friends, whereas Japanese pupils recommended direct action against the bullies, seeking help from others or just putting up with it; some 15% blamed the victim and recommended they reflect on any fault in themselves and try to improve themselves.

Overall, Japanese pupils seemed reluctant to seek help from others; instead they appeared to think taking direct action against bullies was a more useful coping strategy, especially for direct physical and verbal forms of *ijime*. One explanation may be a lack of trust towards teachers and peers as a defender or as an intervener in *ijime* situations in Japan. When asked who they would tell, many more pupils in England reported that they would go to teachers or parents, for example because they could help them deal with the problem; by contrast, more pupils in Japan responded that telling teachers and/or parents could make the situation even worse, and so were more likely only to tell their friends.

These differences may reflect the relative lack of sustained national intervention efforts against *ijime* in Japan. A culture of seeking help for bullying has probably taken some ten years or more to get established in English schools. Pupils in England compared to Japan were more likely to say that their school did something to stop bullying/*ijime* (85% vs. 28%), that schools should do more to stop it (98% vs. 56%) and that bullying/*ijime* in school could be stopped (55% vs. 28%).

Telling others in Vietnamese schools

In his study of bullying (*bat nat*) in two Vietnamese lower secondary schools, Horton (2011a, 2012) combined a survey with extensive ethnographic work. The survey included a question about whom pupils would report bullying to: for girls, they would most often tell an older sibling or friend, then a parent, then a teacher; for boys, the picture was similar, but with older siblings coming after friends and parents; and for both girls and boys, rates for parents and teachers declined rapidly from grades 6 through to 9. Horton's ethnographic work also sheds light on why only relatively few pupils would tell a teacher or parent in the older grades. It was not easy for pupils to communicate with teachers in these schools, as the teachers were very concerned about keeping order and sometimes used strict discipline and physical chastisement. In addition, sometimes if a student told a teacher, who then took clumsy or inconsistent action, the bullying got worse. Pupils also despised other pupils who informed on them to teachers: for example, Horton describes how one girl, Loan, was bullied, in part because she associated with another girl, Yen, who often informed on things to the teacher. At one point the class teacher realised what was happening, and asked Loan in class if certain other pupils were bullying her. Loan stood up and said that they were not. In this way she gained credit in the eyes of the other students, and according to Loan she was not bullied any more.

Effectiveness of coping strategies

The evidence suggests that fighting back is not a successful strategy. In a classic study in this area, using a longitudinal design in US kindergartens, Kochenderfer and Ladd (1997) found that bullying was more persistent for 5–6 year old male victims who peers thought fought back in response to bullying, compared with male victims of the same age who were perceived by peers as having a friend help in bullying situations. In an older age group of 12–13 year old victims in Finland, Salmivalli, Karhunen and Lagerspetz (1996) found that 'counter-aggression' was associated with the initiation or continuation of bullying. Behaviours related to diminished or discontinued bullying were a lack of 'helplessness' for female victims, and 'nonchalance' as well as a lack of 'counter-aggression' for male victims.

There is also some evidence that seeking support can be a good strategy. Smith et al. (2004) interviewed 13–16 years old pupils in English schools with peer support systems. They found the five most frequent coping strategies were talking to someone, followed by ignoring it, sticking up for yourself, avoiding the bullies, and making more/different friends. Over a two-year period, those who had stopped being victims more often had talked to someone about it (67%) compared to those who had stayed victims (46%) or become victims (41%).

A different way of assessing effectiveness was used by Frisén, Hasselblad and Holmqvist (2012). They identified 273 Swedish students, all 18 years old, who had been bullied during their school career. They asked them what had made the bullying stop (if it did) and content analysed the results. Overall, 25% said it was support from school personnel, 23% transition to a new school level, 20% a change of coping strategies, 12% support from parents, 12% a change of appearance or way of being, 11% a change of school or class, 11% making new friends, 8% the bullies changed their attitude, 5% no particular reason, 4% support from peers, and 3% other reasons. Notable here is that fighting back did not appear as one of the themes from the answers elicited. Also, support from peers comes out as being much less effective than support from school or parents.

Coping with cyberbullying

Just as cyberbullying has some special features (see Chapter 4), it may also call for some different coping responses. A thorough review of studies on coping with cyberbullying was reported by Perren et al. (2012) and McGuckin et al. (2013). As well as seeking support, retaliation and avoidant strategies, they also identified technical solution strategies such as using report abuse buttons or blocking an abusive sender.

For example, Smith, Mahdavi et al. (2008) found that 11–16 year old English pupils recommended the following strategies: 'blocking messages/identities' (75%), 'telling someone (parent/teacher)' (63%), 'changing email address/phone number' (57%) and 'keeping a record of offensive emails/texts' (47%), followed by 'ignoring it' (41%), 'reporting to police/other authorities' (39%), 'contact service provider' (31%), and 'asking them to stop' (21%), with the least popular advice being 'fighting back' (20%).

Although telling someone about it is a commonly mentioned strategy, when victims of cyberbullying do tell someone, it appears to be most often friends, followed by parents, with teachers told rather infrequently (Slonje & Smith, 2008; Smith, Mahdavi et al., 2008). Given the generational gap in use and awareness of new technologies, young people may feel that teachers and parents are less aware of the issues involved.

McGuckin et al. (2013) found that there was rather little good evidence on the effectiveness of different strategies. However, the value of support seeking was pointed to in a longitudinal study in 12 Swiss schools by Machmutow, Perren, Sticca and Alsaker. (2012). They examined depression in 13 year olds, in relation to both traditional and cyber victimisation, together with coping. Both traditional and cyber victimisation were associated with higher levels of depression, and cyber victimisation predicted increases in depression by the second time point. Coping strategies rated as helpless were associated with more depression. Longitudinally, support seeking from peers and family was associated with reduced depression, while assertive coping strategies (such as finding and contacting the bully) were associated with increased depression.

Summary on coping strategies

Pupils use a range of coping strategies, and these vary by age, gender, bully/victim status and culture. Smith et al. (2001) hypothesised that much of the apparent age decrement in self-reports of being bullied could be ascribed to an improvement in coping strategies in many older children, as most learn from the experience of coping with milder episodes of bullying and harassment. Non-assertive strategies such as crying are not successful in this respect.

Also, fighting back generally appears to be unproductive. This does not rule out its success in individual cases, but as a rule, the victim is in a weaker position so fighting back is at least risky and often a non-starter. However, being assertive (not aggressive) can be useful: the Paralympic sprinter Ben Rushgrove, who has cerebral palsy, was bullied at school, and he is quoted as saying 'You have to stand up to the people who are bullying you. I think I did that very well' (*Family Guardian*, 23 June 2012, p. 3). Some problem-solving strategies, such as seeking new friends, can be helpful. Steven Frayne (who works as a magician called Dynamo) was small because of being born with Crohn's disease: he was tormented by bullies at school, including being thrown repeatedly into wheelie bins. He used his increasing ability at magic tricks to gain influence in a positive way and stop the bullying (*Guardian*, 2 July 2012, p. 32).

Seeking help consistently appears as a useful strategy and is routinely encouraged by adults. The success of telling teachers will depend on the school context and clearly needs a consistent and effective response from teaching staff. It currently appears to be more problematic in the case of cyberbullying.

The role of parents

Parents or caregivers have an important role, and as demonstrated in Chapter 5, family and parenting characteristics do have an influence on the risks of being in bully or victim roles. Thus in a preventative sense, warm and authoritative parenting – and a generally well-functioning family – will be important factors in reducing the chance of a child getting involved in bullying in any capacity. However, the role of parents beyond this preventative aspect has been rather little studied.

Parent training information nights or teacher–parent meetings have been associated with more effective intervention programmes (Ttofi & Farrington, 2011). Communication between parents and the school will be important in terms of recognising the symptoms of bullying and taking early steps to deal with it. The role of parents was particularly emphasised in the ABC intervention project in Ireland (O'Moore, 2013, and see below). Through parents' evenings, parents were introduced to a discussion of what is bullying, misconceptions of bullying, types of bullying, signs and symptoms, effects of bullying on the victims and aggressors, and the risk factors associated with victims and bullies. In addition, various aspects of parenting were discussed, such as love and care, cruelty, inconsistent discipline, management of aggressive behaviour, excessive physical punishment, and violence between adults.

The importance of parents has come under greater scrutiny in relation to cyberbullying. This is because their role is relatively greater, as much cyberbullying is initiated or responded to outside the school grounds. As a result of the 'digital divide' between young people and adults, parents may feel limited in how they can support their child to effectively prevent and respond to cyberbullying. Furthermore, many young people indicate they are unlikely to report their experiences of cyberbullying to parents/caregivers, largely because they fear having their computers or mobile phones taken away, which would cause them to feel more isolated. Thus, developing parents' awareness about cyberbullying is crucial.

Many guidelines on cyberbullying emphasise the role of parents as role models, talking with their children and helping and monitoring their Information and Communications Technology (ICT) use, and also mention how parents need to develop their own skills. Parents can discuss with their children the use of ICT and, for example, social networking sites, supervise their use, and discuss how to cope with any unpleasant messages or abusive content and the importance in such cases of keeping records. However, fewer guidelines mention how parents can encourage their children to help others, or point out the importance of collaboration with the school (Guidelines, 2012).

School actions against bullying

Some school-based interventions are targeted at the whole school or class, some at the behaviour of those doing the bullying, some at those who are victims, some at bystanders or likely defenders. The following sections discuss particular strategies that can be – and indeed are – used in schools. These are broadly divided into:

- *reactive strategies*, which are ways of dealing with bullying incidents once they have occurred;
- *proactive strategies*, which can be used as a whole school approach and are designed to make bullying less likely to happen;
- *peer support strategies*, which use students themselves to act against and respond to bullying.

These will be particularly illustrated by findings from England. Work against school bullying has been active in England since the 1990s, especially following the Sheffield Project of 1991–1994 (discussed further below). This intervention project produced an anti-bullying pack for schools, *Don't Suffer in Silence* (DfE, 1994, 2nd edition 2000). This pack, and subsequent government advice (DfE, 2013), has not strongly recommended any one programme: instead the philosophy has been to allow schools to use those methods or strategies that they find most useful in their circumstances and according to their school ethos. As a result, a wide variety of methods are used. We have data on these from some national surveys.

Samara and Smith (2008) surveyed schools in England that had used the government pack *Don't Suffer in Silence* in 1996 (after the first edition was published in 1994) and 2002 (after the second edition was published in 2000). In 1996, 109 replies were usable for analysis, and in 2002, 148 replies. Responses were from schools across England, although the response rate on both occasions was low (around 25%). The analysis showed the percentage of schools using a strategy at the two time points, and their satisfaction with this, rated on a five-point scale (1 = not at all satisfied, 2 = not very satisfied, 3 = neutral, 4 = satisfied, 5 = extremely satisfied).

Thompson and Smith (2011) carried out a national survey of schools in England, during 2009–2010, for the then Department for Children, Schools and Families (DCSF, now the DfE), to establish which anti-bullying strategies schools were using and how effective these were rated. In total 1,378 school questionnaires were obtained across England from 888 primary schools, 387 secondary schools, 82 special schools (for children with learning difficulties or disabilities), and 21 Pupil Referral Units (for students with particularly difficult or challenging behaviour). The survey provided data about the use of proactive, peer support and reactive strategies, and ratings of effectiveness by schools on a similar 1–5 scale. More detailed data were obtained from 36 case study schools, where in-depth interviews were held with management, anti-bullying staff and pupils. In addition, 285 bullying incident records were collated (177 provided by staff, 108 from interviews with students involved in bullying incidents). These provided data on the nature of the incident, the strategy used and the outcome; some data from these incident reports are summarised in Table 6.1.

Reactive strategies for teaching staff

Reactive strategies deal with bullying situations when they have arisen. Thompson and Smith (2011) evaluated five main reactive strategies: direct sanctions, school tribunals, restorative approaches, the Support Group Method and the Pikas method. These provided a range from more 'disciplinary' to more 'counselling' or 'no blame' type approaches, and this diversity has been the source of considerable controversy and disagreement. In practice, schools do not always follow a particular method exactly, or for all types of bullying. Often 'serious talks' (which might or might not involve further sanctions) are used as a first step. Also, various reactive strategies may be used depending on the type of bullying and whether the perpetrator(s) have engaged in bullying before.

In England, the DfE recommends that bullying should always incur some form of sanction: 'Schools should apply disciplinary measures to pupils who bully in order to show clearly that their behaviour is wrong' (DfE, 2013: 7). Many professionals, however, prefer less direct approaches, at least for less severe cases of bullying.

Direct sanctions

Direct sanctions cover a range of procedures used by schools, which have some negative consequences for the perpetrator(s) of bullying. Thompson and Smith (2011) found that 92% of schools used some kind of direct sanction. Almost all schools reported using verbal reprimands, or serious talks perhaps with the headteacher, and almost all reported using meetings involving parents. About 80% reported withdrawal of privileges, and about 70% (more secondary schools) reported temporary removal from class. About 60% reported some other disciplinary measures, such as litter-picking or school clean-ups. Some form of internal or short-term external exclusion was reported by most secondary schools (but only a minority of primary schools). About a quarter of secondary schools had resorted to permanent exclusion in one or more cases.

Direct sanctions thus vary in severity and may be used on a graded scale if bullying persists. There are a variety of reasons for advocating or using direct sanctions.

They are expected to impress on the perpetrator that what he/she has done is unacceptable, promote understanding of the limits of acceptable behaviour, and deter him/her from repeating that behaviour. They can also signal to other pupils that the behaviour is unacceptable and deter them from doing it. Direct sanctions also demonstrate publicly that school rules and policies are to be taken seriously. These reasons are often articulated by schools. In the Thompson and Smith (2011) survey, schools were asked why they had used direct sanctions. A content analysis showed that the three most popular reasons stated were that they send a clear message that bullying will not be tolerated, that they are effective for stopping bullying, and that they are in the school policy.

In fact, there is little evidence for the effectiveness of direct sanctions. Thompson and Smith (2011) found an effectiveness rating of 4.14 (out of 5). This was positive, but in fact equal lowest out of ratings for reactive strategies generally. However, some further evidence has come from the KiVa intervention project in Finland (described in detail later). Salmivalli and Poskiparta (2012) summarised findings from an early phase of the KiVa project, in which schools were randomly assigned to 'confronting' and 'non-confronting' approaches when an incident occurred. The confronting approach was one where the bullying child was told that such behaviour was not tolerated and must stop immediately. In the non-confronting approach, the bully was not blamed but instead asked to share the concern of the victim (similar to the Pikas or Support Group methods; see later). Both approaches were found to be successful in stopping the bullying in 79% of cases. However, non-confrontational methods were more effective at a primary rather than secondary level and for long-term victimisation. More detailed analyses (differing in some small aspects) are given by Garandeau, Poskiparta and Salmivalli (2014).

From incident reports, Thompson and Smith (2011) found that direct sanctions were effective in 62% of cases (see Table 6.1) – slightly less than other reactive strategies. Direct sanctions probably work best as a clear set of consequences expressed in the anti-bullying policy and mostly used within the framework of other strategies. Thompson and Smith (2011) found that most schools used them in this way, for example if restorative approaches had not worked.

School tribunals/bully courts

School tribunals/bully courts are an elected court of pupils that meets after an alleged incident has occurred: all concerned are interviewed, including witnesses, and the tribunal decides what punishment (if any) is appropriate. A school staff member chairs the tribunal, but the pupils have (at least in theory) the power to decide the appropriate sanctions. This delegation of power to pupils, and the difficulty of reconciling this with a school policy on bullying, mean that the approach is not popular with teachers and rarely used. Smith et al. (1994) found that teacher attitudes to bully courts were significantly less favourable than were student attitudes. Samara and Smith (2008) found that about 11% of schools had tried these (in 1996 and 2002), while Thompson and Smith (2011) only found it used by about 2% by 2009–2010.

The idea of school tribunals – called bully courts initially – was promulgated in England by Kidscape (1986), a national charity concerned with children's safety. At the time great success was claimed for these, but without any publicly available evidence. Nevertheless, two small-scale evaluations did suggest some promise. Brier and Ahmad (1991) tried out a court in a middle school, over one school term, with year 5/6 pupils (about 9–10 years old). Only two cases were heard by the court during the first half-term, and none in the second half-term. Nevertheless, the presence of the court was felt to have an impact. A survey showed that the bully and victim rates fell in the three year 5/6 classes that took part, but by comparison rose slightly in four non-intervention classes in year 4 and year 7 that did not take part.

In a subsequent case study, Mahdavi and Smith (2002) evaluated the work of a bully court in one English secondary school. Questionnaires and interviews were used in conjunction with observing the bully court in action and accessing excerpts from the school's bully court record. The court was mainly for year 7 pupils. It met 25 times, and of the sanctions given to the bully or bullies, most were warnings or detentions, sometimes with a letter sent home. Altogether 35 year 7 victims were involved: of these, 30 said the bully court was helpful, and 26 that it had stopped the bullying completely. However, the bully court was found to be less effective and less used in year 8 and year 9. This report also discussed the limitations of the evaluation: the school used year 12 pupils to act as mentors to year 7 pupils in the context of a whole school approach to bullying. This mentoring system, and other aspects of the anti-bullying practice in place within the school, could have been important aspects contributing to the success of the bully court in this study.

In sum, school tribunals are rarely used and teachers generally do not like handing so much power over to pupils. Nevertheless, they are one way of directly involving pupils constructively, and if properly handled the indications are that they can have some success in the middle school years. The Thompson and Smith (2011) survey found that they were given a quite high rating of 4.26 by the small number of schools that did use them.

Restorative approaches

Restorative approaches emphasise a restoration of good relationships rather than retribution. The underlying principle is to resolve conflict and repair harm by focusing on the perpetrator, who is made aware of the victim's feelings, encouraged to acknowledge the impact of what they have done, and given an opportunity to make reparation. Those who have suffered have the opportunity to have their harm or loss acknowledged and amends made (Restorative Justice Consortium, 2005).

The ideas of restorative justice originated in the criminal justice system, and have only relatively recently been applied to schools in a substantial way. They were not explicitly mentioned in the assessment of English schools by Samara and Smith (2008) in 2002. However, since then the approach has become very popular in schools for all types of anti-social or inappropriate behaviour, including bullying. Thompson and Smith (2011) found that some forms of restorative approaches were reportedly being used to deal with bullying incidents by 69% of schools (64% of primary schools and 83% of secondary schools) by 2009–2010, and 88% claimed to be 'developing a restorative ethos and culture'.

Restorative approaches as anti-bullying strategies cover a hierarchy of flexible responses, ranging from informal conversations through to formal facilitated meetings or conferences. A basic form is a short or 'mini' conference where an informal meeting is held between the pupils involved, led by a trained member of staff, in which incidents and harm caused are examined and the offender(s) are asked to discuss possible means of reparation. In practice these may not be so very different from the 'serious talks' discussed earlier in direct sanctions, but in a restorative framework – although the bullying children are held responsible for their actions – the emphasis should be less on 'you have broken the school rules and this must stop', and more on 'X (victim) has felt hurt by what you have done; what can you do to help make things better?'.

For more serious or repeated incidents, a full restorative conference might be used. Here, a formal structured meeting takes place involving pupils, along with their parents/carers, friends and school representatives, who are brought together to discuss and resolve an incident. The staff member leading the conference should be highly trained, and prior to this large meeting, should hold individual interviews with the participants to ensure a full conference is appropriate, and that everyone is prepared for it.

Preparation is crucial if restorative justice is to be effective. Pupils need to be able to talk about feelings and relationship issues, and to be accustomed to this rather than suddenly being 'pushed' into a restorative conference. A good preparation for this is problem-solving circles, or circle time, used in the curriculum. Although used more in the primary sector, circle time experiences can facilitate simple restorative approaches such as restorative reminders, restorative discussions and restorative thinking plans.

Some evaluations have reported successful outcomes of restorative practices in schools. In the UK, a national evaluation found that 92% of conferences were resolved successfully, and three months later, 96% of agreements remained intact (Youth Justice Board, 2004). Most school staff reported that their school had benefitted, although no general improvements in pupil attitudes were found at a whole school level.

Thompson and Smith (2011) found that restorative approaches got a satisfaction rating of 4.18 (out of 5). In addition, in their analysis of bullying incident forms from case study schools, restorative approaches were rated as successful for 73% of incidents, being highest for relational bullying; see Table 6.1. In visiting the case study schools where these incident reports were gathered, it was apparent that some schools had trained staff thoroughly in restorative approaches, using one of several recognised schemes, whereas some others had done things on a much more piecemeal basis. Looking at how incidents were dealt with in different schools, it was found that those using restorative approaches with whole staff training and the consistent application of restorative strategies were more successful at stopping bullying (79% of incidents) than those that were less consistent (64%) or schools that were 'non-restorative' – that is, not claiming to use the approach at all (58%). Most practitioners in the area recommend that, to be effective, restorative practice needs to be adopted as a whole school approach fully supported by senior management, and with adequate training in restorative techniques for staff. Without this radical change towards a restorative ethos, tensions can arise between the prevailing practices of the school, often sanction-based, and restorative principles.

Restorative approaches are not a panacea. Cremin (2013) has reviewed some of the concerns: a bully may feign contrition in order to escape punishment; a poorly organised restorative conference can lead the victim to feel their concerns are not being respected – a 'revictimisation'; and restorative meetings move the resolution of bullying incidents from a public to a private forum and may produce outcomes that are inconsistent with a publicly-stated school policy. While restorative approaches may offer a more positive approach to repairing harm, there are significant concerns about them becoming a form of social control, as much of the language is derived from the criminal justice system (for example, offender, perpetrator and victim). However, when properly implemented it appears that restorative approaches have much potential. Schools may still resort to direct sanctions if a pupil refuses 'to restore' or does not abide by the decisions reached, and even then such sanctions can be placed in a restorative framework.

The Shared Concern or Pikas method

The Shared Concern or Pikas method was developed in Sweden by Pikas (1989, 2002) as a non-punitive counselling-based approach used to deconstruct the group dynamics of bullying. It is carried out by a teacher or counsellor who is not the class teacher and has not previously been directly involved with the children concerned, and uses a combination of individual and group meetings, outlined below, structured around five consecutive phases.

Individual talks with suspected bullies: first, the counsellor ascertains who the suspected bullies are, and then arranges to see them individually but in quick succession, starting with the likely 'ringleader'. She or he discusses the plight of the victim with the bully, but does not directly accuse them of involvement; rather, the bully is asked to first recognise the hurt of the victim, and then to come up with a proposal to help the situation.

Individual talk with the victim: following this, the counsellor sees the victim. A primary aim here is to see whether the victim is or is not contributing to the situation by being aggressive or provocative. If not, then the counsellor basically reassures the victim, and mentions that he or she has seen the bullying children, they plan to change their behaviour in agreed ways, and how about meeting them together to discuss this? If the victim contributes to the situation, then the counsellor also discusses this explicitly, and suggests to the victim ways of changing his or her behaviour as well.

Preparatory group meeting: the counsellor meets with the bullies together, and they share what they have agreed to do. They agree on some positive things to say to the victim at the next step.

Summit meeting: the victim is brought in by the counsellor to the full meeting with the bullies. The meeting starts with some positive things being said. Following a thorough and frank discussion, the counsellor moves towards an agreed conclusion of positive steps forward. He or she states that they will return (for example, in a week) to see how things are going.

Follow-up of the results: the counsellor sees each pupil involved, briefly, to ascertain that the agreed steps are being followed.

The rationale behind this approach is that it engages bullying children individually and in a non-hostile way. Pikas believes that seeing them in a group, and in a blaming way, would likely lead to resentment and the reinforcement of each other's anti-social behaviour. The Pikas method thus aims to sensitise bullying children to the harm they are doing to the victim, encourage positive behaviours towards the victim, and also encourage provocative victims to change their behaviour in positive ways.

Thompson and Smith (2011) found that many English schools had no knowledge of the method, but some 5% were using it (4% primary, 8% secondary). For these schools, the overall satisfaction rating was 4.14 (out of 5). It was seen as an 'educative process' for those involved, but there was generally little staff training to support delivery.

More detailed evaluations have been reported from England and Australia. In England, the Sheffield project (see later) carried out an evaluation (Smith et al., 1994) with 21 primary and secondary school teachers, who were trained in the method by Pikas himself. Twelve of the teachers actually used it in practice, and all felt that it was an appropriate and helpful response to bullying. Of 30 pupils who went through the process as victims, three-quarters felt that the situation had improved. However, in some cases the bullying child(ren) had switched their attention from the initial victim to another child outside of the group.

Rigby and Griffiths (2010) carried out an evaluation with 17 primary and secondary schools in Western Australia. Altogether 17 cases of use of the method were studied, including interviews with the pupils involved (bullies and victims). Although most cases followed the standard procedure as outlined above, only 14 of the 17 cases made it to the group meeting, and only 12 to the summit meeting. Nevertheless, most (15 out of 17) of the practitioners thought that the method had been successful. Out of 15 victims interviewed, 12 said that the bullying had stopped, while only 2 said that it had not improved. Of the pupils taking part as suspected bullies, most reported positive effects, such as feeling better that they had stopped bullying.

The Pikas method appears to work well in some circumstances, but like the Support Group/No Blame approach (following), has attracted hostility from some quarters. Olweus (1999a) argues that it is unethical not to give responsibility to the bullying children directly, when there should be a school policy (or class rules) that bullying will not be tolerated. Also, he criticises the lack of involvement of parents in the Pikas procedure.

Support Group Method (Seven Steps approach)

The Support Group Method, sometimes called the Seven Steps approach (Robinson & Maines, 2007), was formerly called the No Blame approach (Maines & Robinson, 1992; Robinson & Maines, 1997). It has a similar non-punitive philosophy to the Pikas method, but sees the bullying children together with more prosocial others, as a group, with more emphasis on peer pressure to elicit a prosocial response

The Seven Steps involve the following: (1) the facilitator talks individually to the victim, who shares some account of his/her suffering; (2) a group meeting of six to eight students is then set up, some suggested by the victim but without his or her presence; (3) the facilitator explains to the group that the victim has a problem, but does not discuss the incidents that have taken place; (4) the facilitator assures the group no punishment will given, but that instead all participants must take joint responsibility to make the victim feel happy and safe; (5) each group member shares their ideas on how the victim can be helped; (6) the facilitator ends the meeting, with the group given responsibility for improving the victim's safety and well-being; (7) follow-up individual meetings are held with group members one week after the meeting to establish how successful the intervention has been.

The name 'No Blame' was unfortunate in the climate of England in the late 1990s and early 2000s. The procedure was attacked by many who felt that bullying children must be held responsible for their actions, including the national charity Kidscape and a number of politicians (see Smith et al., 2007). Government advice at the time, including the revision of the *Don't Suffer in Silence* pack (DfE, 2000), precluded any advocacy of the No Blame approach. However, a change of name to Support Group method ameliorated the situation to some extent, and the approach also has many supporters.

Samara and Smith (2008) found that in 1996 some 34% of schools were using a non-punitive approach (primarily the Support Group method, but also including the Pikas method); this fell slightly to 28% in 2006 (20% of primary schools, 36% of secondary schools). Smith and Thompson (2011) found that in 2009–2010, 10% of primary schools and 14% of secondary schools were using the Support Group Method. Even when combined with the Pikas method (4% and 8% respectively), this indicates a decline in use. This may be due to the earlier adverse publicity, but another factor may well have been the increasing interest in restorative approaches. Although Maines and Robinson saw the Support Group Method as falling within the range of restorative approaches, many practitioners of the latter feel that while a similarity is the emphasis on improving relationships rather than punishment, a crucial difference is whether or not the perpetrator is asked to acknowledge the harm they have caused.

Smith et al. (2007) ascertained the use of and support for the Support Group method across England in 2006. A survey was made of 59 schools that were using it. Just over half rated the effectiveness of the method as very satisfactory, while 30% said it was rather satisfactory and the remainder were neutral. The Support Group Method was found to be adapted considerably in use, so that the Seven Steps were not always followed as earlier. Two issues were commonly mentioned in this respect. One was parental involvement: many schools wanted parents to know what was happening, and to work through any reservations the latter might have. The other was the back-up availability of sanctions should the procedure not work.

No direct evidence was provided in this study as to whether the Support Group Method was able to change behaviour. However, some positive evaluations have been made. Young (1998), in a slight adaptation of the method, reported that of 51 support group sessions studied, 80% resulted in immediate success and 14% in a delayed success, with 6% having only limited success. Smith and Thompson (2011) found that the Support Group method had a mean satisfaction rating of 4.20 (out of 5). Their analysis of bullying incidents (see Table 6.1) showed a success rate of 76%, which is actually the highest of the methods examined.

Summary on reactive strategies

There continues to be some controversy over which reactive strategies are best. In practice, many schools use some form of serious talk with those involved, which may or may not be more 'disciplinary' or 'restorative' in orientation. This may depend also on the history of those involved, and how serious the incident is. The findings from the randomised trial in Finland (Salmivalli & Poskiparta, 2012) suggested that both kinds of approach can be quite successful, and this was where schools were 'assigned' to one or other condition. More usually, schools will choose according to their different philosophies about this.

The evidence from the incident reports in Thompson and Smith (2011) is also that all types of reactive strategy are reasonably successful. As Table 6.1 also shows, success rates may vary by sector and by type of bullying. The Support Group Method appears to be more successful in primary school (in line with the Finnish findings). Serious talks and direct sanctions were relatively more successful for cyberbullying. However, the number of incidents in some cells of Table 6.1 is small, and more evidence is clearly needed in this area.

Gregory et al. (2010) have argued that the contrast between tough disciplinary and soft supportive approaches can become too polarised. They state that safe schools need both clear and enforced rules (which they call structure), while being respectful of students and responsive to their needs (which they call support). In a study of 290 high schools in the USA, they found that measures of both structure and support were associated with lower bully and victim rates, and

Table 6.1 Percentage of bullying incidents where the bullying stopped completely, by sector and type of bullying, from 285 incident report forms in 35 schools (data from Thompson and Smith, 2011)

	Sector			Type of bullying			
	Total	Primary	Secondary	Physical	Verbal	Relational	Cyber
Serious talk	65	58	71	62	61	66	73
Direct sanctions	62	58	65	60	61	60	75
Restorative approaches	73	68	77	67	73	76	73
Support group	76	80	71	60	68	100	60
Overall	67	61	71	62	65	69	70

that their combination – which they call authoritative discipline – will be most effective. This position seems consistent with the findings earlier: it does not totally bypass the debate about confronting or non-confronting reactive strategies, but it does suggest that either inconsistent or extreme positions will have poorer outcomes.

Proactive strategies in the school

Whole school policy on bullying

A whole school policy is a short written handout or brochure, available for everyone in the school community. It should define bullying, state the responsibilities of all concerned in the school if it happens, and clearly explain what actions will be taken to reduce bullying and deal with incidents when they occur. Since 1999, schools in England and Wales have been legally required to have some form of anti-bullying policy. Samara and Smith (2008) found that only 72% of schools in England had a whole school policy on bullying in 1996, but that this had increased to 92% by 2002.

School policies vary greatly in their coverage and quality. Epstein and colleagues (2006) carried out an analysis of 480 anti-bullying policies in Welsh schools. Policies were assigned scores in eight areas, with a final profile of outstanding for 3% of schools, good with some excellent features for 18%, satisfactory for 46%, some significant problems for 24%, and unsatisfactory/ many problems for 9%.

Smith, Smith, Osborn and Samara (2008) carried out a detailed analysis of 142 school anti-bullying policies, gathered in 2002 from 115 primary schools and 27 secondary schools in England. A 31-item scoring scheme was used to assess coverage, and schools averaged about 40% of these items in their policies. Smith,

Kupferberg et al. (2012) reported a follow-up from a sample of 169 primary and 48 secondary schools, from the same county in England but six years later, in 2008. A slightly expanded 34-item scoring scheme was used. Schools now averaged about 49% of the items in their policies – a modest increase. Most included a definition of bullying including reference to physical, verbal, material and relational forms, and clarifying the difference from other kinds of aggressive behaviour, as well as statements about improving school climate, how sanctions will depend on the type or severity of incident, and contact with parents when bullying incidents occurred. But despite some improvement since 2002, there was still low coverage of cyberbullying, homophobic bullying, and bullying based on disabilities or faith; teacher–pupil bullying; responsibilities beyond those of teaching staff; the following up of incidents; and specific preventative measures such as playground work, peer support, inclusiveness issues, and bullying that occurred going to and from school.

There is only modest evidence that having a good policy translates into lower rates of school bullying or violence. In England, Woods and Wolke (2003) obtained policies from 34 primary schools, and scored them low, moderate or high in quality. There were no relationships between quality and measures of direct victimisation or direct bullying: high policy scores did predict fewer pupils reporting being directly bullied in the playground, but more pupils reporting bullying others relationally. In Wales, Lambert and colleagues (2008) found a significant association between lower levels of bullying and pupils reporting that the school had clear rules on bullying, which might be taken as an indirect measure of the actual policy content.

In their analysis of 217 school policies in England, Smith, Kupferberg et al. (2012) had data available on bullying as perceived and experienced by pupils in these schools, from Pupil Attitude Surveys carried out each year in the county. Policy scores could be related to these in 78 of the schools: most correlations were not significant, although in schools whose policies had more strategies to prevent bullying, there were fewer reports of pupils bullying others.

A good school policy should encourage pupils to report bullying, so straightforward correlations to incidence rates at one time point may not be very informative. Rather, policies should be seen as providing a framework for the school's response involving the whole school community: pupils, teachers, learning mentors, school support staff, governors and parents/carers.

Working in the playground

Especially in primary schools, much bullying can occur in the playground (see Chapter 4). Three important proactive strategies here are having a playground policy, training lunchtime supervisors, and the design of the playground environment.

A playground policy includes a strategy for appropriate behaviour in breaks and playtimes, liaison between teaching staff and lunchtime supervisors, and encouraging prosocial playground games and activities. This provides a framework for other actions. Samara and Smith (2008) found that 38% of schools reported having a playground policy in 2002, and Thompson and Smith (2011) found a figure of 46% in 2009.

In some countries, including the UK, playtimes are not supervised by teachers but by lunchtime supervisors. The latter are often volunteers from the local community, without much recognised status in the school, and often receiving little or no training for their role. Yet lunchtime supervisors can have a pivotal role in implementing any playground or school anti-bullying policy. Training sessions can provide them with additional skills in organising games, recognising bullying behaviours, interviewing pupils, and dealing with bullying and conflict situations. A key aspect is distinguishing bullying from playful fighting (Smith, 2010b). Such training can also raise the self-esteem of lunchtime supervisors, as well as their status in the school community. As part of the Sheffield intervention project (see later), Boulton (1994) found that lunchtime supervisor training was well received, and correlated with reductions in playground bullying (although as other interventions were also in place, a causal relationship was not established). Boulton and Flemington (1996) found positive results from using a video illustrating aspects of playground behaviour and interpretation of play fights, real fights and bullying. Samara and Smith (2008) found that 62% and 57% of schools reported training lunchtime supervisors in 1996 and 2002, and Thompson and Smith (2011) found a figure of 80% in 2009–2010.

Work on the physical environment of the playground includes structuring or redesigning it to provide more creative opportunities for pupils during break and lunch times, and reduce boredom and bullying. This can be a participatory and inclusive process for pupils: strategies include playground design exercises, mapping existing use, and identifying danger areas and bullying hotspots (Higgins, 1994). Features of good practice include the efficient checking of the school site, the setting up of safe play areas or quiet rooms, and close supervision at the start and end of the school day. Samara and Smith (2008) found that 60% and 65% of schools reported improving the school grounds as an anti-bullying strategy in 1996 and 2002, and Thompson and Smith (2011) reported a higher figure of 81% in 2009–2010.

Curricular materials/approaches: films, drama, role play

Classroom activities can be used to tackle issues associated with bullying in an age, gender and culturally appropriate way. Such curricular approaches raise awareness of bullying and schools' anti-bullying policies. They can include more passive activities such as literature, audiovisual materials and videos, and can take more active forms such as drama/role play, music, debates and workshops. Samara and Smith (2008) found that in 2002, 53% of schools reported using video films, 64% literature, and 74% drama/role play, as part of their anti-bullying work. 'Curriculum work' as an overall global category was also reported by 96% of schools in 2009–2010 (Thompson & Smith, 2011).

These kinds of activities were used and assessed in detail in the Sheffield project (Cowie & Sharp, 1994). Assessments with teachers and pupils immediately after the film, video or role play showed that pupils generally found the materials interesting and said it made them think about the issues, but follow-up assessments some months later suggested the effects are likely to only be temporary if curriculum work is not backed up by continuing anti-bullying work and policy (Smith & Sharp, 1994).

A more recent development has been the use of computer-based games and virtual learning environments where pupils can act out roles and possible bystander actions and evaluate the consequences. This was shown to have some effect by Sapouna (2010) in a trial of a program called FearNot! in primary schools in England and Germany; although the effects were short-term and only found in the English schools. This kind of approach has been used as part of the KiVa programme (see later; Poskiparta et al., 2012); here it is part of a continuing programme of coordinated activities.

Curriculum interventions for cyberbullying

Guidance on cyberbullying specifically, and/or internet safety more generally, is now being developed in many countries, and there are many sources of advice not only for children and young people but also for parents and schools. These can cover actions young people can take themselves (such as reporting abuse, keeping evidence), information on legal rights and recourse, and information on websites and schemes such as cybermentors. An EU-funded project has provided a training manual on cyberbullying for trainers dealing with different target groups, such as pupils, parents, teachers or whole schools, and this is available online as a user-friendly eBook in several language versions (Jäger, 2009).

An earlier review of three short-term classroom-based interventions by Mishna and colleagues (2009) found scant evidence of effectiveness. A more recent review by Jones and colleagues (2013) of internet safety education programmes points out the need for basing such programmes on research findings, tailoring them to developmental needs and evaluating their effectiveness.

In England, an evaluation was made of two e-safety films used by secondary schools – Childnet International's *Lets Fight It Together* about cyberbullying, and Child Exploitation and Online Protection's (CEOP) *Exposed* about sexting (sending sexually explicit images and texts using mobile phones). Both films and resources were rated as good by the students and staff, although changes in behaviour were not assessed (Thompson et al., 2013; www.bullyingandcyber.net/en/documents/ecip/united-kingdom/).

Personal and Social Skills Education

Education about topics such as relationships, responsibility, emotional health and well-being, and citizenship, can provide school staff with a clear opportunity to work on bullying. Social skills training can also be embedded in such approaches. Social skills-based programmes have had some success in promoting social competence (Durlak et al., 2011), but not all evaluations have been positive.

In schools in England, Personal, Social, Health and Economic Education (PSHEE) is intended (amongst other aims) to include developing awareness of different types of bullying and the consequences of bullying, promoting assertiveness in challenging bullying, developing confidence in coping with bullying, and developing strategies for conflict resolution. One widely used resource is SEAL (Social and Emotional Aspects of Learning), which is a whole school approach to developing social and emotional skills. It has both primary and secondary school programmes. The primary SEAL programme has seven themes, one of which is 'Say No to Bullying'. An evaluation by Humphrey et al. (2008) found a significant impact for the small group work component on the pupils at delivery and at the seven-week follow-up, although this was not supported by parental ratings. The skill and experience of the facilitators were seen as crucial, and recommendations included more standardised training and greater parental involvement.

The Secondary SEAL programme was launched in 2005 under the title Developing Social, Emotional and Behavioural Skills (SEBS). An evaluation by Humphrey and colleagues (2010) reported a lack of structure and consistency in the delivery of the secondary SEAL curriculum, recommending that schools needed greater guidance about maximising the impact of the resource.

In the USA, the PATHS programme has been used quite extensively. This is a 60-lesson intervention, with units on self-control, emotions and problem solving. However, an evaluation of PATHS in the Netherlands, with intervention and control schools, failed to find effects on internalising and externalising behaviours, including victimisation (Goossens et al., 2012). A similar design failed to find any long-term effects of PATHS in Swiss schools (Malti et al., 2012).

Another curriculum programme used in the USA is the Second Step classroom intervention. Espelage and colleagues (2013) described an evaluation of this, in sixth graders, in 36 schools randomly assigned to intervention (18) or control (18). Fifteen weekly lessons covered social emotional skills, including empathy, emotion management, bully prevention and problem-solving skills. There were no significant effects at post-test on bully or victim rates, or on homophobic name-calling or sexual harassment: there was, however, a significant effect of a lesser increase for physical aggression in the intervention schools.

In Austria, the ViSC school programme is one part of a national strategy against violence in schools (Spiel & Strohmeier, 2011). Activities are geared towards the school as a whole, in classrooms, and on the individual level. The class project consists of 13 units, covering alternative ways to perceive, interpret and deal with critical situations using vignette stories, discussions and role plays. An evaluation with the OBVQ using intervention and control classes found greater reductions in victim rates in the intervention classes, post-test and at the follow-up four months later, and a greater reduction in bullying rates at the follow-up only.

In Germany, a fairplayer manual approach has been developed by Scheithauer, Hess, Schultze-Krumbholz and Bull (2012). It involves awareness raising and fostering social-emotional competencies, through methods such as moral dilemma discussion groups and role plays. The authors report on three evaluation studies. The third study included a non-intervention control, and this study especially produced significant decreases in bully and victim rates in intervention classes compared to controls.

In Switzerland, Alsaker and Valkanover (2012) describe a programme called Be-Prox, developed for use with younger, kindergarten age, children. Much of the programme involves intensive training work with teachers. This is then translated into curriculum work with the children. Using eight kindergartens each as intervention and control, the programme had a positive effect on physical and indirect victim rates, although not on bully rates.

Cooperative Group Work

Cooperative Group Work (CGW) provides a format for classroom work which has been regarded as helpful in terms of pupil relationships. In CGW, pupils work together to solve a common task (for example, design a newspaper). It has been referred to as a 'jigsaw classroom', since different pupils provide different parts of the 'jigsaw' to solve the task: each has a distinctive contribution to make. CGW thus has the potential to involve and integrate vulnerable bullied children in the class peer group. Samara and Smith (2008) found that 73% of schools reported using some form of this in 2002, and in 2009–2010 this was 89% (Thompson & Smith, 2011), although it is likely that such usage is occasional rather than part of the normal curriculum format.

Cowie et al. (1994) specifically evaluated the extensive use of CGW in several middle schools in England. The teachers using it reported some beneficial effects on relationships, including integrating pupils at risk of being victimised, but a difficulty experienced in several classes was that pupils who might be involved in bullying could disrupt the activities and make the approach difficult to sustain.

Quality Circles

Quality Circles (QCs) are problem-solving groups of pupils formed for regular classroom sessions. They deal with a particular topic – and one such topic very suitable for QCs is bullying. There are a set of procedures to follow about group formation, data gathering and the presentation of outcomes. QCs were used in the Sheffield project in England, and Samara and Smith (2008) reported 33% of schools using it in 1996, but this fell to 20% in 2002. Thompson and Smith (2011) found only 16% of schools using it in 2009–2010.

Paul and colleagues (2010, 2012) reported on the use of QCs in one English secondary school, in the context of understanding and reducing bullying and cyberbullying. QCs were found to be an effective means of gathering information on bullying and cyberbullying in the school. The use of the QCs was an engaging process for pupils, and encouraged young people to provide a realistic perspective on the bullying problems occurring in school. Pupils suggested a range of solutions to these problems, and the information gained was useful to staff in understanding how bullying was changing over time (for example, new forms of cyberbullying), and gave them some suggestions for intervention.

Overall QCs seem a promising approach, though not so much for reducing bullying directly as for finding out about specific issues in a school and involving pupils in problem solving about it. In this context the relatively low take-up in schools in England is surprising and perhaps a missed opportunity.

Assertiveness training

Assertiveness training provides a means for enhancing coping strategies for victims or those pupils who might be victimised. Through regular in-class or after school sessions, pupils learn specific strategies for dealing with difficult situations, such as attempts to bully them, in assertive rather than passive or aggressive ways. They can talk about their experiences, and learn and practise effective responses. Various skills/techniques are taught, such as the 'broken record' or 'fogging'.

Samara and Smith (2008) found that 32% of schools reported using this in 1996, down to 24% on 2002. The evidence from the Sheffield project (Sharp & Cowie, 1994) was that it could be expensive and time-consuming to carry out properly. Nevertheless, the training did help victims develop useful strategies. According to pupils, it worked best with periodic refresher sessions. While helpful for some pupils (and indeed useful for everyone), it is clear that assertiveness training does not solve bullying and should not be expected to do so.

Summary of proactive strategies

Proactive strategies have strong face validity. It seems almost obvious that a school should have a clear policy on bullying and that curriculum work will help prevent bullying. However, policies in themselves only provide a framework, and with curriculum activities, a lot seems to depend on the quality of what is done. Short-term initiatives have little lasting effect, and the success for longer-term initiatives is patchy, although certain programmes have had some good outcomes. Empathy and responsibility training may be challenging for certain children, for example for those exhibiting callous-unemotional traits (Frick & White, 2008).

It is likely that these proactive strategies must be used as part of a more comprehensive programme in order to be really effective. Some particular initiatives – such as CGW, assertiveness training and QCs – may be useful in particular circumstances or for particular objectives.

Peer support schemes

Peer support uses the knowledge, skills and experience of children and young people themselves in a planned and structured way; it can be used for a variety of purposes, but a prominent one has been to help deal with or reduce bullying. Cowie and Smith (2010) proposed that there are four essential aspects of peer support:

1. *Selected peers are trained to be peer supporters.* An immediate aim here is to give peer supporters certain skills: communication skills, sharing information, developing perspective-taking and empathic abilities, and dealing with interpersonal conflicts, social exclusion, violence and bullying in proactive and non-violent ways.
2. *Certain peers will be users of the peer support scheme(s).* The aim here – usually the main aim of such schemes – is that they will be helped, either directly by the peer supporter, or by the peer supporter arranging or encouraging other forms of help to be sought and/or given to them.
3. A longer-term aim is to *improve peer relationships generally* and to *reduce rates of unresolved conflicts and bullying* among pupils in the school.
4. The workings of peer support scheme(s) in a school might *raise the profile of the school as a caring and moral institution, and have effects on the school climate or ethos*, as manifested, for example, in increased liking of school and playtimes, and increased feelings of safety in school.

Peer support has been quite widely used in Canada and Australia since the 1980s. It has grown in popularity in recent years and is now used in many countries (Cowie & Smith, 2010). Samara and Smith (2008) found that 52% of their sample of English schools were using some peer support method in 2002, and Houlston et al. (2009) carried out a national survey, with an adjusted estimation (which made correction for non-response error) that 62% of English schools were using a structured peer support scheme in 2007. The most popular types of peer support schemes differed by sector. In primary schools, befriending and mediation were reported most: buddies and befrienders generally look out for pupils at break-times who are upset or lonely, and playleaders or playground pals lead structured games activities. In secondary schools, mentoring and befriending were most used: peer supporters – usually from older year groups – can support younger students at transition and can also provide one-to-one mentoring/counselling for bullied students.

There are various ways by which peer supporters can be contacted. Primary schools might have a bench in the playground where children can sit and then a trained peer supporter will go and talk to them. In secondary schools there is more commonly a confidential area such as a private room, manned by peer supporters at lunchtimes, or alternatively contact can be made through a worry/bully box or the school intranet. Peer supporters can be identified by badges, a special notice board with their photographs, and introductory assemblies.

Thompson and Smith (2011) used six categories of peer support, summarised below. They found that in 2009–2010, some 69% of schools were using befriending schemes, 68% circles of friends, 48% peer mentoring, 34% peer listening, 27% peer mediation and 4% bystander training.

Befriending

In befriending schemes, peer supporters are trained to offer support and friendship to pupils in everyday situations. Some schemes are based on playground buddies (clearly identifiable by special caps/clothing) helping lonely or bullied children during breaktimes or lunchtimes. Other schemes focus on organising playground games or on running lunchtime clubs which are open to all but offer companionship to lonely pupils. Befrienders can be the same age or older than their target group. They are supported or supervised by school staff and need training in listening skills, confidentiality issues, assertiveness and leadership. Playground buddy schemes can be helpful but may be underused if their users feel exposed or stigmatised. Buddies may also be teased about their special caps/clothes. Running lunchtime activities can usually avoid these problems (Smith & Watson, 2004).

Circles of friends/Circles of support/Supportive friends

In these circles, volunteer pupils are trained to befriend and support other pupils who are identified as isolated or rejected by their peers and hence vulnerable to bullying. Training involves increasing empathic skills, developing a flexible and creative method to form positive relationships with peers, and ingenuity in devising practical strategies to support victims.

Peer mentoring

Peer mentoring schemes aim for a supportive relationship between two pupils, combining practical advice and encouragement. They are especially used for supporting a pupil at challenging times (for example, joining a new school, bereavement or bullying). In secondary schools, older pupil mentors can help train younger ones. Mentoring is most effective when agreed ways of working are clear and there is good staff supervision and support of the mentors (Cowie & Wallace, 2000; Smith & Watson, 2004).

Peer listening

Peer listeners are older students who provide a sympathetic ear for younger students when troubled. Listeners provide both emotional and academic support. Listening is a more discrete form of peer support and not so much a reporting system for problems such as bullying. In the primary sector peer listeners are accessible in the playground at breaktimes, identified by a badge or ribbon. In the secondary sector listeners may attend Form Groups on a weekly basis, or run lunchtime sessions or clubs in a designated room where they are available on demand.

Peer mediation

Peer mediation is a problem-solving process. Pupil mediators are trained in conflict resolution skills and in helping individuals resolve disputes. A peer mediator will encourage a pupil to define the problem, identify and agree on key issues, discuss and brainstorm possible options, negotiate a plan of action and agreement, and follow-up and evaluate outcomes. As one secondary school peer mediator put it, 'I'd recommend it because children don't really want to talk to adults so they can talk to anyone of the peer mediators. They give advice, not help. They help the children come up with their own ideas' (Smith & Watson, 2004). Training for this should emphasise boundaries of expertise and when referral to an adult is necessary.

Bystander (defender) training

This involves intervention action on the part of pupil bystanders when they witness peer victimisation: defenders will try to intervene and stop the bullying or comfort pupils who experience bullying.

Evaluation of peer support schemes

Smith and Watson (2004) carried out a detailed study of 20 schools that were implementing peer support, using the CHIPS (ChildLine in Partnership with Schools) training programme. They identified a number of issues: these included how peer supporters are selected (there is often a gender imbalance, with more girls than boys volunteering), how they are trained (training schemes are usually well planned and received), how they can be contacted (this should be discreet to avoid stigmatising users), how well the scheme is known in the school and whether there is sufficient take-up that peer supporters can feel positive in their role, how much ongoing support is available to the peer supporters from designated staff members, and how much the scheme is supported by senior management.

Cowie and Smith (2010) assessed the outcomes of peer support schemes in the four main areas mentioned earlier: for those trained in peer support, for users of peer support, for peer relationships in the school, and for the general school ethos or climate. Many evaluations are impressionistic 'in-house' case studies, often carried out by enthusiastic practitioners who have introduced and implemented the intervention, but others have used independent evaluation, some with quantitative surveys of attitudes and outcomes.

Cowie and Smith (2010) concluded that the most well-established finding is the benefits of peer support systems for the peer supporters: improved self-esteem, increased social and communication skills, greater empathy, and a sense of responsibility and doing something worthwhile in the school have been commonly reported. These benefits probably stem from the high quality of training usually received, continuing supervision, and the practice of skills in a context generally valued by other pupils and the school. Problems identified in some schools were a lack of status in the school community, gender imbalance and a lack of usage for the scheme. James and colleagues (2014) identified the opportunities and challenges facing 16–17 year old peer mentors, from a focus group in an English secondary school. As one peer mentor said, 'I always find at first they're all sort of closed up but then after that I can get onto talking to them. And then they open up and I can always help with their problems'; and another, 'When you actually just see the looks on their faces and you know like before and then after. And you're like yeah, it actually is all worth it'.

Generalising over a number of studies, most users of peer support systems report it as being helpful. The degree of helpfulness varies, but a majority would use the service again and would recommend it to a friend in need. For example, Smith and Watson (2004) found that of those students who had made use of a peer support scheme, 96% of primary pupils and 89% of secondary pupils felt it had helped them either 'a bit' or 'a lot', and 75% and 67% in primary and secondary schools, respectively, said they would use peer support again should the situation arise. In a study in an all girls' secondary school, Houlston and Smith (2009) found that over 30% of year 7 students had used the peer support service at least once, but only 11% had done so in year 8 (the two years the programme was targeted at). In year 7, 33% of pupils said the scheme had helped 'a lot' and 50% 'a bit', while 17% said it had not helped. However, in year 8, no-one said it had helped 'a lot', 75% said 'a bit' and 25% said it had not helped. In general, it seems that younger pupils are often more receptive to peer support schemes.

But does the use of peer support schemes actually stop experiences of being bullied, or improve peer relationships in the school generally or the school climate? There are anecdotal reports of how individual pupils have benefited. In the Smith and Watson (2004) study, 52% of staff and 43% of pupils felt that the peer support scheme was having a positive effect in helping to stop bullying in schools, with many pupils being unsure about this even though it might have helped them personally. These uncertainties are illustrated by these quotes from primary school pupils: 'I think that befrienders are making lots of children's lives easier at school'; 'When I went to a buddy it really helped me because I used to get bullied a lot'; 'Befrienders are helping people with no friends, but they are not really making an influence on bullying'.

Some studies have used pre- and post-tests to assess outcomes – such as levels of victimisation – on a wider basis. Cowie and Olafsson (2001), in a study of one secondary school in England with high levels of violence, gave a bullying questionnaire before the introduction of a peer support service and 7.5 months later. The high incidence of bullying in the school showed little change: the pupils' estimate of the number of victims in their own class was 2.64 in November and 2.63 in the following June, while the estimated number of bullies was 2.39 in November and 2.46 in June. The authors concluded that it was unrealistic to expect that a small number of peer supporters could solve the problem of bullying in such a challenging context, especially when there was little evidence of supervision, monitoring and support from adults in order to sustain the intervention over time.

Houlston and Smith (2009), in their study of an all girls' secondary school, used pre- and post-test assessments of levels of bullying with pupils in grades 7, 8 and 9. There was no significant change in levels of reported victimisation or bullying, although perceptions that the school was doing something about bullying did increase, most notably in year 7 pupils.

Perhaps the most encouraging findings regarding peer support, from studies including non-intervention control classes, have come from work by Menesini and colleagues in Italy. Menesini et al. (2003) assessed a class-based befriending intervention in the sixth, seventh and eighth grades of two Italian middle schools over one year. Across the two schools, nine classes were in the programme condition and five were controls. Experimental classes showed a decrease in bullying and outsider roles, and less of an increase in reinforcer and assistant bullies, compared to controls, and especially for boys. There were no significant changes in the defender or victim roles overall. Attitudinal data showed an increase in anti-bullying attitudes only in sixth graders.

Menesini, Nocentini and Palladino (2012) reported two studies on a web-based project called *Noncadiamointrappola* [Let's not fall into a trap]. In the first study (2009–2010), students developed a website to promote peer-to-peer content against bullying and cyberbullying. Peer educators were trained, and monitored the website, answering questions and monitoring discussions. An evaluation at eight high schools found that cyberbullying others decreased more significantly (especially for boys) for those in the programme, compared with those who only experienced awareness-raising or no-treatment control. However, cyber victim and traditional bully or victim rates did not show differential effects. In the second study, *Noncadiamointrappola* was expanded to involve bystanders and teachers to a greater degree and included a Facebook page to integrate the web forum. An evaluation in four high schools over a five-month period found significant reductions in traditional bully and victim rates and cyber victim rates for the experimental group, compared to some increases in the control group: this time, no effect was found on cyberbullying others. The decreases were found both for the peer educators and for other children in the experimental classes.

As the Menesini, Nocentini and Palladino (2012) work indicates, new technologies can be used productively in peer support. Another development in this respect has been cybermentors.

CyberMentors

A UK charity, Beatbullying, launched a new form of virtual peer support called CyberMentors in 2009 (Kaenel-Platt & Douglas, 2012). Students are trained in two-day workshops, while staff are briefed separately by the Beatbullying trainers. Cybermentors and mentees log on to the CyberMentors' website and mentor on demand. The website, moderated by Beatbullying staff, has a software filter to protect the identity of mentors and mentees and screen online dialogue. Cybermentors can refer mentees on to senior cybermentors and counsellors for further support if necessary.

The CyberMentor scheme was evaluated by Banerjee, Robinson and Smalley (2010) and Thompson and Smith (2011), and more recently as part of a DAPHNE III project on cyberbullying (www.bullyingandcyber.net/en/). The latter evaluation found that the training was rated highly by students. A sample of cybermentors and cybermentees completed an online evaluation questionnaire: most were 11–18 years old. Cybermentors and mentees who reported cyberbullying incidents said that most lasted several weeks, involved social networking sites and that the victims knew the perpetrators, who were about the same age. The website was rated as easy to use and safe, and cybermentors as easy to contact and talk to. Of 106 online questionnaires completed by cybermentees, most found the cybermentors' advice helpful (40%) or very helpful (40%) and said they would use the CyberMentor scheme again: 'The good part about the session was being able to tell someone I don't know everything and just let it out without getting criticised' (cybermentee, aged 15). Most cybermentors and cybermentees were female so, as with many peer support schemes, ways to encourage more participation by males is clearly important.

General evaluation of peer support schemes

Peer support schemes have become popular in a number of countries, and they have potential for harnessing pupil involvement in productive ways. Nevertheless, there can be problems in using such schemes as an anti-bullying measure, especially if they are not well thought out or supported. Problems can include a gender imbalance in peer supporters, under-use of schemes, and stigmatisation of users or even of peer supporters themselves. These and other problems are not inevitable, but they can occur.

Nevertheless, schools using well-managed peer support schemes are seen as being more caring and concerned about pupil well-being, and the schemes are known and supported by pupils and staff. In addition, there is good evidence that the peer supporters themselves generally benefit from the experience. In individual cases pupils who use peer support schemes for reasons of being bullied report being helped. There is mixed evidence regarding whether schemes produce significant changes on their own in general levels of bullying behaviour. Peer support schemes can, however, be integrated into wider programmes, as has been done successfully in the KiVa progamme in Finland (see later).

Red Balloon Learner Centres

For some children and young people, trying to cope with bullying at school becomes a continual ordeal which they literally cannot cope with any longer.

Such children may be withdrawn from school and some will be educated at home: at times this can be satisfactory, but such children are also likely to need help in recovering from the trauma they have experienced at school.

In England, Dr Carrie Herbert started up Red Balloon Learner Centres (RBLC) which provide an intensive care and learning environment for pupils who have been very severely bullied at school. In fact, she started up the first such centre in her own house, in Cambridge in 1996, following a desperate call from the parents of a 13 year old girl who had taken an overdose following very severe bullying. She hired teachers and offered a full-time curriculum with much personal and social education and therapy to 12 secondary school-aged local children. Seven years later she moved the Centre from her home into a similar domestic property to make sure the small-scale and cosy environment was retained. In 2004 the Red Balloon Group was established and further centres were set up. As well as Red Balloon-Cambridge there are now Centres in Norwich, NW London and Reading. In addition a virtual Centre, Red Balloon of the Air, with online curricula and regular local face-to-face support, has been instituted.

An RBLC takes up to 15 young people, who will have been severely traumatised by bullying at school. Here is a description from one former RBLC student, of how she wanted to die following cyber victimisation:

> I cut myself like mad that night and didn't leave the house for the next month or two fearing for my life. People sent me the pictures on MSN. The girl started messaging me, that she would find me and get me. I would sit under my desk sometimes praying to God even though I didn't believe in him. My mum took me out of school when I started having nightmares of the girl killing me. I had therapy and was put on antidepressants but they didn't work, it was too late.

For such young people RBLCs provide a safe haven, therapeutic care, and the opportunity to continue studies in a form tailored to their needs. There is a high staff-to-pupil ratio, and the centre provides a therapeutic community with clear guidelines for behaviour, which aims to build up confidence and self-esteem. Pastoral issues are an important part of the curriculum, but academic work is not neglected. The aim of RBLCs is to return young people to a mainstream school (whether their previous school, or a different school) or, if old enough, to a college of further education. The median length of stay at an RBLC is three terms: 95% of the children who stay at a Red Balloon longer than six weeks return to school or move on to college. After successfully completing college many of the students go on to university.

Hayes and Herbert (2011) provide eight case studies of young people who came to an RBLC. Each one had been severely bullied, for a variety of reasons – such as obesity, dyslexia, wearing the wrong clothes, being gay. Even from the children's own accounts, it is apparent that many factors were at play – some had problems with anger management, and some would certainly appear as bully/victims if assessed in the traditional research format. However, all are success stories in that all describe how the RBLC experience helped them to recover their self-esteem and well-being and get back on track academically in order to continue their studies.

Knights (2011) carried out her doctoral thesis examining the effectiveness of RBLCs. She compared the change or recovery of victims in RBLCs with similar pupils who had been victimised in mainstream schools in Hertfordshire Local Authority. She used quantitative methods to measure bullying experiences and depression, self-esteem, trauma, and academic engagement and self-concept, at baseline and after three, six and nine months; plus interviews as qualitative data. The quantitative analyses showed that the RBLC children improved, but not significantly more than those in the mainstream schools. However, the qualitative data, as in the case studies in Hayes and Herbert (2011), clearly show how some very troubled young people benefitted from RBLCs. Although Knights attempted to match her control children for aspects such as length and severity of bullying experiences, such matching is difficult to achieve, and it is clear that RBLCs can effectively help some very disturbed children make a good recovery from what seem to be desperate situations. As one former pupil wrote:

> Coming to the Red Balloon was the best thing that's happened to me. When I stopped going to school and before I came to the Red Balloon I always thought I was a loser, a no hoper, but thanks to the teachers I now believe I have something worth living for.

Anti-bullying programme interventions

Many schools use a variety of methods in combination. Samara and Smith (2008) found that in 2006 numerous English schools reported using not only a whole school policy, but also, for example, 80% used circle time, 74% used drama/role play, 57% used trained playground supervisors, and 28% used either the Support Group or Pikas (that is, non-punitive) methods.

Internationally, there are programmes available with a structured set of components and sequence of activities. Many pre-/post-test studies have examined their effect, usually with standard questionnaires such as the OBVQ. A possible issue in interpreting pre-/post-test comparisons is response shift – do pupils become sensitised to bullying issues and change their responses to questions about bullying experiences, after an intervention (irrespective of any changes in behaviour)? However, Shaw, Cross and Zubrick (submitted) tested for response shift bias in evaluating anti-bullying programmes in two ways: using retrospective pre-test scores and confirmatory factor analysis. In general, neither approach found much evidence for a response shift.

A common design for assessing programme effects is to compare intervention schools (or classes) with control classes in which no intervention took place. There may be issues about why some schools elect to have the intervention, however – perhaps they were more motivated to tackle bullying anyway. The best design for evaluating programmes is generally considered to be the randomised control trial (RCT), where schools or classes are assigned randomly to intervention or control. This largely removes other alternative explanations for the differences found, although there may be an element of artificiality in requiring schools or classes to follow a certain procedure they have not chosen completely voluntarily.

Sometimes control schools are not feasible (for example if there is a national anti-bullying campaign), and then an age-cohort or extended selection cohort design (explained below for the OBPP) can be used to control for age effects. Detailed descriptions of many studies can be found in Smith, Pepler and Rigby (2004), a special issue of the *International Journal of Behavioral Development* (Spiel, Salmivalli & Smith, 2011), a collection edited by Strohmeier and Noam (2012), and a special issue of the *International Journal of Conflict and Violence* that has a broader focus on violence prevention (Eisner & Malti, 2012). Some of these programmes are discussed in the following sections in approximate chronological order.

The Olweus Bullying Prevention Programme (OBPP) in Norway

As noted in Chapter 1, western action on school bullying started in Norway, and it was accelerated by the publicity given to the suicides of three 10–14 year old boys in late 1982, attributed in large part to their experiences of severe bullying. This, together with Olweus's existing research findings (Olweus, 1973/1978), helped bring about the first Norwegian National Anti-Bullying campaign, starting in autumn 1983. This campaign involved a 32-page booklet for school personnel, giving detailed suggestions about what teachers and school could do to counteract bullying; a four-page folder with information and advice for parents; a 25-minute video cassette showing episodes from everyday lives of two bullied children, as a basis for class discussion; and a short survey given to pupils, to ascertain the level and nature of bully/victim problems in each school.

As part of the nationwide campaign, Olweus carried out a large-scale intervention project in the city of Bergen (see below), and developed a first version of what later became known as the Olweus Bullying Prevention Programme (OBPP). The fully-evolved OBPP has school-level components (such as a Bullying Prevention Coordinating Committee, introducing school rules against bullying, doing a questionnaire survey), classroom-level components (such as class meetings and meetings with parents), individual-level components (such as serious talks and intervention plans for involved students), and community-level components (such as supportive partnerships with community members); for full details see Olweus and Limber (2010). The overall philosophy is for adults to act as responsible and authoritative role models; to be warm and supportive to students, but set firm limits to unacceptable behaviour such as bullying; and to 'consistently use non-physical, nonhostile negative consequences when rules are broken' (Olweus & Limber, 2010: 377).

Olweus's evaluation of the original version of the OBPP, in the First Bergen Project (1983–1985), was carried out in 42 primary and junior high schools, with some 2,500 students in grades 4, 5, 6 and 7, followed over two-and-a-half years. At that time children only started school at 7 years old, so these students were around

11–14 years old in May 1983, shortly before the intervention campaign was started. Measurements were taken at this point (time 1), and again in May 1984 (time 2) and May 1985 (time 3). The measurements made at the three time points were based on questionnaires measuring the frequency of being bullied and bullying others, spending playtime alone, antisocial behaviour, and satisfaction with school life.

To evaluate the success of the intervention, it would not be valid to simply see whether victimisation decreased for a particular cohort of students (for example, comparing students in grade 5 at the start and grade 7 at the end): victim rates decrease with time anyway (see Chapter 4). A common way around this is to compare intervention and control (no-intervention) schools, but as the first Norwegian National Anti-Bullying campaign was on a national basis, there could not be any 'no-treatment' control groups.

To overcome this problem, Olweus made use of time-lagged contrasts between age-equivalent groups, in which schools serve as their own controls. For example, the children who were grade 4 at time 1, and moved into grade 5 at time 2, had now experienced one year of intervention: they could be compared with those who had been at grade 5 at time 1, before the intervention started. And as they moved into grade 6 at time 2, their scores could now be compared with those who had been in grade 6 at time 1. Olweus calls this an 'extended selection cohorts' design and it has been used in many of his, and some other, studies. This design overcomes the absence of conventional no-treatment control groups, and controls for age changes. However, the comparisons do not control for possible historical effects. For example, suppose some other events had happened in 1984, such as a severe economic depression, or increased racial tension – these might influence the comparisons. The comparisons are in effect measuring the effects of the intervention programme (itself an historical effect!) and any other large-scale effects felt in 1983–1985. Nevertheless, there were no other such obviously important effects in Norway in the period concerned.

Using this methodology the effect on rates of bullying was dramatic, with reported victim rates falling by around 50% (see Table 6.2) for both boys and girls. There were also reductions in anti-social behaviour and increases in satisfaction with school. A 'dosage–response' relationship was found: that is, greater teacher involvement in the programme and implementation correlated ($r = 0.51$) with reductions in levels of being bullied. The bullying was not just displaced elsewhere – there were no changes in reports of bullying on the way to and from school. These findings were very significant in encouraging researchers and inspiring the next wave of research.

A decade later, a second New Bergen project (1997–1998) did use a more conventional intervention/control school design. Surveys were carried out in 14 intervention and 16 comparison schools. After six months, victim and bully rates had decreased in intervention schools, with little change or increase in comparison schools. The outcomes are shown in Table 6.2, both as straightforward reductions in the intervention schools (but confounded by age) and as changes relative to the control schools. Soon after this, an Oslo project (1999–2000) was used in 37 schools, and a cohort analysis again showed substantial effects (see Table 6.2).

Table 6.2 Effects of six evaluations of the Olweus Bullying Prevention Programme; percentage changes (rounded to whole numbers)

Study, date and type	Victim: percentage reduction	Bully: percentage reduction
First Bergen project: 1983–1985 cohort	64	53
New Bergen project 1997–1998: intervention/control	24 (28 relative to controls)	21 (58 relative to controls)
Oslo project: 1999–2000 cohort	42	52
New National Initiative: 2001–2002 cohort	33	37
New National Initiative: 2002–2003 cohort	34	48
New National Initiative: 2003–2004 cohort	34	49

Subsequent to this, a New Norwegian National Initiative against Bullying (Manifesto-I) was launched in autumn 2001. All schools were expected to develop a plan for anti-bullying work, but could decide their own strategy or adopt the OBPP. From the spring of 2003, the Zero programme of Roland (later) could also be chosen. From an evaluation perspective, the new national initiative provided a unique opportunity to examine the effects of the OBPP with very large samples of students and schools. Olweus and Limber (2010) have reported findings associated with the use of the OBPP in this context, using several consecutive cohorts with a total of 160 schools and 21,000 students. Consistently, substantial reductions have been found, as shown in Table 6.2. The use of large consecutive cohorts of schools also makes explanations of the findings in terms of historical effects unlikely. The considerable success of the OBPP in Norway is thus both substantial and well-replicated.

Of course, as in all programmes, schools using the OBPP vary in implementation and outcome. Olweus (2004) reported on teacher-level and school-level predictors of implementation of the OBPP in the First Bergen project. He found the most important predictors at the teacher level were Perceived Staff Importance (influence and responsibility), Read Programme Information and Perceived Level of Bullying; less important predictors were Affective Involvement and Self-Victimised as a Child. The most important predictors at the school level were Openness in Communication and School Attention to Bullying Problems. Interestingly, two factors which did not predict implementation were Teacher–Leadership Collaboration and Teacher–Teacher Collaboration (which in fact did predict weakly, but in a negative direction).

The OBPP in other European countries

The programme has been used outside Norway, but with less consistent success. In Germany, a project in Schleswig-Holstein was reported by Hanewinkel (2004). This used the OBPP school-, class- and individual-level interventions in 37 primary and secondary schools during 1994–1996. Over a period of one-and-a-half to two years, there were small decreases in victim and bully rates up to age 16, but some increase at ages 17–18. It is not clear from this report that a cohort design was used, so the reported figures may be confounded with age changes.

In the Netherlands, Fekkes, Pijpers and Verloove-Vanhorick (2006) worked with 15 intervention and 30 control schools from 1999–2000, with a follow-up in 2001. They used a programme modelled on the OBPP with an emphasis on written anti-bullying policy. They found that victim rates decreased by 25% in intervention compared to control schools in the first year, and also some relative improvement in rates of bullying others. However, no significant effects remained at the second year follow-up.

Olweus and Limber (2010) argue that these studies cannot be seen as replications of the OBPP, since the interventions used deviated considerably from the original model in terms of both programme content and implementation. However, Olweus (personal communication, 3 October 2013) states that as yet unpublished results from evaluations in Lithuania, and also in Iceland, are showing positive findings.

The OBPP in the USA

Several studies have been carried out in the USA (see also Olweus & Limber, 2010).

Limber et al. (2004) reported on a project in South Carolina, from 1994–1995, with 11 intervention schools and 28 control schools. This used the OBPP with added peer community involvement measures. No significant effects were found in victim rates, but bullying rates were reduced by some 25% in intervention schools compared to some increase in control schools.

Bauer and colleagues (2007) reported on a project in Seattle, from 2003–2005, with 10 intervention schools and three control schools, using the OBPP. There were no significant main effects on victim rates, attitudes to intervene, or perceptions of safety, but there was a significant improvement in intervention schools in perceptions of other students as likely to intervene.

Black and Jackson (2007) reported a study of the OBPP in six elementary and middle schools in Philadelphia. It is not clear that a cohort design was used, so the reported figures may be confounded with age changes. Two kinds of evaluation were adopted. Pupil surveys using the OBVQ gave unpromising findings: more prominence in the discussions is given to a Bullying Incident Density (BID) measure, based on observations. This gave promising outcomes, although there was no dose–response relationship found with implementation. However the BID measure has faults. One recognised by the authors is that it mainly assesses physical attacks (not verbal and relational). A second is that play fights were included in BID: this ignores research showing that most play fights do not escalate into real fights, and that these are distinguishable from real fighting (Smith, 2010b). A third difficulty is that aggressive acts in BID may not involve repetition or an imbalance of power, and thus may not be bullying (in terms of the definition recognised by the authors).

As Olweus and Limber (2010: 397) comment on these studies in the USA: 'Although these findings are clearly encouraging, it should also be noted that the results from these studies have not been uniformly positive.' However, Olweus (personal communication, 3 October 2013) has stated that 'We have – at long last – some very good intervention data from Pennsylvania, USA, with more than 300 schools, followed over two–four years, and with 70,000 students. Most of the statistical analyses are completed and we see quite good and systematic results in the different cohorts. We are eagerly looking forward to get the findings published'.

In summary, the OBPP has proved highly effective in Norway, but so far its success in other countries is more variable.

Programmes with more limited similarity to OBPP

In Canada, the Toronto project, 1991–1993 (Pepler, Craig, O'Connell, Atlas & Charach, 2004), used a programme largely modelled on the OBPP with a range of school, class and individual level interventions in four elementary (primary) schools. A peer mediation programme was also used in three schools. Rates of victimisation showed a reduction of about 5%, and rates of bullying actually showed a small increase of about 2%.

In Belgium, the Flanders project, from 1995–1997, used a programme modelled on the Bergen (early OBPP) and Sheffield projects (Stevens, Van Oost & De Bourdeaudhuij, 2004). It worked with 18 schools, three primary and three secondary schools each in Treatment with Support (from the research team), Treatment without Support and Treatment to Control. Comparing the Treatment to Control schools, the finding was a mixed pattern of positive changes in primary school and zero outcomes in secondary schools. Support by the research team made little difference.

The Sheffield project (England)

In England the main programme intervention was the Sheffield project, from 1991–1993 (Smith & Sharp, 1994; Smith, Sharp, Eslea & Thompson, 2004). This used 23 intervention schools and four control schools. It embodied developing a whole school policy, plus a choice from a range of other intervention components. The most used were curriculum work (videos, drama, literature, quality circles), assertiveness training, the Pikas method, the playground environment and supervisor training, and peer support. Over a two-year period, and using the extended selected cohorts design, in the intervention schools there was a reduction in victimisation rates. This was around 17% in being bullied for primary schools, but only around 3–5% in secondary schools. For bullying others, reductions were around 12% in both sectors. Furthermore there were high positive correlations (around 0.6, 0.7) between measures of the amount of effort put in by schools (assessed by teachers and pupils), and measures of the outcomes achieved. It was difficult to draw conclusions from the small number of control schools (which showed varied results) as during the period some of these had responded to national government initiatives on bullying and could not be regarded as no-treatment controls.

Spain: SAVE and ConRed

The SAVE (Sevilla Anti-Violencia Escolar) project was carried out in Seville between 1995–1996 and 1999–2000, inspired by the Sheffield and Bergen projects but developed independently. It had four parts: the democratic management of interpersonal relationships; cooperative group work and the curriculum; training in emotions, attitudes and values; and direct interventions for pupils at risk or involved in bullying (Ortega et al., 2004). Ten schools participated in the intervention programme, with pupils aged 8–18 years, and five took part in a post-intervention survey four years later. Three different schools participated as control schools.

For numbers of pupils involved, in the intervention schools there were reductions of 57% for victimisation and 16% for bullying. The proportion of bully/victims (those taking part in bullying and also being bullied) decreased by 57% and that of bystanders increased by 7%. The post-test results showed a significantly lower incidence of bullying problems at intervention schools, compared with control schools. There was an increase of 16% of children reporting that relationships with their peers were positive, and a reduction in long-term victims (those reporting being victimised for a year or more) of 41%. Unfortunately, despite these promising results, support for further rollouts of the programme was not forthcoming.

More recently, a programme called ConRed has been developed, more specifically to address cyberbullying (Ortega, del Rey & Casas, 2012). This was carried out with three secondary schools in Cordoba. The programme involved an awareness raising campaign, clear policies and procedures in the schools, a three-month period of weekly sessions with pupils with a curriculum on internet safety and responsible use, advice for teachers and families, and joint activities to foster school–family–community partnerships.

Within the three schools, some classes acted as intervention and some as controls. After three months the intervention classes showed significant decreases in both victim and bully rates, for both traditional and cyberbullying, whereas the control classes showed no change or much smaller decreases. There were also relative increases in affective empathy (for girls only), and decreases in internet addiction in the intervention classes.

Norway: the ZERO programme

Roland had worked with Olweus at the time of the first Norwegian National Anti-Bullying campaign in 1983. During 1996–1997 he started to develop a programme with more emphasis on classroom management than on work with individual pupils. By the time of the Norwegian Manifesto against Bullying (Manifesto-I) launch in autumn 2002, the ZERO programme was fully developed, and (along with the OBPP, earlier) recommended for use by the Norwegian government. The programme and results are described in Roland and colleagues (2010), Roland (2011) and Roland and Midthassel (2012).

A main focus of ZERO is training the teachers to set up classroom rules about bullying and exercise authoritative classroom leadership. The role of the pupil bystanders and the importance of telling adults are also emphasised. After a bullying incident, the class teacher will talk with the victim, and then with the bullying pupils individually, leading up to a meeting with all those involved in the bullying. (This sequence of meetings resembles that used in the Pikas method earlier, but ZERO is different, first in that the bullying children are told directly and authoritatively that the bullying must stop, and second, in that parents are informed promptly about the situation).

According to Roland and Midthassel (2012), more than 370 schools have used the ZERO programme since 2003. A survey of 146 primary schools from 2003 to 2004 showed significant decreases in bullying, but no more so than control schools (which were part of a national campaign broader than either the OBPP or ZERO programmes).

Overall, according to national surveys, there was a reduction in Norwegian schools generally between 2001 and 2004 from 6.3–4.9% for victims, and 2.3–1.9% for bullies. Unfortunately, by 2008 at the next national survey, the percentages had risen again to 6.2% (victims) and 3.7% (bullies) (Roland, 2011). Roland attributes this in large part to two main factors. One was the ending of the Manifesto-I initiative: this was succeeded by a Manifesto-II in 2005, which, however, had a relatively weak focus on anti-bullying work. The government put much more emphasis on general curriculum reform in the schools. The second was the advent of cyberbullying, which became a serious issue around 2004–2008.

Clearly, an important lesson in the Norwegian experience is about the sustainability of interventions. An intervention or campaign, even a national one, may have immediate positive effects, but it is also necessary to lay a basis for ensuring these effects continue after the initial enthusiasm for the 'campaign', and to stay on top of new developments.

Ireland: The Donegal project and ABC project

O'Moore and Minton (2004) carried out an intervention project in primary schools in Donegal, a predominantly rural county in north-west Ireland. The programme included training a network of professionals, a teacher's resource pack, a parent's resource pack, and curriculum work with pupils. The OBVQ was given in 1999 and one year later in 2000. Although 42 schools took part, only 22 returned pre- and post-test survey questionnaires.

The analysis of results did not use a cohort design, so, as the authors acknowledge, there is a confound with age in interpreting the findings. However, age-related decreases in victim or bully rates were not significant in this data set. Over the year, there were significant decreases of 20% in victim rates and (marginally significant) 17% in bully rates over the last school term.

Following the success of the project in Donegal, some funding was obtained to try out the intervention on a more national basis. Coordinated by the Anti Bullying Centre at Trinity College Dublin, this involved teaching a network of trainers during 2004 (O'Moore & Minton, 2004), and running an in-service professional development day for school staff, prior to implementing the programme. Emphasis was placed on reporting strategies and on the role of parents (see earlier section). Peer support strategies were also encouraged. Training was carried out in 58 schools.

Evaluation involved using the OBVQ in 2004–2005 and again in 2005–2006 after one year of intervention. Unfortunately, only 18 of the 58 schools which had received training returned pre-programme questionnaires, and only 27 of the 53 control schools. The situation was even worse at post-test, when only seven programme schools and 12 control schools returned questionnaires. The results obtained suggested significant decreases in victim rates but not in bully rates, but the poor response rates really prevented reliable conclusions being reached (O'Moore, 2013), and further funding was not forthcoming to continue the programme.

Finland: the KiVa project

A recent and ongoing programme in Finland, 2006–2009, the KiVa antibullying project is both innovative in its methods and producing encouraging and replicable findings (Salmivalli et al., 2010). KiVa is short for *Kiusaamista Vastaan*, which means *against bullying* (but the acronym KiVa also means nice or good in Finnish). The programme was developed around 2006, and a randomised control trial (RCT) evaluation was carried out in the 2007–2008 academic year. Following that, KiVa has been rolled out generally across the country. A national launch in autumn 2009 involved 1,450 schools, and by 2011 this had risen to some 2,500 schools, which is 90% of all comprehensive schools in the country.

KiVa includes universal interventions (for example, via the classroom), including an anti-bullying virtual learning environment, and targeted interventions (individual discussions with victims and bullying children, and using prosocial, high-status peers to be defenders). KiVa is in part based on the participant role approach to bullying (Salmivalli, Lagerspetz et al., 1996; see Chapter 3), and the views that the peer context is an essential part of effective anti-bullying work, and that peer bystanders (or defenders) have a crucial role in how much bullying happens in the school. It thus aims to provide evidence-based strategies to enhance self-efficacy to support victimised peers and positive outcome expectations regarding such behaviours.

The *universal actions* involve student lessons (primary school) and theme days (secondary school), including discussion, video films, and exercises done in dyads or small groups. These cover topics such as group interaction, the dynamics and consequences of bullying, and the actions students can take in order to counter bullying and support victimised peers. There are also a parents' guide and posters.

The virtual learning environment comprises an anti-bullying computer game for primary school students, and an internet forum 'KiVa Street' for secondary school students. These are closely connected to the topics of the student lessons and themes (Poskiparta et al., 2012). Each level of the KiVa computer game includes three modules: I Know, I Can and I Do. In the *I Know* module, students are presented with new facts about bullying and examine what they have learnt during the lessons so far. In the *I Can* module, students practise the skills they have learnt. In a virtual school environment, they face a number of challenging situations in the playground, lunchroom and school corridors, and decide on how to respond to these situations, receiving feedback based on the choices they have made. The third module, *I Do*, encourages students to transfer their knowledge and skills acquired in the virtual environment to real-life interactions with peers: they report which of the KiVa-rules (taught in the lessons) they have put into practice – for instance, whether they have treated others with respect, resisted negative group pressure or supported a victimised peer.

The targeted interventions utilise school-based KiVa teams, consisting of three adults working in the school. Any incident of bullying is referred to this team, who discuss the situation with the children involved and provide support for the victimised student. In addition, the classroom teacher meets with selected high-status classmates of the victimised children, asking them to provide support for these peers; the reasoning here is that high-status peers can have much more influence and impact as defenders than those with a lower status. The programme provides annual online surveys answered by students, and each school gets feedback on their own situation and the changes that have taken place since the implementation of KiVa.

The academic year 2007–2008 provided an opportunity for an RCT evaluation of KiVa, and this was reported on by Kärnä, Voeten, Little, Poskiparta et al. (2011) for grades 4–6 (about ages 11–13 in Finland), and by Kärnä et al. (2012) for grades 1–3 and 7–9 (ages 8–10 and 14–16 years).

Kärnä, Voeten, Little, Poskiparta et al. (2011) reported on data from 78 schools, randomly assigned to intervention (39) or control (39), with about 4,000 pupils from some 200 classrooms in each condition. Bully and victim rates were assessed at three time points over an academic year, using both self-report (global items from the OBVQ) and peer nomination (Salmivalli PRS). In addition, measures were taken of attitudes to bullying, empathy toward victims, self-efficacy for defending, and general well-being at school.

By the end of the year, the control schools showed modest reductions in bully and victim rates from self-report, and not much change on peer report. However, the KiVa intervention schools showed significantly greater reductions on the self-report measures, and also significant reductions on peer reports of being a victim (a reduction for bully reports did not reach significance). Peer reports also showed reductions in bully assistant and reinforcer roles (but not significant for defending role) compared to controls. There were improvements in self-efficacy for defending, and in well-being; trends in anti-bullying attitudes and empathy were not significant by the end of the year.

In percentage terms, at the end of the year the KiVa schools compared to control schools showed a 30% reduction in self-reports of being a victim, and 17% reduction in self-reported bullying of others. Translated into odds ratios, the findings are shown in Table 6.3 (so for example the odds ratio of 1.47 for victim self-report means that a pupil had a 1.47 greater chance of being a victim in a control school than in a KiVa school).

Encouragingly, these reductions were found for all kinds of bullying (Salmivalli et al., 2011). For victims, the odds ratios ranged from 1.94 for physical victimisation down to 1.32 for social exclusion. There was a large effect for cyberbullying, with an odds ratio of 1.80.

Kärnä et al. (2012) reported corresponding analyses for grades 1–3 (38 intervention and 36 control schools), and grades 7–9 (38 intervention and 35 control schools). For grades 1–3, again encouraging and significant findings were found for reductions in victim and bully rates, although for victim rates the reduction was only significant for girls. (Peer nominations were not used for these younger children.) The findings were more mixed for the oldest age group, grades 7–9. There were no significant intervention effects for self-reports of victim or bully in this age group. There was a reduction in peer reports of victims, though only for the younger pupils in this age range, but no significant effect on peer-reported bullying. Peer-reported assisting the bully decreased, for reinforcing there was no effect, and for defending – surprisingly – a negative effect (a relative decrease in KiVa schools).

Overall, Kärnä and colleagues calculated that for the entire age range, the odds ratios were 1.28 for victim and 1.30 for bully – corresponding to about a 20% reduction in prevalence. However, this is clearly considerably larger in the younger age groups but smaller and/or non-significant in older adolescents.

Kärnä, Voeten, Little, Alanen et al. (2011) reported on a further evaluation carried out over the academic year 2009–2010. By now an RCT was impossible as KiVa was being carried out across most Finnish schools, so a cohort-sequential design was used. The sample was very large, with 888 schools and some 150,000 students, across grades 1–9. Only self-reports were used in this study. Generally, the KiVa programme reduced bully and victim rates, and the odds ratios are shown by grade level in Table 6.3. Overall, the odds ratios were 1.21 for victim and 1.18 for bully – highly significant, but somewhat less than in the RCT trials. The authors suggest that this might be because the RCT trial attracted more motivated schools than in the larger national sample.

Programme fidelity has emerged as a key issue in KiVa and is well documented in the evaluations. For example, in the primary schools, teachers delivered on average 8.7 out of 10 lessons in the RCT trial, but this fell to 7.8 during the first year of the national rollout, and to 7.2 in the second year. Schools not only varied greatly in implementation, but in addition this did correlate as expected with victim and bully reductions (Salmivalli & Poskiparta, 2012).

Table 6.3 Odds ratios for reductions in victim and bully rates, for the KiVa programme in Finland

Study	Type	Grade level	Victim	Bully
Kärnä et al., 2012	RCT, KiVa vs. control	1–3	1.63 (self – girls) 1.04 (self – boys)	1.43 (self)
Kärnä, Voeten, Little, Poskiparta et al., 2011	RCT, KiVa vs. control	4–6	1.47 (self) 1.83 (peer)	1.22 (self) 1.29 (peer)
Kärnä et al., 2012	RCT, KiVa vs. control	7–9	1.04 (self)	1.08 (self)
Kärnä, Voeten, Little, Poskiparta et al., 2011	KiVa schools, cohort-sequential		(all self-reports)	(all self-reports)
		1	1.17	1.15
		2	1.23	1.30
		3	1.23	1.28
		4	1.33	1.34
		5	1.30	1.23
		6	1.22	1.19
		7	1.11	1.05
		8	1.15	1.05
		9	1.13	1.07
		All grades	1.21	1.18

KiVa is now being tried out in the Netherlands as KiVa+ with the addition of using social network analysis (see Chapter 3; and Huitsing & Veenstra, 2012) to better identify targeted interventions. RCT trials are also under way in Estonia, Italy and Wales in Europe, and in Delaware in the USA (Salmivalli, personal communication, 23 September 2013).

An overview of large-scale interventions, and meta-analyses

There have been several reviews and meta-analyses of the anti-bullying programme studies, such as those reviewed above. The most thorough have been by Ttofi, Farrington and Baldry (2008) and Ttofi and Farrington (2011): in the latter review, a meta-analysis of 44 school-based intervention programmes internationally found that, on average, these reduced bullying by around 20–23% and victimisation by around 17–20%. This overall conclusion of reductions of around 20% appears to be a robust finding and also encouraging. For example, the OBPP – and the KiVa programme – now have well-replicated successes at or above this level.

As seen in the examples detailed earlier, these programmes have varied in both design and outcomes. So which aspects of the programmes are most important, or useful? Some information on this has come from looking at variations in how schools implement the programmes; and from meta-analyses across programmes.

Variations in implementation

A study carried out with 39 Swedish schools between 2007 and 2010 by Flygare et al. (2011) aimed to compare the success of eight anti-bullying programmes, including the OBPP, the Farsta Method (a variant of the Pikas method), and Second Step. Both quantitative and qualitative assessments were used with teachers and pupils, over a two-year period. A surprising finding was that all the 'intervention' schools actually used components from more than one programme; and even eight schools selected as non-intervention 'controls' were doing so! Thus the focus of their evaluation changed from comparing programmes to comparing programme components.

According to their analyses, the most successful components were training for the majority of staff; having clear procedures for dealing with bullying incidents; having a cooperative anti-bullying team of staff with differing expertise; doing regular follow-up and evaluation of anti-bullying measures; and having pupils participate actively in preventing bullying (not as peer mediators, but 'running activities aimed at creating a good atmosphere').

In addition, some measures were found to work better for girls, some for boys. For girls, monitoring school break times, and for boys, enhancing relationships, having clear rules, and using disciplinary strategies. Finally, some components were identified as having possible negative effects. These included special lessons on bullying (which in this study were found to be often uninteresting and counter-productive), and using pupils as peer mediators (rather than as active participants in anti-bullying activities).

This study in Sweden did not include the KiVa programme in its comparisons. Following the rollout of KiVa in Finland, Saarento and colleagues (2014) have analysed variations at the student, classroom and school level, from their RCT evaluation of 2007–2008 (Kärnä, Voeten, Little, Poskiparta et al., 2011; see earlier). Their findings varied slightly depending on whether self- or peer-report outcome data were used. At the student level, antibullying attitudes and perceptions about defending by peers (for self-report only) predicted reductions in bullying behaviour. At the classroom level, student's collective perception that the classroom teacher was opposed to bullying was a significant predictor for reductions in bullying, whereas perceptions that peers might reinforce bullying had the opposite effect. Interestingly, a measure of affective empathy for the victim was not a significant independent predictor. From this study, then, the effect of general attitudes, and of perceptions of reinforcing and defending in the peer group and of classroom teacher commitment, seem more influential than just feeling sorry for victims.

Meta-analyses across programmes

In their meta-analyses, as well as just looking at success rates, Ttofi and Farrington examined, across programmes, which programme components and design features were most associated with success. For reducing both bully and victim rates, the elements most associated with success were parent training/

meetings, disciplinary methods, and cooperative group work, as well as the greater duration and intensity of the programme both for teachers and children. In addition, bully rates were reduced more in programmes with improved playground supervision, classroom management, teacher training, classroom rules, a whole school policy and school conferences. Victim rates were reduced more in programmes with a greater use of videos. Work with peers was associated negatively with victim rates. Finally, for both bully and victim rates, programmes were more effective for older pupils.

Ttofi and Farrington (2011) drew some policy recommendations from these analyses. For example, they stated that 'New anti-bullying initiatives should … be modified in light of the key programme elements that we have found to be most effective (or ineffective). For example, it seems from our results that work with peers should not be used' (2011: 44). Regarding findings from design features, they argued that 'Programmes should be targeted on children aged 14 years or older rather than on younger children' (2011: 46).

While recognising this attempt to draw conclusions about individual component effectiveness and design features as an important step forward, Smith, Salmivalli and Cowie (2012) criticised some aspects of this report. A weakness of the analytic method used by Ttofi and Farrington (2011) is that their arguments were based on 'across-programme' comparisons. Programme elements and design features were dichotomised, and their presence or absence in different programmes were associated with the amount of decrease (or increase) in rates of bullying, and rates of victimisation (being bullied). This procedure is essentially correlational, and thus suffers from the associated weaknesses of correlational designs. Programmes vary in many aspects, and an association of one element or feature with bully or victim rates may actually be brought about by a variation in some other feature. A stronger design for examining the impact of programme elements and design features would be 'within-programme' comparisons, where most or all other elements or features are held constant.

A surprising result reported from the Ttofi and Farrington (2011) meta-analyses was that programmes worked better with older children. In fact, Smith (2010a) had found that a within-programme comparison of effects on older and younger pupils strongly suggested that greater effects are obtained with younger pupils. This is very evident in the KiVa project (see Table 6.3), and has also been found by Olweus with the OBPP: Olweus and Limber (2010: 393) remarked that 'it may take a longer time to achieve consistently good results in grades 8–10 than in lower grades'.

Within-programme comparisons also do not point to a superiority of disciplinary methods. This was not found in the KiVa project (Salmivalli & Poskiparta, 2012), or by Thompson and Smith (2011; see also Table 6.1), in both cases basing analyses on reports of actual outcomes from incidents.

As regards work with peers, as seen earlier the effectiveness of peer support depends very much on the type of scheme used, how it is supported, and many other factors. Some schemes have not been successful and might even be counterproductive. However, the KiVa project uses a form of peer support successfully, and Menesini et al. (2012) found quite beneficial results in an experimental study. Peer support schemes are developing, schools are learning from past experience, and new methods (such as websites designed by peers, cybermentors) are evolving. The Ttofi and Farrington analysis in 2011 was inevitably reflecting a large number of programmes, many dating back to the 1990s or early 2000s. The wider point here is that, necessarily, conclusions are limited to prior studies using a range of programme elements that are evolving and developing quite rapidly, and thus considerable caution is necessary when drawing policy implications from a body of data that may not well reflect current practice. Restorative approaches (see earlier, and Cremin, 2013) have grown rapidly in recent years, but were not evaluated by Ttofi and Farrington due to small numbers at the time of their analysis.

Ttofi and Farrington (2012) replied to this critique with detailed analyses of the studies relevant to age effects, disciplinary practices, and work with peers. Their analysis of age effects using within-programme comparisons now demonstrated that seven out of eight comparisons showed greater effects in younger pupils: the only study with the opposite finding had just two middle schools and one high school in the sample. Regarding disciplinary methods, they agreed that punitive and non-punitive approaches are not mutually exclusive, and their success can vary depending on student age. They reiterated the possible dangers of peer support systems, but agreed that these may be useful as long as they were carefully implemented, adding that future research should focus on the very careful training of peer supporters.

Summary

Many pupils learn to cope successfully with attempts to bully them. Strategies such as seeking support – including telling teachers provided they will help effectively, being assertive rather than shy, and staying with friends, can be helpful. However, some children cannot cope, or can go through very difficult and painful times before the bullying stops. Schools have a responsibility to provide a safe environment.

Part of this responsibility involves responding to bullying incidents effectively. A theoretical debate about the relative virtues of more disciplinary measures or more counselling-based approaches remains unresolved, but in practice many schools now use some version of initial serious talks and restorative approaches, or what in the US might be called 'authoritative discipline'. Perhaps most important here is that a school follows through on its chosen approach both consistently and on a whole school basis.

Part of this responsibility involves proactive strategies, such as having a clear and comprehensive anti-bullying policy that is acted on. Perceptions of teacher commitment, and a school climate generally opposed to bullying, are important. Sustained curriculum work can help, and is best integrated with other features of anti-bullying work and within the broader curriculum; some 'special' lessons on bullying could be counter-productive (Flygare et al., 2011), although the KiVa use of virtual learning environments appears successful. Quality circles may be good for finding out more about the nature of bullying problems in a school, and for involving pupils constructively.

Peer support schemes are a more optional feature, but many schools choose to use them. There can be pitfalls in peer support schemes, but some forms appear to be effective at least for individual pupils, and are a positive feature of the school ethos. In general, encouraging more pupil participation in anti-bullying activities is a promising avenue, perhaps especially so far as cyberbullying is concerned.

Over the last twenty years many anti-bullying programmes have been implemented, inspired by the initial work in Norway. Both methods and success have been varied, but most programmes have had some success. Two programmes – the OBPP in Norway and KiVa in Finland – have shown repeated and consistent positive outcomes, at least in their home countries. We are beginning to understand something of the components of those programmes that are most effective, although continuing developments in the phenomenon of bullying itself (such as the advent of cyberbullying) and ideas for intervention (such as virtual learning environments and restorative approaches) mean that any implications from such analyses must still be tentative.

SEVEN

Acting to reduce bullying and reflections on the research programme

When I was at school we all knew that bullying went on, but nobody talked about it. It was often, wrongly, seen as an inevitable part of growing up. Thankfully, that culture has now changed. All the schools I visit take bullying seriously, with young people themselves drawing up their anti-bullying policies. Bullies are cowards and all of us have a responsibility to speak up against it. It should not be tolerated. (Ed Balls, former UK Minister of Education, quoted in *Education Guardian*, 16 February 2010, p. 13, reprinted with permission)

Acting to reduce bullying

The comment above by a former Minister of Education in the UK throws up many important points. One is that the culture regarding bullying in schools has changed – not only in the UK, but also in many other countries. A second is that a change in culture brings openness in talking about it, including victims feeling more able to seek help. A third is that schools take the issue seriously. A fourth is that often pupils are involved in actions against bullying. A fifth point, however, is more debatable: that 'bullies are cowards'. This view has a long history, going back to the quotation from the book *Tom Brown's School Days* given in Chapter 2.

Bullying is not necessarily maladaptive for those who bully

Unfortunately, the view that bullies are cowards is at best a half-truth and may be quite misleading. It is true that they are picking on a weaker opponent, but the reason for doing so may lie in the rewards this action might bring, for example in prestige in the peer group, extortion of money or valuables, or reinforcing a vulnerable self-esteem (defensive egotism). The research clearly shows that some children bully others for these reasons, and some (especially in secondary schools) may be quite popular, or at least perceived as popular and powerful, because of this.

The view of bullies as cowards has some similarity to the view of bullies or aggressive children as lacking social skills. This is also a half-truth, and again may be quite misleading. Some bullying children at least seem to be quite adept at manipulating social situations for their own ends – it is just that these ends are hurtful to others.

The broader point here is that antisocial behaviour, of which we disapprove as concerned citizens, may not be maladaptive for the perpetrator (Smith, 2007). Indeed, Volk and colleagues (2012) have argued that adolescent bullying can be thought of as an evolutionary adaptation, or at least as an adaptive pathway of behaviour in some circumstances. They argue that some genetic basis for bully-ing, perhaps via temperament (see Chapter 5), plus its universal prevalence at appreciable rates in all societies examined, points to this, and that bullying can bring benefits in resources (ultimately for growth/survival) and attraction to the opposite sex (ultimately for increased mating opportunities), primarily by means of gaining dominance and social status in peer groups. Although some assertions that they make are very debatable (for example, that bullies have better mental health or greater cognitive empathy), it is clear from much research that children who bully others can use good theory of mind skills and acquire prestige in peer groups through their actions.

Volk et al.'s argument is strengthened when they separate pure bullies from bully/victims. Their adaptive argument is focused on pure bullies – they believe that many bully/victims may indeed be acting in dysfunctional and maladaptive ways.

The negative effects of bullying are well established

Although bullying others can in some circumstances bring benefits to the perpetrators, this does not in any way lessen the moral imperative to act to reduce bullying. Foremost, of course, is the suffering of the victim. Although the causal direction may not be entirely one way, there is now a great deal of evidence that experiences of victimisation, especially if prolonged or involving many forms of bullying, can have severe impacts on self-esteem, trust in others and mental health. It is a fundamental issue of human rights that individuals should not have to suffer this kind of torment in their school years (Greene, 2006; Olweus, 1993).

Beyond the individual effects on the victim, bullying that is not challenged will adversely affect the ethos of a school. The 'hidden curriculum' for witnesses and bystanders will be that abuses of power are tolerated. Furthermore, those who do the bullying, even if they obtain some short-term benefits from doing so, are more likely to be involved in antisocial and criminal behaviour in later life, probably with adverse consequences for them, but certainly with adverse consequences for the society in which they operate.

Some negative effects can be long-lasting

The negative effects of involvement in bullying can extend well beyond the school years. One theme from a number of studies is that of difficulties in later relationships. For example, in a retrospective study, Schäfer et al. (2004) surveyed 884 adults (university students and teachers) from Spain, Germany and the UK. They were asked about experiences of bullying at primary and secondary school, and about their current self-esteem and relationship quality. Former victims at school, and especially those who had been victims at both primary and secondary levels, were low on general self-esteem and high on feelings of loneliness, and reported more difficulties in maintaining friendships than did non-victims at school.

Depression is a well-established correlate and outcome of being a victim at school. But being a victim at school also predicts depression in later life. Farrington and colleagues (2012) carried out a meta-analysis of 75 reports from 49 longitudinal studies giving information on this: the average time interval for assessment of depression was seven years later, after the victim experiences at school. As a comparison, they also looked at the relationship between bullying behaviour at school and later offending. Here they had 48 reports from 29 longitudinal studies, with an average time interval of six years. They calculated unadjusted odds ratios, and also odds ratios when adjusting wherever possible for a range of other factors, including child covariates such as impulsivity, parent and parenting covariates such as parent criminality and parent–child conflict, family covariates such as income, and others such as neighbourhood crime. The findings are shown in Table 7.1. Ttofi, Farrington and Lösel (2012) also looked at how bullying at school predicted aggression and violence later in life (an average of six years later): this was based on around 14 studies. The odds ratios, also shown in Table 7.1, are similar to that for offending.

All the odds ratios in Table 7.1 are statistically significant, except for the adjusted value of 1.14 for victim role and offending. Thus, even after adjusting for many associated factors, it is clear that victims at school especially, but also bullies, are at greater risk of later depression, and bullies are at considerably greater risk for later offending and violent behaviour.

Suicide attempts and completed suicides are the most tragic possible outcomes of victimisation. As mentioned in Chapter 5, Klomek et al. (2009) gathered data in Finland on suicide attempts or completed suicides by the age of 25 years. Associations with frequent bully or victim experiences at 8 years old were very

Table 7.1 Unadjusted odds ratios (adjusted ratios in brackets) for long-term associations between victim or bully role at school, and depression and offending later in life (data from Farrington et al., 2012 and Ttofi et al., 2012)

Role in school/odds ratio	Depression	Offending	Violent behaviour
Victim	2.05 (1.71)	1.40 (1.14)	1.65 (1.42)
Bully	1.61 (1.41)	2.64 (1.89)	2.97 (2.04)

high for boys (odds ratios were 9.1 for bullies and 6.5 for victims). When controlling for depression and conduct measures present at 8 years old, the associations for boys became non-significant statistically (although the odds ratio for victims was still at a quite high level of 3.8). For girls there was no association with bullying others, but there was with frequent victimisation (odds ratio 4.2) that remained significant when adjusted (odds ratio now 6.3).

There can also be long-term effects on educational achievement and earnings. Using data from the National Child Development Study (NCDS) in the UK (of all children born during one week in 1958), Brown and Taylor (2008) related victim involvement at 7 and 11 years old, and bully involvement at 16 years old, to educational attainment and earnings at ages 23, 33 and 42. Both the victims and perpetrators of school bullying had lower educational attainment throughout the lifespan, even after controlling for some school and family characteristics. Victims (but not bullies) also had lower earnings. Ammermueller (2012) confirmed the relationship between being a victim at school and later educational attainment, re-analysing the NCDS data with more factors controlled for. These analyses also confirmed the association of school victimisation with earnings as an adult; however, this was not as a direct effect, but an indirect one through the effect on educational attainment.

Wolke, Copeland, Angold and Costello (2013) analysed data from the Great Smoky Mountains study in North Carolina, USA. This obtained bully and victim measures at 9, 11 and 13 years old, together with a range of outcome measures – health, wealth (financial and educational), risky/illegal behaviours, quality of social relationships – that were assessed between 19 and 26 years old. Analyses controlled for childhood hardships and childhood psychiatric problems. The straightforward longitudinal associations showed that in early adulthood being a victim (only) was related to poorer health, wealth and social relationships. Being a bully (only) was related to greater risky/illegal behaviour and poorer wealth and social relationships. Being a bully/victim was associated with poorer outcomes in all domains. When the childhood risk factors were controlled for, the associations for bullies (only) became non-significant; the experience of bullying others did not add to the risk coming from other factors (such as parental maltreatment, ADHD, etc.). However, the associations for victims (only) and bully/victims remained significant, strongly suggesting the additional negative impact of victim experience in all these domains.

Of course, all these findings should not lead to the pessimistic conclusion that the experience of being a victim at school cannot be overcome. Many people can cope with adversity, especially with support from partners, friends and peers. But the negative and often long-lasting effects documented by research do make even stronger the moral imperative to try to reduce levels of school bullying.

Bullying is decreasing – why?

As discussed in Chapter 4, in most countries over the last two decades, there appears to have been some modest but not insignificant decreases in bully and victim rates. This is encouraging news, but why has it happened?

In actual fact this decrease appears to be part of a much larger pattern of decline, since the 1990s, of many forms of childhood victimization. These include child physical and sexual abuse and maltreatment, crimes against juveniles, and juvenile homicides. Finkelhor (2008) documents these declines and discusses possible explanations. Two of the most plausible ones are what he calls agents of social intervention and changing norms and practices. Agents of social intervention refers to how, over this period, more professionals have been trained and active in child welfare and safety services. Along with this, changing norms and practices refers to how awareness of the harmful effects of childhood victimisation has increased, together with less tolerance of such behaviours.

Finkelhor (2008) does not focus strongly on childhood bullying in discussing decline, but his analysis certainly could apply to it. The last twenty years have seen a great increase in awareness of the harm bullying causes, and also in resources for teachers and programmes to reduce bullying. Norms have changed (as Ed Balls stated in 2010). I witnessed this change of ethos myself in the UK. At the time of the Sheffield project, which started in 1991, many schools denied having a bullying problem, and some teachers did not see it as an important issue. But in the years since then this has totally changed. Most schools now recognise the problem, they do something about it, and indeed in many countries are required to do so. How effectively they do this varies, but the requirement to do something is, by and large, accepted.

What schools can do about bullying

We have seen (in Chapter 6) that schools can take action to reduce bullying. They will never eliminate it, but it can be reduced substantially, and it should be possible to prevent most serious or chronic cases of bullying if reporting systems are good and action is taken promptly and effectively. A range of resources is now available for teachers and educators. Over the next few years, we should learn more about the extent to which the two most well-replicated programmes, OBPP and KiVa, can be translated outside their home countries of Norway and Finland. Key issues remain to be studied further, however.

There is still much to be learnt about the effectiveness of specific intervention components. We need more information on the relative effectiveness of more sanctions-based or disciplinary approaches, compared to more non-punitive approaches. Can authoritative discipline (Gregory et al., 2010) bypass this issue? Can restorative approaches fulfil the promise that some hold out for it, and which many schools claim to be adopting? Volk et al. (2012) suggest that (if we accept the argument that there are some immediate benefits to children who bully) effective strategies need to also find alternative pathways for bullying children to receive rewards for changing their behaviour, perhaps through sporting activities or popular prosocial activities which give them prestige in the peer group.

Another controversial issue is peer support. Whatever the other benefits, its effects on bullying have been mixed at best. Should it be discouraged, as Ttofi and Farrington (2011) appear to suggest? Or is it rather a matter of improving the schemes used and using new and innovative methods, as in virtual learning environments and cybermentors?

Another issue is whether we should pursue mainly 'bullying-focused' solutions or work in more general ways. Finkelhor (2008: 178) has proposed that there should be 'a comprehensive, integrated, and developmental curriculum to prevent child victimization at every age'. This would embrace a broader concept of victimisation than just bullying – therefore other forms of aggression, abuse and maltreatment, and not just in the school. However, the curriculum he suggests, covering skills such as self-assertion, empathy, negotiation and seeking help, does not seem dissimilar to what is already available in a range of personal and social educational curricula. Others have argued that we should focus more generally on relationships and school climate and improve *convivencia* – the Spanish word that is the opposite of bullying and implies respect and co-existence (Ortega et al., 2003).

Cyberbullying has provided new challenges, as being a relatively new form of bullying with its own characteristics (Mora-Merchán & Jäger, 2010). There is a considerable overlap in involvement in traditional forms of bullying and cyberbullying, and many standard procedures will help, but cyberbullying also calls for other specific forms of intervention, including education on rights and responsibilities online (Bauman, 2011).

Not just schools – individuals, families, the wider community

Schools can take positive steps to reduce bullying, but it is not just a problem for schools. Individuals have some responsibility, including young people themselves, especially as they get older and are more aware of the consequences and implications of their actions. Families – namely parents, but also siblings and other family members – can act as supporters and help protect against bullying involvement, or they can themselves be risk factors if they are using abusive behaviours in their own relationships. The wider community has an impact too, including through levels of community violence and attitudes to bullying. Abusive behaviours are often portrayed in the media, including computer games and the internet, sometimes in ways that make these seem attractive and successful. Politicians especially have a role to play, in their public pronouncements and in the extent to which they support research and encourage and support schools in anti-bullying work. The perceived legitimacy and effectiveness of school actions against bullying may well be affected by these wider issues. All citizens bear some shared responsibility in a democratic country.

Is reducing bullying cost-effective?

Anti-bullying programmes in school cost money – they need materials and resources, and use up teacher time. So are they worth it? One attempt to address this question directly was made by Persson and Svensson (2013). They took two

Swedish anti-bullying programmes, one called Friends and the other the OBPP, as exemplars, for which the cost of implementation in a school of 300 pupils has been estimated at between around 98,000 to 417,000 Swedish kronor (about 11,000 to 46,000 euros) per year. Is this worthwhile? They surveyed a random sample of households in the district of Örebro, Sweden, and asked them to imagine a school of 4,800 pupils where 10% were being bullied (that is, 480 pupils). They asked them if, as taxpayers, they would be willing to pay amounts between 200 to 5,000 kronor to reduce the number of bullied pupils by 100, 240 or 380: 'yes' votes were very high for 200 kronor (about 22 euros), even for the lower reductions in victims.

From the overall figures, Persson and Svensson calculated a 'willingness to pay' (WTP) metric, which even on a conservative estimate translated into a figure of around 585,000 kronor for the district – more than the cost of a programme. Assuming an actual reduction in victims of 20% (as in Ttofi & Farrington, 2011), they calculated a benefit–cost ratio of 8.4 in investing in an anti-bullying programme. They also compared the costs favourably with the actual costs of court settlements brought by individuals against schools or education authorities for being bullied in school, and for actual compensation costs for injuries. Overall, this first study points to the cost-effectiveness of anti-bullying programmes, although calculations based on estimated costs of the damage done to victims in terms of (for example) mental health, education and earnings could be another and perhaps more convincing approach.

Reflections on the research programme

If we date the substantial onset of bullying as a research programme from 1989 (see Chapter 2), then what is the state of this programme after some 25 years? An indisputable fact is that the volume of research has grown enormously. Olweus (2013, see his Figure 3) analysed citations from the PsycINFO data base, showing that citations for bully, bullying or bullied rose from around 5 (1990) to 104 (2000) to 566 (2010) on a steadily rising curve.

As a result of this, we now know very much more about the types of bullying, roles in bullying, how it develops through childhood and adolescence, the risk and protective factors for involvement, and ways of intervening to reduce it, especially in schools. The methods for analysing quantitative data have become increasingly sophisticated, and the large number of studies has recently facilitated many meta-analyses which give us a firmer basis for conclusions than do individual studies. One area perhaps under-developed is the use of mixed methods research. The number of qualitative or mixed methods studies is relatively small, but they do have great potential. Quantitative studies can throw up quite complicated interactions or associations, and qualitative data can help us understand better the meanings of these and the processes involved, from the viewpoints of participants. For example, why did a particular intervention fail to reduce bullying, maybe for one sex or one age group particularly? Quantitative studies generally come up with some suggestions to explain such results, but interviews or focus groups with young people who participated in the interventions could also throw a lot of light on these kinds of findings.

Greater use of young people as researchers might also be considered. Traditionally, children/young people give their opinions via questionnaires, interviews, focus groups – but they could be involved further, helping to gather data in a project, being involved in the planning and implementation of a project, or even designing a project. Such approaches may be especially useful for cyberbullying where young people are the 'digital natives' (Spears & Kofoed, 2013).

But how about the core of the research programme? Do we really need 'bullying' as a separate category? A challenge to this comes from Finkelhor and colleagues (2012) in an article entitled *'Let's prevent peer victimization, not just bullying'*. They argue that the focus on bullying can lead to the neglect of serious one-off aggressive acts, and an undue focus on the school as a context. They do not propose abandoning the bullying concept, but they do propose that it should be part of a broader domain of 'peer victimisation and aggression'. To some extent this is an argument about focus of effort, and reflects concerns mentioned earlier about the breadth and scope of anti-bullying work in schools.

Finkelhor et al. (2012) also argue that there are difficulties in definition and construing the imbalance of power in bullying. Such issues were discussed in Chapter 2. On the whole, it can be argued that bullying has emerged as a useful and viable construct over the period of the research programme. Although there may not be words for it in some other languages, the concept appears to be grasped readily, and the word has been adopted into other languages such as Italian and Spanish.

A more specific challenge of this type has come from Bauman, Underwood and Card (2013), who argue that bullying is particularly difficult to define in the cyber domain. They propose that cyber-aggression more broadly would be a better focus of research. Smith et al. (2013) defended the concept of cyberbullying, while acknowledging that cyber-aggression should also be studied more generally. Researchers should be clear on what they are assessing, and studies on aggression should not just be labelled as studies on bullying because of the bandwagon effect of the bullying research programme.

In Table 2.1 I suggested some aspects of the study of bullying as a research programme. Looking at the examples I gave there of auxiliary hypotheses, the progress is encouraging: these hypotheses have been tested out and found useful. I think also that there are signs that it has been a progressive research programme. For example, delineation of participant roles has led to new and consistent findings related to attitudes, behaviour and adjustment. Also, our increasing knowledge about roles in bullying and risk and protective factors is beginning to help us in designing more effective interventions (as, for example, the KiVa project building on knowledge of peer-group influences).

One sign of a degenerating research programme could be continuing unresolved arguments about definition. Definitions are always going to be a bit 'fuzzy' around the boundaries, but my view is that the bullying concept is robust and defensible. This is quite compatible with a view that other kinds of victimisation, and aggression, must be taken seriously as well.

Another sign of a degenerating research programme would be if we fail to design more effective interventions. Success rates at present are encouraging, but generally for even the most successful programmes they are below 50%. We should be able to make increasing use of the burgeoning knowledge base to improve interventions further.

To end on a personal note, I have been involved in this research programme myself since 1989, and have seen how it has developed and changed. It has been an exciting and satisfying period. Exciting because of the interest it has generated, in the wider public and in the media, both at national and also international levels; satisfying because of working with many supportive and stimulating colleagues, but beyond that because there have been tangible effects on practice. I think it is reasonable to say that many schools are safer places, and many children and young people are happier, because of what has been done over this period. But that success is partial, and the programme has many challenges for the next generation of researchers to grapple with.

APPENDIX A

Record sheet for incidents of bullying

School name:..

[This sheet should be filled in for any incident of bullying that was reported and dealt with. An 'incident' refers to what may have been a series of events, but where there is a definite outcome in terms of trying to get the bullying to stop.

There is no need to identify any individual by name, pseudonyms can be used, e.g. 'boy X in year 7 was attacked by two older boys, Y and Z, from year 8'.]

A: What happened?

Date of incident (month/year): ....

Who was directly involved? [Indicate age and gender]
[As perpetrator]

☐ One boy ☐ One girl ☐ Several boys ☐ Several girls ☐ Both boys and girls

Year group? ....

[As victim]
☐ One boy ☐ One girl ☐ Other: [specify] ....

Year group? ....

Were there any bystanders? If so, about how many (if known)?
☐ No ☐ Yes – if so about how many? ....

What happened? What kind of bullying?
☐ Physical Verbal ☐ Relational ☐ Cyber
☐ Other (specify)............

What was the sequence of events in the bullying – brief details?

....
....
....

How often had this happened?
☐ Once ☐ 2–3 times ☐ 4–5 times ☐ Many times

Over how long a period?
☐ A few days ☐ A week ☐ A month ☐ Several months

How serious was this incident judged to be?
☐ Not very serious ☐ Average ☐ More serious than usual ☐ Very serious

How was the bullying found out about? [Who first told about it?]
☐ Victim ☐ Peer supporter ☐ Other pupil ☐ Parent ☐ Observed by staff
☐ Other (specify)...

B: What was done about it?

What was initially done about the bullying in this case?

☐ Serious Talk with bully or bullies
☐ Restorative Approaches
☐ Pikas Method
☐ Support Group Method
☐ Bully Court
☐ Negative Sanctions – if so what kind?...

Did this work? ☐ Yes ☐ Partially ☐ No

What was the outcome?

....
....
....
....

Was any follow-up work with the bullying student(s) carried out?
☐ No ☐ Yes – how?

....
....
....
....

What was the outcome of that?

....
....
....
....

Was the victim supported in any way?
☐ No ☐ Yes – how?

....
....
....
....

What was the outcome of that?

....
....
....
....

Any other comments on this incident and how it was dealt with?

....
....
....
....

References

Ahmad, Y. & Smith, P.K. (1990). Behavioural measures: bullying in schools, *Newsletter of the Association for Child Psychology & Psychiatry*, 12: 26–27.

Ahmad, Y., Whitney, I. & Smith, P.K. (1991). A survey service for schools on bully/victim problems. In P.K. Smith & D.A. Thompson (eds), *Practical Approaches to Bullying*. London: David Fulton, pp. 103–111.

Ahmed, E. (2001). Shame management: regulating bullying. In E. Ahmed, N. Harris, J. Braithwaite & V. Braithwaite (eds), *Shame Management through Reintegration*. Cambridge: Cambridge University Press, pp. 211–314.

Ahmed, E. & Braithwaite, V. (2004a). Bullying and victimization: cause for concern for both families and schools, *Social Psychology of Education*, 7: 35–54.

Ahmed, E. & Braithwaite, V. (2004b). 'What, me ashamed?': shame management and school bullying, *Journal of Research in Crime and Delinquency*, 41: 245–269.

Alderson, P. & Morrow, V. (2004). *Ethics, Social Research and Consulting with Children and Young People*. Available at www.barnados.org.uk

Alsaker, F.D. & Valkanover, S. (2012). The Bernese program against victimization in kindergarten and elementary school, *New Directions for Youth Development*, 133: 15–28.

Ammermueller, A. (2012). Violence in European schools: a widespread phenomenon that matters for educational production, *Labour Economics*, 19: 908–922.

Anderson, C.A., Shibuya, A., Ihori, N., Swing, E.L., Bushman, B.J., Sakamoto, A., Rothstein, H.R. & Saleem, M. (2010). Violent video game effects on aggression, empathy, and prosocial behavior in Eastern and Western countries: a meta-analytic review, *Psychological Bulletin*, 136: 151–173.

Andreou, E. (2004). Bully/victim problems and their association with Machiavellianism and self-efficacy in Greek primary school children, *British Journal of Educational Psychology*, 74: 297–309.

Andreou, E. & Bonoti, F. (2009). Children's bullying experiences expressed through drawings and self-reports, *School Psychology International*, 31: 164–177.

Ang, R.P. & Goh, D.H. (2010). Cyberbullying among adolescents: the role of affective and cognitive empathy, and gender, *Child Psychiatry and Human Development*, 41: 387–397.

Anti-Bullying Alliance (ABA) (2011). 'Tackling bullying in schools: a governors guide'. Available at www.anti-bullyingalliance.org.uk

Aoyama, I., Utsumi, S. & Hasegawa, M. (2012). Cyberbullying in Japan. In Q. Li, D. Cross & P.K. Smith (eds), *Cyberbullying in the Global Playground: Research from International Perspectives*. Chichester, England: Wiley-Blackwell, pp. 183–201.

Arora, C.M.J. & Thompson, D.A. (1987). Defining bullying for a secondary school, *Education and Child Psychology*, 14: 110–120.

Arora, T. (1994). Measuring bullying with the 'Life in School' checklist, *Pastoral Care in Education*, 12: 11–15.

Arseneault, L., Milne, B.J., Taylor, A., Adams, F., Delgado, K., Caspi, A. & Moffitt, T.E. (2008). Being bullied as an environmentally mediated contributing factor to children's internalizing problems: a study of twins discordant for victimization, *Archives of Pediatrics and Adolescent Medicine*, 162: 145–150.

Arslan, S., Savaser, S., Hallett, V. & Balci, S. (2012). Cyberbullying among primary school students in Turkey: self-reported prevalence and associations with home and school life, *Cyberpsychology, Behavior, and Social Networking*, 15: 525–533.

Atria, M., Strohmeier, D. & Spiel. C. (2007). The relevance of the school class as social unit for the prevalence of bullying and victimization, *European Journal of Developmental Psychology*, 4: 372–387.

Ball, H.A., Arsenault, L., Taylor, A., Maughan, B., Caspi, A. & Moffitt, T.E. (2008). Genetic and environmental influences on victims, bullies and bully-victims in childhood, *Journal of Child Psychology and Psychiatry*, 49: 104–112.

Bandura, A. (2002). Selective moral disengagement in the exercise of moral agency, *Journal of Moral Education*, 312: 101–119.

Banerjee, R., Robinson, C. & Smalley, D. (2010). *Evaluation of the Beatbullying Peer Mentoring Programme: Report for Beatbullying*. Sussex: University of Sussex.

Barker, E.D., Arsenault, L., Brendgen, M., Fontaine, N. & Maughan, B. (2008). Joint development of bullying and victimization in adolescence: relations to delinquency and self-harm, *Journal of the American Academy of Child and Adolescent Psychiatry*, 47: 1030–1038.

Barter, C. (2011). Peer violence in residential children's homes: a unique experience. In C. Monks & I. Coyne (eds), *Bullying in Different Contexts*. Cambridge: Cambridge University Press, pp. 61–86.

Bauer, N.S., Lozano, P. & Rivara, F.P. (2007). The effectiveness of the Olweus bullying prevention program in public middle schools: a controlled trial, *Journal of Adolescent Health*, 40: 266–274.

Bauman, S. (2011). *Cyberbullying: What Counselors Need To Know*. Alexandria, VA: American Counseling Association.

Bauman, S. (2012). Cyberbullying in the United States. In Q. Li, D. Cross & P.K. Smith (eds), *Cyberbullying in the Global Playground: Research from International Perspectives*. Chichester, England: Wiley-Blackwell, pp. 143–179.

Bauman, S., Toomey, R.B. & Walker, J. (2013). Associations among bullying, cyberbullying, and suicide in high school students, *Journal of Adolescence*, 36: 341–350.

Bauman, S., Underwood, M.K. & Card, N. (2013). Definitions: another perspective and a proposal for beginning with cyberaggression. In S. Bauman, J. Walker & D. Cross (eds), *Principles of Cyberbullying Research: Definition, Methods, and Measures*. New York & London: Routledge, pp. 87–93.

Bauman, S., Walker, J. & Cross, D. (2013). *Principles of Cyberbullying Research: Definition, Methods, and Measures*. New York & London: Routledge.

Beckman, L., Hagquist, C. & Hellstrom, L. (2012). Does the association with psychosomatic health problems differ between cyberbullying and traditional bullying?, *Emotional and Behavioural Difficulties*, 17: 421–434.

Belsey, B. (2004). Retrieved from www.cyberbullying.ca, 15 July 2004.

Benton, T. (2011). 'Sticks and stones may break my bones, but being left on my own is worse': An analysis of reported bullying at school within NFER attitude survey. Slough: NFER. Available at www.nfer.ac.uk

Berne, S., Frisén, A., Schultze-Krumbholz, A., Scheithauer, H., Naruskov, K., Luik, P., Katzer, C., Erentaite, R., & Zukauskiene, R. (2013). Cyberbullying assessment instruments: a systematic review, *Aggression and Violent Behavior*, 18: 320–334.

Besag, V. (1989). *Bullies and Victims in Schools*. Milton Keynes: Open University Press.

Besag, V. (2006). *Understanding Girls' Friendships, Fights and Feuds*. Maidenhead: Open University Press.

Bibou-Nakou, I., Tsiantis, J., Assimopoulos, H. & Chatzilambou, P. (2012). Bullying/victimization from a family perspective: a qualitative study of secondary school students' views, *European Journal of Psychology of Education*, 28: 53–71.

Bijttebier, P. & Vertommen, H. (1998). Coping with peer arguments in school-age children with bully/victim problems, *British Journal of Educational Psychology*, 68: 387–394.

Birkett, M., Espelage, D.L. & Koenig, B. (2009). LGB and questioning students in schools: the moderating effects of homophobic bullying and school climate on negative outcomes, *Journal of Youth and Adolescence*, 38: 989–1000.

Björkqvist, K., Lagerspetz, K. M. J. & Kaukainen, A. (1992). Do girls manipulate and boys fight? Developmental trends in regard to direct and indirect aggression, *Aggressive Behavior*, 18: 117–127.

Black, S.A. & Jackson, E. (2007). Using bullying incident density to evaluate the Olweus Bullying Prevention Programme, *School Psychology International*, 28: 623–638.

Boivin, M., Brendgen, M., Vitaro, F., Dionne, G., Girard, A., Perusse, D. & Tremblay, R. (2012). Strong genetic contribution to peer relationship difficulties at school entry: findings from a longitudinal twin study: *Child Development*, 84: 1098–1114.

Bosacki, S.L., Marini, Z.A. & Dane, A.V. (2006). Voices from the classroom: pictorial and narrative representations of children's bullying experiences, *Journal of Moral Education*, 35: 231–245.

Boulton, M.J. (1992). Rough physical play in adolescence: does it serve a dominance function?, *Early Education and Development*, 3: 312–333.

Boulton, M.J. (1994). Understanding and preventing bullying in the junior school playground. In P.K. Smith & S. Sharp (eds), *School Bullying: Insights and Perspectives*. London. Routledge, pp. 132–159.

Boulton M.J. (1999). Concurrent and longitudinal relations between children's playground behavior and social preference, victimization, and bullying, *Child Development*, 70: 944–954.

Boulton M.J. (2013). The effects of victim of bullying reputation on adolescents' choice of friends: mediation by fear of becoming a victim of bullying, moderation by victim status, and implications for befriending interventions, *Journal of Experimental Child Psychology*, 114: 146–160.

Boulton M.J. & Flemington I. (1996). The effects of a short video intervention on secondary school pupils' involvement in definitions of and attitudes towards bullying, *School Psychology International*, 17: 331–345.

Boulton, M.J. & Smith, P.K. (1992). Ethnic preferences and perceptions among Asian and White British middle school children, *Social Development*, 1: 55–66.

Boulton, M.J. & Smith, P.K. (1994). Bully/victim problems among middle school children: stability, self-perceived competence, and peer acceptance, *British Journal of Developmental Psychology*, 12: 315–329.

Boulton, M.J., Smith, P.K. & Cowie, H. (2010). Short-term longitudinal relationships between children's peer victimization/bullying experiences and self-perceptions: evidence for reciprocity, *School Psychology International*, 31: 296–311.

Bouman, T., van der Meulen, M., Goossens, F.A., Olthof, T., Vermande, M.M. & Aleva, E.A. (2012). Peer and self-reports of victimization and bullying: their differential association with internalizing problems and social adjustment, *Journal of School Psychology*, 50: 759–774.

Bovaird, J.A. (2010). Scales and surveys: some problems with measuring bullying behavior. In S.R. Jimerson, S.M. Swearer & D.L. Espelage (eds), *Handbook of Bullying in Schools: An International Perspective*. New York & London: Routledge, pp. 277–292.

Bowen, R. & Holcom, D. (2010). *A Survey into the Prevalence and Incidence of School Bullying in Wales*. Cardiff: Welsh Assembly Government. Available at http://dera.ioe.ac.uk/563/

Bowers, L., Smith, P.K. & Binney, V. (1992). Family relationships as perceived by children involved in bully/victim problems at school, *Journal of Family Therapy*, 14: 371–387.

Bowes, L., Arsenault, L., Maughan, B., Taylor, A., Caspi, A. & Moffitt, T.E. (2009). School, neighborhood, and family factors are associated with children's bullying involvement: a nationally representative longitudinal study, *Journal of the American Academy of Child and Adolescent Psychiatry*, 48: 545–553.

Bowes, L., Maughan, B., Caspi, A., Moffitt, T.E. & Arseneault, L. (2010). Families promote emotional and behavioural resilience to bullying: evidence of an environmental effect, *Journal of Child Psychology and Psychiatry*, 51: 809–817.

Brendgen, M., Boivin, M., Dionne, G., Barker, E.D., Vitaro, F., Girard, A., Tremblay, R. & Perusse, D. (2011). Gene–environment processes linking aggression, peer victimisation and the teacher–child relationship, *Child Development*, 82: 2021–2036.

Brendgen, M., Boivin, M., Vitaro, F., Girard, A., Dionne, G., & Perusse, D. (2008). Gene–environment interaction between peer victimisation and child aggression, *Development & Psychopathology*, 20: 455–471.

Brewin, C.R., Andrews, B. & Gotlib, I.H. (1993). Psychopathology and early experience: a reappraisal of retrospective reports, *Psychological Bulletin*, 113: 82–89.

Brier, J. & Ahmad, Y. (1991). Developing a school court as a means of addressing bullying in schools. In P.K. Smith & D.A. Thompson (eds), *Practical Approaches to Bullying*. London: David Fulton, pp. 25–36.

Brown, S. & Taylor, K. (2008). Bullying, education and earnings: evidence from the National Child Development Study, *Economics of Education Review*, 27: 387–401.

Burk, F.L. (1897). Teasing and bullying, *Pedagogical Seminary*, 4: 336–371.

Butchart, A. & Kahane, T. (2006). *Preventing Child Maltreatment: A Guide to Taking Action and Generating Evidence*. Geneva: World Health Organisation.

Calvete, E., Orue, I., Estévez, A., Villardón, L. & Padilla, P. (2010). Cyberbullying in adolescents: modalities and aggressors' profile, *Computers in Human Behavior*, 26: 1128–1135.

Campbell, M., Spears, B., Slee, P., Butler, D. & Kift, S. (2012). Victims' perceptions of traditional and cyberbullying, and the psychosocial correlates of their victimisation, *Emotional and Behavioural Difficulties*, 17: 389–401.

Caravita, S., DiBlasio, P. & Salmivalli, C. (2009). Unique and interactive effects of empathy and social status on involvement in bullying, *Social Development*, 18: 140–163.

Carlyle, K.E. & Steinman, K.J. (2007). Demographic differences in the prevalence, co-occurrence, and correlates of adolescent bullying at school, *Journal of School Health*, 77: 623–629.

Carragher, D.J. & Rivers, I. (2002). Trying to hide: a cross-national study of growing up for non-identified gay and bisexual male youth, *Clinical Child Psychology and Psychiatry*, 7: 457–474.

Cassidy, W., Jackson, M. & Brown, K.N. (2009). Sticks and stones can break my bones, but how can pixels hurt me?, *School Psychology International*, 30: 383–402.

Chan, J.H.F., Myron, R. & Crawshaw, M. (2005). The efficacy of non-anonymous measures of bullying, *School Psychology International*, 26: 443–458.

Chaux, E., Molano, A. & Podlesky, P. (2009). Socio-economic, socio-political and socio-emotional variables explaining school bullying: a country-wide multilevel analysis, *Aggressive Behavior*, 35: 520–529.

ChildLine (2006). *Casenotes: Calls to ChildLine about Sexual Orientation, Homophobia and Homophobic Bullying*. Available at: www.nspcc.org.uk/inform/publications/downloads/WD_CasenotesSexualOrientation_gf37413.pdf

Christensen, L.L., Fraynt, R.J., Neece, C.L. & Baker, B.L. (2012). Bullying adolescents with intellectual disability, *Journal of Mental Health Research in Intellectual Disabilities*, 5: 49–65.

Cole, J.C.M., Cornell, D.G. & Sheras, P. (2006). Identification of school bullies by survey methods. *Professional School Counseling*, 9: 305–313.

Collishaw, S., Pickles, A., Messer, J., Rutter, M., Shearer, C. & Maughan, B. (2007). Resilience to adult psychopathology following childhood maltreatment: evidence from a community sample, *Child Abuse & Neglect*, 31: 211–229.

Cook, C.R., Williams, K.R., Guerra, N.G. & Kim, T.E. (2010). Variability in the prevalence of bullying and victimization: a cross-national and methodological analysis. In S.R. Jimerson, S.M. Swearer & D.L. Espelage (eds), *Handbook of Bullying in Schools: An International Perspective.* New York & London: Routledge, pp. 347–362.

Cook, C.R., Williams, K.R., Guerra, N.G., Kim, T.E. & Sadek, S. (2010). Predictors of bullying and victimization in childhood and adolescence: a meta-analytic investigation, *School Psychology Quarterly*, 25: 65–83.

Cornell, D.G. & Brockenbrough, K. (2004). Identification of bullies and victims: a comparison of methods, *Journal of School Violence*, 3: 63–87.

Cowie, H., & Olafsson, R. (2001). The role of peer support in helping the victims of bullying in a school with high levels of aggression, *School Psychology International*, 21: 79–95.

Cowie, H. & Sharp, S. (1994). Tackling bullying through the curriculum. In P.K. Smith & S. Sharp (eds), *School Bullying: Insights and Perspectives.* London: Routledge, pp. 84–107.

Cowie, H. & Smith, P.K. (2010). Peer support as a means of improving school safety and reducing bullying and violence. In B. Doll, W. Pfohl & J. Yoon (eds), *Handbook of Youth Prevention Science.* New York: Routledge. pp. 177–193.

Cowie, H., Smith, P.K., Boulton, M.J. & Laver, R. (1994). *Co-operative Group Work in the Multi-ethnic Classroom.* London: David Fulton.

Cowie, H. & Wallace, P. (2000). *Peer Support in Action – From Bystanding to Standing By.* London: SAGE.

Coyne, I. (2011). Bullying in the workplace. In C. Monks & I. Coyne (eds), *Bullying in Different Contexts.* Cambridge: Cambridge University Press, pp. 157–184.

Coyne, I., Chesney, T., Logan, B. & Madden, N. (2009). Griefing in a virtual community: an exploratory study of second life residents, *Zeitschrift für Psychologie/Journal of Psychology*, 217: 214–221.

Craig, W., Harel-Fisch, Y., Fogel-Grinvald, H., Dostaler, S., Hetland, J., Simons-Morton, B., Molcho, B., Gaspar de Mato, M., Overpeck, M., Due, P., Pickett, W., HBSC Violence & Injuries Prevention Focus Group, and HBSC Bullying Writing Group (2009). A cross-national profile of bullying and victimization among adolescents in 40 countries, *International Journal of Public Health*, 54 (Suppl 2): 216–224.

Cremin, H. (2013). Critical perspectives on Restorative Justice/Restorative Approaches to educational settings. In E. Sellman, H. Cremin & G. McCluskey (eds), *Restorative Approaches to Conflict in Schools: Interdisciplinary Perspectives on Whole School Approaches to Managing Relationships.* London: Routledge.

Crick, N.R. & Dodge, K.A. (1999). 'Superiority' is in the eye of the beholder: a comment on Sutton, Smith and Swettenham, *Social Development*, 8: 128–131.

Crick, N. R., & Grotpeter, J.K. (1995). Relational aggression, gender, and social-psychological adjustment, *Child Development*, 66: 710–722.

Cross, J.E. & Newman-Gonchar, R. (2004). Data quality in student risk behavior surveys and administrator training, *Journal of School Violence*, 3: 89–108.

Cullerton-Sen, C. & Crick, N.R. (2005). Understanding the effects of physical and relational victimization: the utility of multiple perspectives in predicting social-emotional adjustment, *School Psychology Review*, 34: 147–160.

Currie, C. et al. (eds) (2012). *Social Determinants of Health and Well-being among Young People: Health Behaviour in School-aged Children (HBSC) Study: International report from the 2009/2010 survey.* Copenhagen: WHO Regional Office for Europe.

Debarbieux, E., Blaya, C. & Vidal, D. (2003). Tackling violence in schools: a report from France. In P.K. Smith (ed.), *Violence in Schools: The Response in Europe.* London & New York: RoutledgeFalmer. pp. 17–32.

Del Barrio, C., Martín, E., Montero, I., Gutiérrez, H., Barrios, A. & de Dios, M.J. (2008). Bullying and social exclusion in Spanish secondary schools: national trends from 1999 to 2006, *International Journal of Clinical and Health Psychology*, 8: 657–677.

Department for Education (DfE) (1994). *Bullying: Don't Suffer in Silence: An Anti-bullying Pack for Schools*. London: HMSO. (2nd edition, 2000.)

Department for Education (DfE) (2013). *Preventing and Tackling Bullying: Advice for Head Teachers, Staff and Governing Bodies*. Available at www.education.gov.uk/publications

Dixon, R. (2011). *Rethinking School Bullying: Towards an Integrated Model*. Cambridge: Cambridge University Press.

Dixon, R., Smith, P.K. & Jenks, C. (2004). Bullying and difference: a case study of peer group dynamics in one school, *Journal of School Violence*, 3: 41–58.

Dooley, J.J., Cross, D., Hearn, L. & Treyvaud, R. (2009). *Review of Existing Australian and International Cyber-safety Research*. Perth, Australia: Child Health Promotion Research Centre, Edith Cowan University.

Dooley, J.J., Pyżalski, J. & Cross, D. (2009). Cyberbullying versus face-to-face bullying: a theoretical and conceptual review, *Zeitschrift für Psychologie/Journal of Psychology*, 217: 182–188.

Due, P., Merlo, J., Harel-Fisch, Y. et al. (2009). Socioeconomic inequality in exposure to bullying during adolescence: a comparative, cross-sectional, multilevel study in 35 countries, *American Journal of Public Health*, 99: 907–914.

Duncan, N. (1999). *Sexual Bullying: Gender Conflict and Pupil Culture in Secondary Schools*. London: Routledge.

Duncan, N. (2002). Girls, bullying and school transfer. In T.V. Sunnari, J. Kangasvuo & M. Heikkinen (eds), *Gendered and Sexualised Violence in Educational Environments*. Oulu: University of Oulo Press, pp. 110–126.

Duncan, R.D. (1999). Peer and sibling aggression: an investigation of intra- and extra-familial bullying, *Journal of Interpersonal Violence*, 14: 871–886.

Durlak, J.A., Weissberg, R.P., Dymnicki, A.B., Taylor, R.D., & Schellinger, K.B. (2011). The impact of enhancing students' social and emotional learning: a meta-analysis of school-based universal interventions, *Child Development*, 82: 405–432.

Egan, S.K. & Perry, D.G. (1998). Does low self-regard invite victimization?, *Developmental Psychology*, 34: 299–309.

Eisner, M. & Malti, T. (2012). The future of research on evidence-based developmental violence prevention in Europe – Introduction to the Focus Section, *International Journal of Conflict and Violence*, 6: 166–175.

Elgar, F. J., Craig, W., Boyce, W., Morgan, A. & Vella-Zarb, R. (2009). Income inequality and school bullying: multilevel study of adolescents in 37 countries, *Journal of Adolescent Health*, 45: 351–359.

Ellis, V. & High, S. (2004). Something more to tell you: gay, lesbian or bisexual young people's experiences of secondary schooling, *British Educational Research Journal*, 30: 213–225.

Encarta World English Dictionary (1999). London: Bloomsbury Publishing.

Endresen, I.M. & Olweus, D. (2001). Self-reported empathy in Norwegian adolescents: sex differences, age trends, and relationship to bullying. In A.C. Bohart, C. Arthur & D.J. Stipek (eds), *Constructive and Destructive Behavior: Implications for Family, School and Society*. Washington, DC: American Psychological Association, pp. 147–165.

Engström, K., Hallqvist, J., Möller, J. & Laflamme, L. (2005). Do episodes of peer victimization trigger physical injury? A case-crossover study of Swedish school children, *Scandinavian Journal of Public Health*, 33: 19–25.

Epstein, D., Dowler, A., Mellor, D. J. & Madden, L. (2006). *Evaluation of Anti-bullying Policies in Schools in Wales: Final Report*. Cardiff: Welsh Assembly Government.

Eslea, M., Menesini, E., Morita, Y., O'Moore, M., Mora-Merchan, J.A., Pereira, B., Smith, P.K. & Wenxin, Z. (2003). Friendship and loneliness among bullies and victims: data from seven countries, *Aggressive Behavior*, 30: 71–83.

Eslea, M. & Mukhtar, K. (2000). Bullying and racism among Asian children in Britain, *Educational Research*, 42: 207–217.

Espelage, D.L., Low, S., Polanin, J.R. & Brown, E.C. (2013). The impact of a middle school program to reduce aggression, victimization, and sexual violence, *Journal of Adolescent Health*, 30: 1–7.

Espelage, D.L. & Swearer, S.M. (eds) (2004). *Bullying in American schools: A Socio-ecological Perspective on Prevention and Intervention*. Mahwah, NJ: Erlbaum.

Fanti, K.A., Demetriou, A.G. & Hawa, V.V. (2012). A longitudinal study of cyberbullying: examining risk and protective factors, *European Journal of Developmental Psychology*, 9: 168–181.

Faris, R. & Felmlee, D. (2011). Status struggles: network centrality and gender segregation in same- and cross-gender aggression, *American Sociological Review*, 76: 48–73.

Farrington, D.P., Lösel, F., Ttofi, M.M. & Theodorakis, N. (2012). *School Bullying, Depression and Offending Behaviour Later in Life: An Updated Systematic Review of Longitudinal Studies*. Stockholm: Swedish National Council for Crime Prevention.

Fekkes, M., Pijpers, F.I.M. & Verloove-Vanhorick, P.S. (2006). Effects of antibullying school program on bullying and health complaints, *Archives of Pediatrics and Adolescent Medicine*, 160: 638–644.

Ferguson, C.J. & Kilburn, J. (2010). Much ado about nothing: the misestimation and overinterpretation of violent video game effects in Eastern and Western nations: comment on Anderson et al. (2010), *Psychological Bulletin*, 136: 174–178.

Finkelhor, D. (2008). *Childhood Victimization: Violence, Crime and Abuse in the Lives of Young People*. Oxford: Oxford University Press.

Finkelhor, D., Turner, H. & Hamby, S. (2012). Let's prevent peer victimization, not just bullying, *Child Abuse & Neglect*, 36: 271–274.

Finkelhor, D., Turner, H., Ormrod, R. & Hamby, S.L. (2009). Trends in childhood violence and abuse exposure: evidence from two national surveys, *Archives of Pediatrics and Adolescent Medicine*, 164: 238–242.

Finnegan, R.A., Hodges, E.V.E. & Perry, D.G. (1998). Victimization by peers: associations with children's reports of mother–child interaction, *Journal of Personality and Social Psychology*, 75: 1076–1086.

Fisher, H.L., Moffitt, T.E., Houts, R.M., Belsky, D.W., Arsenault, L. & Caspi, A. (2012). Bullying victimisation and risk of self harm in early adolescence: longitudinal cohort study, *British Medical Journal*, 344.

Fleming, L.C. & Jacobsen, K.H. (2009). Bullying and symptoms of depression in Chilean middle school students, *Journal of School Health*, 79: 130–137.

Flouri, E. & Buchanan, A. (2002). Life satisfaction in teenager boys: the moderating role of father involvement and bullying, *Aggressive Behavior*, 28: 126–133.

Flouri, E. & Buchanan, A. (2003). The role of mother involvement and father involvement in adolescent bullying behaviour, *Journal of Interpersonal Violence*, 18: 1–11.

Flygare, E., Frånberg, G-M., Gill, P., Johansson, B., Lindberg, O., Osbeck, C. & Söderström, Å. (2011). *Evaluation of Anti-bullying Methods*. Report 353, National Agency for Education, Stockholm. Available at www.skolverket.se

Fonzi, A. (ed.) (1997). *Il Bullismo in Italia: Il fenomeno delle prepotenze a scuola dal Piemonte alla Sicilia*. Firenze: Giunti.

Fonzi, A., Genta, M.L., Menesini, E., Bacchini, D., Bonino, S. & Costabile, A. (1999). Italy. In P.K. Smith, Y. Morita, J. Junger-Tas, D. Olweus, R. Catalano & P. Slee (eds), *The Nature of School Bullying: A Cross-national Perspective*. London & New York: Routledge, pp. 140–156.

Foshee, V.A. & Matthew, R.A. (2007). Adolescent dating abuse perpetration: a review of findings, methodological limitations, and suggestions for future research. In D.J. Flannery, A.T. Vazsonyi & I.D. Waldman (eds), *The Cambridge Handbook of Violent Behavior and Aggression*. Cambridge: Cambridge University Press, pp. 431–449.

Fox, C.L. & Boulton, M.J. (2006). Friendship as a moderator of the relationship between social skills problems and peer victimisation, *Aggressive Behavior*, 32: 110–121.

Fraczek, A. (1996). Violence and aggression in children and youth: a socio-psychological perspective, *European Review*, 4: 75–90.

Frey, K.S. (2005). Gathering and communicating information about school bullying: overcoming 'secrets and lies', *Health Education*, 105: 409–413.

Frick, P.J. & White, S.F. (2008). Research review: the importance of callous-unemotional traits for developmental models of aggressive and antisocial behavior, *Journal of Child Psychology and Psychiatry*, 49: 359–375.

Frisén, A., Berne, S., Schultze-Krumbholz, A., Scheithauer, H., Naruskov, K., Luik, P., Katzer, C., Erentaite, R., & Zukauskiene, R. (2013). Measurement issues: a systematic review of cyber-bullying instruments. In P.K. Smith & G. Steffgen (eds), *Cyberbullying through the New Media: Findings from an International Network*. Hove: Psychology Press, pp. 37–62.

Frisén, A., Hasselblad, T. & Holmqvist, K. (2012). What actually makes bullying stop? Reports from former victims, *Journal of Adolescence*, 35: 981–990.

Furlong, M.J., Sharkey, J.D., Felix, E.D., Tanigawa, D. & Green, J.G. (2010). Bullying assessment: a call for increased precision of self-reporting procedures. In S.R. Jimerson, S.M. Swearer & D.L. Espelage (eds), *Handbook of Bullying in Schools: An International Perspective*. New York & London: Routledge, pp. 329–345.

Galen, B.R. & Underwood, M.K. (1997). A developmental investigation of social aggression among children, *Developmental Psychology*, 33: 589–600.

Gámez-Guadix, M., Orue, I., Smith, P.K. & Calvete, E. (2013). Longitudinal and reciprocal rela-tions of cyberbullying with depression, substance use, and problematic internet use among adolescents, *Journal of Adolescence*, 53: 446–452.

Garandeau, C. F., Poskiparta, E., & Salmivalli, C. (2014). Tackling acute cases of school bullying in the KiVa anti-bullying program : A comparison of two approaches. *Journal of Abnormal Child Psychology*.

Gehring T.M., Debry M. & Smith P.K. (eds) (2001). *The Family System Test (FAST): Theory and Application*. London and Philadelphia: Brunner-Routledge.

Gendron, B.P., Williams, K.R. & Guerra, N. (2011). An analysis of bullying among students within schools: estimating the effects of individual normative beliefs, self-esteem, and school climate, *Journal of School Violence*, 10: 150–164.

Genta, M.L. (ed.) (2002). *Il Bullismo: Bambini aggressivi a scuola*. Roma: Carocci.

Genta, M.L., Smith, P.K., Ortega, R., Brighi, A., Guarini, A., Thompson, F., Tippett, N., Mora-Merchan, J. & Calmaestra, J. (2012). Comparative aspects of cyberbullying in Italy, England and Spain: findings from a DAPHNE project. In Q. Li, D. Cross & P.K. Smith (eds), *Cyberbullying in the Global Playground: Research from International Perspectives*. Chichester, England: Wiley-Blackwell, pp. 15–31.

Gholsen, B. & Barker, P. (1985). Kuhn, Lakatos and Laudan: applications in the history of physics and psychology, *American Psychologist*, 40: 755–769.

Gini, G. (2006). Social cognition and moral cognition in bullying: what's wrong? *Aggressive Behavior*, 32: 528–539.

Gini, G., Albiero, P., Benelli, B. & Altoè, G. (2008). Determinants of adolescents' active defending and passive bystanding behaviour in bullying, *Journal of Adolescence*, 31: 93–105.

Gini, G. & Pozzoli, T. (2009). Association between bullying and psychosomatic symptoms: a meta-analysis, *Pediatrics*, 123: 1059–1065.

Gini, G. & Pozzoli, T. (2013). Bullied children and psychosomatic problems: a meta-analysis, *Pediatrics*, 132: 720–729.

Gini, G., Pozzoli, T. & Hauser, M. (2011). Bullies have enhanced moral competence to judge rela-tive to victims, but lack moral compassion, *Personality and Individual Differences*, 50: 603–608.

Gini, G., Pozzoli, T. & Hymel, S. (2014). Moral disengagement among children and youth: a meta-analytic review of links to aggressive behavior, *Aggressive Behavior*, 40: 56–68.

Gittins, C. (ed.) (2006). *Violence Reduction in Schools – How to Make a Difference*. Strasbourg: Council of Europe.

Goldbaum, S., Craig, W.M., Pepler, D. & Connolly, J. (2003). Developmental trajectories of victimization: identifying risk and protective factors, *Journal of Applied School Psychology*, 19: 139–156.

Goossens, F.A., Olthof, T. & Dekker, P.H. (2006). New participant role scales: comparison between various criteria for assigning roles and indications for their validity, *Aggressive Behavior*, 32: 343–357.

Goossens, F.X., Gooren, E.M.J.C., de Castro, B.C., van Overveld, K.W., Buijs, G.J., Monshouwer, K., Onrust, S.A. & Paulussen, T.G.W.M. (2012). Implementation of PATHS through Dutch municipal health services: a quasi-experiment, *International Journal of Conflict and Violence*, 6: 234–248.

Gradinger, P., Strohmeier, D. & Spiel, C. (2009). Traditional bullying and cyberbullying: identification of risk groups for adjustment problems, *Zeitschrift für Psychologie/Journal of Psychology*, 217: 205–213.

Greene, M.B. (2006). Bullying in schools: a plea for a measure of human rights, *Journal of Social Issues*, 62: 63–79.

Gregory, A., Cornell, D., Fan, X., Sheras, P., Shih, T-H. & Huang, F. (2010). Authoritative school discipline: high school practices associated with lower bullying and victimization, *Journal of Educational Psychology*, 102: 483–496.

Grigg, D. (2010). Cyber-aggression: definition and concept of cyberbullying, *Australian Journal of Guidance and Counselling*, 20: 143–156.

Guerin, S. & Hennessy, E. (2002). Pupils' definitions of bullying, *European Journal of Psychology of Education*, 17: 249–261.

Guerra, N., Williams, K.R. & Sadek, S. (2011). Understanding bullying and victimization during childhood and adolescence: a mixed methods study, *Child Development*, 82: 295–310.

Guidelines for preventing cyber-bullying in the school environment: a review and recommendations (2012). COST IS0801. Available at http://sites.google.com/site/costis0801/

Hamburger, M.E., Basile, K.C. & Vivolo, A.M. (2011). *Measuring Bullying, Victimisation, Perpetration, and Bystander Experiences: A Compendium of Assessment Tools*. Atlanta, GA: Centers for Disease Control and Prevention, National Center for Injury Prevention and Control. Available at www.cdc.gov/violenceprevention/pub/measuring_bullying.html

Hamer, A. den, Konijn, E.A. & Keijer, M.G. (2014). Cyberbullying behavior and adolescents' use of medias with antisocial content: a cyclic process model, *Cyberpsychology, Behavior, and Social Networking*, 17: 74–81.

Hamiwka, L.D., Yu, C.G., Hamiwka, L.A., Sherman, E.M.S., Anderson, B. & Wirrell, E. (2009). Are children with epilepsy at greater risk for bullying than their peers?, *Epilepsy & Behavior*, 15: 500–505.

Hanewinkel, R. (2004). Prevention of bullying in German schools: an evaluation of an anti-bullying approach. In P.K. Smith, D. Pepler & K. Rigby (eds), *Bullying in Schools: How Successful Can Interventions Be?* Cambridge: Cambridge University Press, pp. 81–97.

Hawker, D.S.J. & Boulton, M.J. (2000). Twenty years' research on peer victimization and psychosocial maladjustment: a meta-analytic review of cross-sectional studies, *Journal of Child Psychology and Psychiatry*, 41: 441–455.

Hawkins, D.L., Pepler, D.J. & Craig, W.M. (2001). Naturalistic observations of peer interventions in bullying, *Social Development*, 10: 512–527.

Hay, C. & Meldrum, R. (2010). Bullying, victimization and adolescent self-harm: testing hypotheses from General Strain theory, *Journal of Youth and Adolescence*, 39: 446–459.

Hayes, R. & Herbert, C. (2011). *Rising Above Bullying: From Despair to Recovery*. London and Philadelphia: Jessica Kingsley.

Heinemann, P.P. (1972). *Mobbning – Gruppvåld bland barn och vuxna*. Stockholm: Natur och Kultur.

Helsper, E.J., Kalmus, V., Hasebrink, U., Sagvari, B. & De Haan, J. (2013). *Country Classification: Opportunities, Risks, Harm and Parental Mediation*. London: LSE/EU Kids Online.

Herba, C.M., Ferdinand, R.F., Stijnen, T., Veenstra, R., Oldehinkel, A.J., Ormel, J. & Verhulst, F.C. (2008). Victimisation and suicide ideation in the TRAILS study: specific vulnerabilities of victims, *Journal of Child Psychology and Psychiatry*, 49: 867–876.

Higgins, C. (1994). Improving the school ground environment as an anti-bullying intervention. In P.K. Smith & S. Sharp (eds), *School Bullying: Insights and Perspectives*. London: Routledge. pp. 160–192.

Hinduja, S. & Patchin, J.W. (2008a). *Bullying beyond the Schoolyard: Preventing and Responding to Cyberbullying*. Thousand Oaks, CA: SAGE (Corwin Press).

Hinduja, S. & Patchin, J.W. (2008b). Cyberbullying: an exploratory analysis of factors related to offending and victimization, *Deviant Behavior*, 29: 1–29.

Hinduja, S. & Patchin, J.W. (2010). Bullying, cyberbullying, and suicide, *Archives of Suicide Research*, 14: 206–221.

Hinduja, S. & Patchin, J.W. (2012a). Cyberbullying: neither an epidemic nor a rarity?, *European Journal of Developmental Psychology*, 9: 539–543.

Hinduja, S. & Patchin, J.W. (2012b). *School Climate 2.0: Preventing Cyberbullying and Sexting One Classroom at a Time*. Thousand Oaks, CA: SAGE (Corwin Press).

Hodges, E.V.E., Boivin, M., Vitaro, F. & Bukowski, W.M. (1999). The power of friendship: protection against an escalating cycle of peer victimization, *Developmental Psychology*, 35: 94–101.

Hodges, E.V.E., Malone, M.J. & Perry, D.G. (1997). Individual risk and social risk as interacting determinants of victimization in the peer group, *Developmental Psychology*, 33: 1032–1039.

Hodges, E.V.E. & Perry, D.G. (1999). Personal and interpersonal antecedents and consequences of victimisation by peers, *Journal of Personality and Social Psychology*, 76: 677–685.

Hofstede, G. (2001). *Culture's Consequences: Comparing Values, Behaviours, Institutions, and Organizations Across Nations* (2nd edition). London: SAGE.

Holmberg, K. & Hjern, A. (2008). Bullying and attention-deficit-hyperactivity disorder in 10-year-olds in a Swedish community, *Developmental Medicine & Child Neurology*, 50: 134–138.

Horton, P. (2011a). 'School Bullying and Power Relations in Vietnam'. PhD dissertation. Linköping, Sweden: Linköping Studies in Arts and Science, no. 541.

Horton, P. (2011b). School bullying and social and moral orders, *Children & Society*, 25: 268–277.

Horton, P. (2012). *Bullied Into It: Bullying, Power and the Conduct of Conduct*. Gloucestershire: E&E Publishing.

Houlston, C. & Smith, P.K. (2009). The impact of a peer counselling scheme in an all girl secondary school, *British Journal of Educational Psychology*, 79: 69–86

Houlston, C., Smith, P.K. & Jessel, J. (2009). Investigating the extent and use of peer support initiatives in English schools, *Educational Psychology*, 29: 325–344.

House of Commons (2004). *Elder Abuse*. London: HMSO.

Hugh-Jones, S. & Smith, P.K. (1999). Self-reports of short- and long-term effects of bullying on children who stammer, *British Journal of Educational Psychology*, 69: 141–158.

Hughes, T. (1857). *Tom Brown's School Days*. Cambridge: Macmillan.

Huitsing, G. & Veenstra, R. (2012). Bullying in classrooms: participant roles from a social network perspective, *Aggressive Behavior*, 38: 494–509.

Humphrey, N., Kalambouka, A., Bolton, J., Lendrum, A., Wigelsworth, M., Leenie, C. & Farrell, P. (2008). *Primary Social and Emotional Aspects of Learning (SEAL): Evaluation of Small Group Work*. DCSF RB064. London: DCSF.

Humphrey, N., Lendrum, A. & Wigelsworth, M. (2010). *Social and Emotional Aspects of Learning (SEAL) Programme in Secondary Schools: A National Evaluation*. DFE-RB049. London: DfE.

Hunt, C., Peters, L. & Rapee, R.M. (2012). Development of a measure of the experience of being bullied in youth, *Psychological Assessment*, 24: 156–165.

Hunt, R. & Jensen, J. (2007). *The School Report: The Experiences of Young Gay People in Britain's Schools*. London: Stonewall.

Hunter, S.C. & Boyle, J.M.E. (2004). Appraisal and coping strategy use of victims of school bullying, *British Journal of Educational Psychology*, 74: 83–107.

Hunter, S.C., Boyle, J.M.E. & Warden, D. (2007). Perceptions and correlates of peer-victimization and bullying, *British Journal of Educational Psychology*, 77: 797–810.

Hussey, J.M., Chang, J.J. & Kotch, J.B. (2010). Child maltreatment in the United States: prevalence, risk factors, and adolescent health consequences, *Pediatrics*, 118: 933–942.

Hymel, S., Schonert-Reichl, K.A., Bonnano, R.A., Vaillancourt, T. & Henderson, N.R. (2010). Bullying and morality: how good kids can behave badly. In S.R. Jimerson, S.M. Swearer & D.L. Espelage (eds), *Handbook of Bullying in Schools: An International Perspective*. New York & London: Routledge. pp. 101–118.

Ireland, J.L. (2011). Bullying in prisons: bringing research up to date. In C. Monks & I. Coyne (eds), *Bullying in Different Contexts*. Cambridge: Cambridge University Press. pp. 137–156.

Jäger, T. (2009). CyberTraining: a research-based European training manual on cyberbullying, *Zeitschrift für Psychologie/Journal of Psychology*, 217: 234.

James, A., Smith, P.K. & Radford, L. (2014). Becoming grown-ups: a qualitative study of the experiences of peer mentors, *Pastoral Care in Education*, forthcoming.

Janowski, A. (1999). Sweden. In P.K. Smith, Y. Morita, J. Junger-Tas, D. Olweus, R. Catalano & P. Slee (eds), *The Nature of School Bullying: A Cross-national Perspective*. London & New York: Routledge, pp. 264–275.

Japanese Ministry of Education, Culture, Sports, Science and Technology (2012). *Heisei 22nenndo Jidou seito no mondaikoudoutou seitoshidou jou no shomondai ni kansuru chousa* [2010 Annual fact-finding survey on problematic behavior in school]. Tokyo: Ministry of Education, Culture, Sports, Science & Technology.

Jennifer, D. (2013). Girls and indirect aggression. In I. Rivers & N. Duncan (eds), *Bullying: Experiences and Discourses of Sexuality and Gender*. London and New York, Routledge, pp. 47–59.

Jimerson, S., Swearer, S. & Espelage, D. (eds) (2010). *Handbook of Bullying in Schools: An International Perspective*. New York: Routledge.

Jolliffe, D. & Farrington, D.P. (2006). Examining the relationship between low empathy and bullying, *Aggressive Behavior*, 32: 540–550.

Jolliffe, D. & Farrington, D.P. (2011). Is low empathy related to bullying after controlling for individual and social background variables?, *Journal of Adolescence*, 34: 59–71.

Jones, L.M., Mitchell, K.J. & Finkelhor, D. (2012). Trends in youth internet victimization: findings from three youth internet safety surveys 2000–2010, *Journal of Adolescent Health*, 50: 179–186.

Jones, L.M., Mitchell, K.J. & Walsh, W.A. (2013). *Evaluation of Internet Child Safety Materials used by ICAC Task Forces in School and Community Settings: Final Report*. Washington, DC: US Department of Justice.

Juvonen, J. & Graham, S. (eds) (2001). *Peer Harassment at School: The Plight of the Vulnerable and Victimised*. New York: Guilford.

Juvonen, J., Nishina, A. & Graham, S. (2001). Self-views versus peer perceptions of victim status among early adolescents. In J. Juvonen & S. Graham (eds), *Peer Harassment at School: The Plight of the Vulnerable and Victimised*. New York: Guilford, pp. 105–124.

Kanetsuna, T. & Smith, P.K. (2002). Pupil insights into bullying, and coping with bullying: a bi-national study in Japan and England, *Journal of School Violence*, 1: 5–29.

Kanetsuna, T., Smith, P.K. & Morita, Y. (2006). Coping with bullying at school: children's recommended strategies and attitudes to school-based interventions in Japan and England, *Aggressive Behavior*, 32: 570–580.

Karch, D.L., Logan, J., Daniel, D.D., Floyd, C.F. & Vagi, K.J. (2013). Precipitating circumstances of suicide among youth aged 10–17 years by sex: data from the National Violent Death Reporting System, 16 states, 2005–2008, *Journal of Adolescent Health*, 53: S51–S53.

Kärnä, A., Voeten, M., Little, T., Alanen, E., Poskiparta, E. & Salmivalli, C. (2011). Going to scale: a nonrandomized nationwide trial of the KiVa antibullying program for comprehensive schools, *Journal of Consulting and Clinical Psychology*, 79: 796–805.

Kärnä, A., Voeten, M., Little, T., Alanen, E., Poskiparta, E., & Salmivalli, C. (2012). Effectiveness of the KiVa antibullying program: Grades 1–3 and 7–9, *Journal of Educational Psychology*, 105: 535–551.

Kärnä,A.,Voeten, M., Little,T., Poskiparta, E., Kaljonen,A., & Salmivalli, C. (2011).A large-scale evaluation of the KiVa anti-bullying program: Grades 4–6, *Child Development*, 82: 311–330.

Kärnä,A.,Voeten, M., Poskiparta, E. & Salmivalli, C. (2010).Vulnerable children in varying class-room contexts: Bystanders' behaviors moderate the effects of risk factors on victimization, *Merrill-Palmer Quarterly*, 56: 261–282.

Kaukiainen,A., Björkqvist, K., Lagerspetz, K., Österman, K., Salmivalli, C., Rothberg, S. & Ahlbom, A. (1999).The relationship between social intelligence, empathy, and three types of aggression, *Aggressive Behavior*, 25: 81–89.

Kendal, R.L. (2008).Animal 'culture wars', *The Psychologist*, 21: 312–315.

Kert, A.S., Codding, R.S., Tryon, G.S. & Shiyko, M. (2010). Impact of the word 'bully' on the reported rate of bullying behavior, *Psychology in the Schools*, 47: 193–204.

Khoury-Kassabri, M., Benbenishty, R.,Astor, R.A. & Zeira,A. (2004).The contributions of com-munity, family, and school variables to student victimization, *American Journal of Community Psychology*, 34: 187–204.

Kidscape (1986). *Bully Courts*. London: Kidscape.

Kim,Y.S., Koh,Y-J. & Leventhal, B.L. (2004). Prevalence of school bullying in Korean middle school students, *Archives Journal of Adolescent Mental Health*, 158: 737–741.

Kim,Y.S., Koh, Y-J. & Leventhal, B.L. (2005). School bullying and suicidal risk in Korean middle school students, *Pediatrics*, 115: 357–363.

Kim,Y-S., Leventhal, B., Koh,Y-J. & Boyce,W.T. (2009). Bullying increased suicide risk: prospective study of Korean adolescents, *Archives Journal of Adolescent Mental Health*, 20, 133–154.

King, M., McKeown, E.,Warner, J., Ramsay, A., Johnson, K., Cort, C., Davidson, O. & Wright, L. (2003). Mental health and social wellbeing of gay men, lesbians and bisexuals in England and Wales: controlled, cross-sectional study, *British Journal of Psychiatry*, 183: 552–558.

Klomek,A.B., Kleinman, M.,Altschuler, E., Marrocco, F.,Amakawa, L. & Gould, M.S. (2011). High school bullying as a risk for later depression and suicidality, *Suicide and Life Threatening Behavior*, 41: 501–516.

Klomek, A.B., Sourander, A., Niemelä, S., Kumpulainen, K., Piha, J., Tamminen, T., Almqvist, F. & Gould, M.S. (2009). Childhood bullying behaviours as a risk for suicide attempts and com-pleted suicides: a population-based cohort study, *Journal of the American Academy of Child and Adolescent Psychiatry*, 48: 254–261.

Knights, K. (2011). 'Evaluating a Recovery Programme for Children & Adolescents Who Have Been Bullied: A Mixed Method Study'. Unpublished PhD thesis, University of Hertfordshire.

Knox, E. & Conti-Ramsden, G. (2003). Bullying risks of 11-year-old children with specific lan-guage impairment (SLI): does school placement matter?, *International Journal of Language and Communication Disorders*, 38: 1–12.

Kochenderfer-Ladd, B. (2003). Identification of aggressive and asocial victims and the stability of their peer victimization, *Merrill-Palmer Quarterly*, 49: 401–425.

Kochenderfer, B. & Ladd, G.W. (1997). Victimized children's responses to peers' aggres-sion: behaviors associated with reduced versus continued victimization, *Development and Psychopathology*, 9: 59–73.

Koo, H. (2004). 'The Nature of School Bullying in South Korea'. Unpublished PhD thesis, Goldsmiths, University of London.

Koo, H., Kwak, K. & Smith, P.K. (2008). Victimization in Korean schools: the nature, inci-dence and distinctive features of Korean bullying or *wang-ta*, *Journal of School Violence*, 7: 119–139.

Kowalski, R.M., Limber, S.P. & Agatston, P.W. (2008). *Cyber Bullying*. Malden, MA: Blackwell.

Kristensen, S.M. & Smith, P.K. (2003).The use of coping strategies by Danish children classed as bullies, victims, bully/victims, and not involved, in response to different (hypothetical) types of bullying, *Scandinavian Journal of Psychology*, 44: 479–488.

Kyriakides, L., Kaloyirou, C. & Lindsay, G. (2006). An analysis of the Revised Olweus Bully/Victim Questionnaire using the Rasch measurement model, *British Journal of Educational Psychology*, 76: 781–801.

Ladd, G.W. & Kochenderfer-Ladd, B. (1998). Parenting behaviors and parent–child relationships: correlates of peer victimization in kindergarten?, *Developmental Psychology*, 34: 1450–1458.

Ladd, G.W. & Kochenderfer-Ladd, B. (2002). Identifying victims of peer aggression from early to middle childhood: analysis of cross-informant data for concordance, estimation of relational adjustment, prevalence of victimization, and characteristics of identified victims, *Psychological Assessment*, 14: 74–96.

Lakatos, I. (1970). *Falsification and the Methodology of Scientific Research Programmes.* In I. Lakatos & A. Musgrave (eds), *Criticism and the Growth of Knowledge.* Cambridge: Cambridge University Press, pp. 91–106.

Lam, L.T. & Li, Y. (2013). The validation of the E-victimization Scale (E-VS) and the E-Bullying Scale (E-BS) for adolescents, *Computers in Human Behavior*, 29: 3–7.

Lam, O.B. & Liu, W.H. (2007). The path through bullying – a process model from the inside story of bullies in Hong Kong secondary schools, *Child and Adolescent Social Work Journal*, 24: 53–75.

Lambert, P., Scourfield, J., Smalley, N. & Jones, R. (2008). The social context of school bullying: evidence from a survey of children in South Wales, *Research Papers in Education*, 23: 269–291.

Law, D.M., Shapka, J.D. & Olson, B.F. (2010). To control or not to control? Parenting behaviours and adolescent online aggression, *Computers in Human Behavior*, 26: 1651–1656.

Lee, E. & Kim, M. (2004). Exposure to media violence and bullying at school: Mediating influences of anger and contact with delinquent friends, *Psychological Reports*, 95: 659–672.

Lee, S., Smith, P.K. & Monks, C. (2011). Perception of bullying-like phenomena in South Korea: a qualitative approach from a lifespan perspective, *Journal of Aggression, Conflict and Peace Research*, 3: 210–221.

Lee, S-H., Smith, P.K. & Monks, C. (2012). Meaning and usage of a term for bullying-like phenomena in South Korea: a lifespan perspective, *Journal of Language and Social Psychology*, 31: 342–349.

Leff, S.S., Kupersmidt, J.B., Patterson, C.J. & Power, T.J. (1999). Factors influencing teacher identification of peer bullies and victims, *School Psychology Review*, 28: 505–517.

Lereya, S.T., Samara, M. & Wolke, D. (2013). Parenting behavior and the risk of becoming a victim and a bully/victim: a meta-analysis study, *Child Abuse & Neglect*, 37: 1091–1108.

Lester, L., Cross, D. & Shaw, T. (2012). Problem behaviours, traditional bullying and cyberbullying among adolescents: longitudinal analyses, *Emotional and Behavioural Difficulties*, 17: 435–447.

Leymann, H. (1996). The content and development of mobbing at work, *European Journal of Work and Organisational Psychology*, 5: 165–184.

Li, Q. (2007). Bullying in the new playground: research into cyberbullying and cyber victimisation, *Australasian Journal of Educational Technology*, 23: 435–454.

Li, Q., Cross, D. & Smith, P.K. (2012). *Cyberbullying in the Global Playground: Research from International Perspectives.* Chichester, England: Wiley-Blackwell.

Limber, S.P., Nation, M., Tracy, A.J., Melton, G.B., & Flerx, V. (2004). Implementation of the Olweus Bullying Prevention Programme in the Southeastern United States. In P.K. Smith, D. Pepler & K. Rigby (eds), *Bullying in Schools: How Successful Can Interventions Be?* Cambridge: Cambridge University Press, pp. 55–79.

Livingstone, S., Haddon, L., Görzig, A. & Ólafsson, K. (2011). *Risks and Safety on the Internet: The Perspective of European Children: Full findings.* London: LSE/EU Kids Online.

Ma, L., Phelps, E., Lerner, J.V. & Lerner, R.M. (2009). The development of academic competence among adolescents who bully and who are bullied, *Journal of Applied Developmental Psychology*, 30: 628–644.

Machmutow, K., Perren, S., Sticca, F. & Alsaker, F.D. (2012). Peer victimisation and depressive symptoms: can specific coping strategies buffer the negative impact of cybervictimisation?, *Emotional and Behavioural Difficulties*, 17: 403–420.

Madsen, K.C. (1996). Differing perceptions of bullying and their practical implications, *Educational and Child Psychology*, 13: 14–22.

Mahdavi, J. & Smith, P.K. (2002). The operation of a bully court and perceptions of its success: a case study, *School Psychology International*, 23: 327–341.

Mahdavi, J. & Smith, P.K. (2007). Individual risk factors or group dynamics? An investigation of the scapegoat hypothesis of victimisation in school classes, *European Journal of Developmental Psychology*, 4: 353–371.

Maines, G. & Robinson, B. (1992). *Michael's Story: The 'No Blame' Approach*. Bristol: Lame Duck.

Malti, T., Ribeaud, D. & Eisner, M. (2012). Effectiveness of a universal school-based social competence program: the role of child characteristics and economic factors, *International Journal of Conflict and Violence*, 6: 249–259.

Martin, P., & Bateson, P. (2007). *Measuring Behaviour: An Introductory Guide* (3rd edn). Cambridge: Cambridge University Press.

May-Chahel, C. & Cawson, P. (2005). Measuring child maltreatment in the United Kingdom: a study of the prevalence of child abuse and neglect, *Child Abuse & Neglect*, 29: 969–984.

Mayeux, L., Underwood, M. & Risser, S. (2007). Perspectives on the ethics of sociometric research with children: how children, peers and teachers help to inform the debate, *Merrill-Palmer Quarterly*, 53: 53–78.

McGrath, H. & Noble, T. (eds) (2006). *Bullying Solutions: Evidence-based Approaches to Bullying in Australian Schools*. Frenchs Forest, NSW: Pearson, pp. 189–201.

McGuckin, C., Lewis, C.A., Cummins, P.K. & Cruise, S.M. (2011). The stress and trauma of school victimization in Ireland: a retrospective account, *Psychology, Society & Education*, 3: 55–67.

McGuckin, C., Perren, S., Corcoran, L., Cowie, H., Dehue, F., Ševčiková, A., Tsatsou, P. & Vollink, T. (2013). Coping with cyberbullying: how we can prevent cyberbullying and how victims can cope with it. In P.K. Smith & G. Steffgen (eds), *Cyberbullying through the New Media: Findings from an International Network*. Hove: Psychology Press, pp. 121–135.

Menesini, E. (2000). *Bullismo: Che fare? Prevenzione e strategie d'intervento nella scuola*. Firenze: Giunti.

Menesini, E., Codecasa, E., Benelli, B. & Cowie, H. (2003). Enhancing children's responsibility to take action against bullying: evaluation of a befriending intervention in Italian middle schools, *Aggressive Behavior*, 29: 1–14.

Menesini, E., Eslea, M., Smith, P.K., Genta, M.L., Giannetti, E., Fonzi, A. & Costabile, A. (1997). A cross-national comparison of children's attitudes towards bully/victim problems in school, *Aggressive Behavior*, 23: 245–257.

Menesini, E., Fonzi, A. & Smith, P.K. (2002). Attribution of meanings to terms related to bullying: a comparison between teachers' and pupils' perspectives in Italy, *European Journal of Psychology of Education*, 17: 393–406.

Menesini, E., Nocentini, A. & Palladino, B.E. (2012). Empowering students against bullying and cyberbullying: evaluation of an Italian peer-led model, *International Journal of Conflict and Violence*, 6: 313–320.

Menesini, E., Nocentini, A., Palladino, B.E., Frisén, A., Berne, S., Ortega Ruiz, R., Calmaestra, J., Scheithauer, H., Schultze-Krumbholz, A., Luik, P., Naruskov, K., Blaya, C., Berthaud, J. & Smith, P.K. (2012). Cyberbullying definition among adolescents: a comparison across six European countries, *Cyberpsychology, Behavior and Social Networking*, 15: 455–463.

Mishna, F. (2003). Learning disabilities and bullying: double jeopardy, *Journal of Learning Disabilities*, 36: 336–347.

Mishna, F., Cook, C., Saini, M., Wu, M-J. & MacFadden, R. (2009). *Interventions for Children, Youth and Parents to Prevent and Reduce Cyber Abuse*. Oslo, Norway: Campbell Systematic Reviews.

Molcho, M., Craig, W., Due, P., Pickett, W., Harel-Fisch, Y., Overpeck, M. & the HBSC Bullying Writing Group (2009). Cross-national time trends in bullying behaviour 1994–2006: findings from Europe and North America, *International Journal of Public Health*, 54: S1–S10. Available at http://springerlink.com/content/j15430j1x087r023/fulltext.pdfol

Monks, C. & Coyne, I. (eds) (2011). *Bullying in Different Contexts*. Cambridge: Cambridge University Press.

Monks, C., Ortega-Ruiz, R. & Rodríguez-Hidalgo, A.J. (2008) Peer victimization in multi-cultural schools in Spain and England, *European Journal of Developmental Psychology*, 5: 507–535.

Monks, C. & Smith, P.K. (2006). Definitions of 'bullying': age differences in understanding of the term, and the role of experience, *British Journal of Developmental Psychology*, 24: 801–821.

Monks, C. & Smith, P.K. (2010). Peer, self and teacher nominations of participant roles taken in victimization by five- and eight-year-olds, *Journal of Aggression, Conflict and Peace Research*, 2: 4–14.

Monks, C. & Smith, P.K. (2011). Bullying, aggression and victimization in young children: measurement, nature and prevention. In M. Veisson, M. Maniganayake, E. Hujala, E. Kikas & P.K. Smith (eds), *Global Perspectives in Early Childhood Education: Diversity, Challenges and Possibilities*. Frankfurt: Peter Land, pp. 457–475.

Monks, C., Smith, P.K., Naylor, P., Barter, C., Ireland, J.L. & Coyne, I. (2009). Bullying in different contexts: commonalities, differences and the role of theory, *Aggression and Violent Behavior*, 14: 146–156.

Monks, C., Smith, P.K. & Swettenham, J. (2003). Aggressors, victims and defenders in preschool: peer, self and teacher reports, *Merrill-Palmer Quarterly*, 49: 453–469.

Monks, C., Smith, P.K. & Swettenham, J. (2005). The psychological correlates of peer victimiza-tion in preschool: social cognitive skills, executive function and attachment profiles, *Aggressive Behavior*, 31: 571–588.

Mora-Merchan, J. & Jäger, T. (eds) (2010). *Cyberbullying: A Cross-national Comparison*. Landau, Germany: Verlag Empirische Pädagogik.

Moran, S., Smith, P.K., Thompson, D. & Whitney, I. (1993). Ethnic differences in experiences of bullying: Asian and white children, *British Journal of Educational Psychology*, 63: 431–440.

Morita, Y. (1985). *Ijime shuudan no kouzo ni kansuru shakaigakuteki kenkyu* [Sociological study on the structure of bullying group]. Osaka: Department of Sociology, Osaka City University.

Morita, Y. (2001). *Ijime no kokusai hikaku kenkyu* [Cross-national comparative study of bullying]. Japan: Kaneko Shobo.

Morita, Y., Soeda, H., Soeda, K. & Taki, M. (1999). Japan. In P.K. Smith, Y. Morita, J. Junger-Tas, D. Olweus, R. Catalano & P. Slee (eds), *The Nature of School Bullying: A Cross-national Perspective*. London & New York: Routledge, pp. 309–323.

Muñoz, L.C., Qualter, P. & Padgett, G. (2011). Empathy and bullying: exploring the influence of callous-unemotional traits, *Child Psychiatry & Human Development*, 42: 183–196.

Nabuzoka, D. & Smith, P.K. (1993). Sociometric status and social behaviour of children with and without learning difficulties, *Journal of Child Psychology and Psychiatry*, 34: 1435–1448.

Nakamoto, J. & Schwartz, D. (2010). Is peer victimization associated with academic achieve-ment? A meta-analytic review, *Social Development*, 19: 221–241.

Nansel, T.R., Craig, W., Overpeck, M.D., Saluja, G., & Ruan, W.J. (2004). Cross-national consist-ency in the relationship between bullying behaviors and psychosocial adjustment, *Archives of Pediatrics and Adolescent Medicine*, 158: 730–736.

Nansel, T.R., Overpeck, M.D., Pilla, R.S., Ruan, W.J., Simons-Morton, B. & Scheidt, P.C. (2001). Bullying behaviors among US youth: prevalence and association with psychosocial adjustment, *Journal of the American Medical Association*, 285: 2094–2100.

National Family Week Survey (2010). *Facebook is a major influence on girls, says survey*. Retrieved 19 May 2010, from http://news.bbc.co.uk/1/hi/education/10121931.stm

Naylor, P., Cowie, H. & del Rey, R. (2001). Coping strategies of secondary school children in response to being bullied, *Child Psychology and Psychiatry Review*, 6: 114–120.

Naylor, P., Petch, L. & Ali, A. (2011). Domestic violence: bullying in the home. In C. Monks & I. Coyne (eds), *Bullying in Different Contexts*. Cambridge: Cambridge University Press, pp. 87–112.

Nesdale, D., Durkin, K., Maass, A., Kiesner, J. & Griffiths, J.A. (2008). Effects of group norms on children's intentions to bully, *Social Development*, 17: 889–907.

Nickerson, A.B., Mele, D. & Princiotta, D. (2008). Attachment and empathy as predictors of roles as defenders or outsiders in bullying interactions, *Journal of School Psychology*, 46: 687–703.

O'Connell, P., Pepler, D.J. & Craig, W.M. (2001). Peer involvement in bullying: insights and challenges for intervention, *Journal of Adolescence*, 22: 437–452.

OFSTED (2012). *No Place For Bullying*. Available at www.ofsted.gov.uk

Olafsen, R.N. & Viemerö, V. (2000). Bully/victim problems and coping with stress in school among 10- to 12-year-old pupils in Åland, Finland, *Aggressive Behavior*, 26: 57–65.

Oliver, C. & Candappa, M. (2003). *Tackling Bullying: Listening to the Views of Children and Young People*. Nottingham: Department for Education and Skills.

Olweus, D. (1973/1978). *Forskning om skolmobbning*. Stockholm, Sweden: Almqvist & Wiksell. (English translation, *Aggression in Schools: Bullies and Whipping Boys*. Washington, DC: Hemisphere.)

Olweus, D. (1986). *Mobbning – vad vi vet och vad vi kan göra*. Stockholm: Liber.

Olweus, D. (1993). *Bullying at School: What We Know and What We Can Do*. Oxford: Blackwell.

Olweus, D. (1999a). Sweden. In P.K. Smith, Y. Morita, J. Junger-Tas, D. Olweus, R. Catalano & P. Slee (eds), *The Nature of School Bullying: A Cross-national Perspective*. London & New York: Routledge, pp. 7–27.

Olweus, D. (1999b). Norway. In P.K. Smith, Y. Morita, J. Junger-Tas, D. Olweus, R. Catalano & P. Slee (eds), *The Nature of School Bullying: A Cross-national Perspective*. London & New York: Routledge, pp. 28–48.

Olweus, D. (2004). The Olweus Bullying Prevention Programme: design and implementation issues and a new national initiative in Norway. In P.K. Smith, D. Pepler & K. Rigby (eds), *Bullying in Schools: How Successful Can Interventions Be?* Cambridge: Cambridge University Press, pp. 13–36.

Olweus, D. (2012a). Cyberbullying: an overrated phenomenon?, *European Journal of Developmental Psychology*, 9: 520–538.

Olweus, D. (2012b). Comments on cyberbullying article: a rejoinder, *European Journal of Developmental Psychology*, 9: 559–568.

Olweus, D. (2013). School bullying: development and some important challenges, *Annual Review of Clinical Psychology*, 9: 751–780.

Olweus, D. & Endresen, I.M. (1998). The importance of sex-of-stimulus object: age trends and sex differences in empathic responsiveness, *Social Development*, 7: 370–388.

Olweus, D. & Limber, S. (2010). The Olweus Bullying Prevention Program: implementation and evaluation over two decades. In S. Jimerson, S. Swearer & D. Espelage (eds), *Handbook of Bullying in Schools: An International Perspective*. New York: Routledge, pp. 377–401.

O'Moore, M. (2000). Critical issues for teacher training to counter bullying and victimisation in Ireland, *Aggressive Behavior*, 26: 99–111.

O'Moore, M. (2013). ABC whole-school approach to bullying prevention. In M. O'Moore & P. Stevens (eds), *Bullying in Irish Education*. Cork: Cork University Press, pp. 338–374.

O'Moore, M. & Minton, S.J. (2004). *Dealing with Bullying: A Training Manual for Teachers, Parents and Other Professionals.* London: Paul Chapman.

O'Moore, M. & Minton, S.J. (2009). Cyber-bullying: the Irish experience. In C. Quin & S. Tawse (eds), *Handbook of Aggressive Behavior Research.* Nova Scotia: Nova Scotia Publishers, Inc, pp. 269–292.

Ortega, R., del Rey, R. & Casas, J.A. (2012). Knowing, building and living together on internet and social networks: the ConRed cyberbullying prevention program, *International Journal of Conflict and Violence,* 6: 303–313.

Ortega, R., del Rey, R. & Fernández, I. (2003). Working together to prevent school violence: the Spanish response. In P.K. Smith (ed.), *Violence in Schools: The Response in Europe.* London and New York: RoutledgeFalmer, pp. 135–152.

Ortega, R., del Rey, R. & Mora-Merchan, J. (2004). SAVE model: an anti-bullying intervention in Spain. In P.K. Smith, D. Pepler & K. Rigby (eds), *Bullying in Schools: How Successful Can Interventions Be?* Cambridge: Cambridge University Press, pp. 167–185.

Ortega, R., Elipe, P., Mora-Merchan, J.A., Genta, M.L., Brighi, A., Guarini, A., Smith, P.K., Thompson, F. & Tippett, N. (2012). The emotional impact of bullying and cyberbullying on victims: a European cross-national study, *Aggressive Behavior,* 38: 342–356.

Ortega, R. & Sánchez, V. (2011). Juvenile dating and violence. In C. Monks & I. Coyne (eds), *Bullying in Different Contexts.* Cambridge: Cambridge University Press, pp. 113–136.

Ostrov, J.M. (2008). Forms of aggression and peer victimisation during early childhood: a short-term longitudinal study, *Journal of Abnormal Child Psychology,* 36: 311–322.

Ostrov, J.M. & Keating, C.F. (2004). Gender differences in preschool aggression during free play and structured interactions: An observational study, *Social Development,* 13: 255–277.

Ouellet-Morin, I., Danese, A., Bowes, L., Shakoor, S., Ambler, A., Pariante, C.M., Papadopoulos, A.S., Caspi, A., Moffitt, T.E. & Arsenault, L. (2011). A discordant monozygotic twin design shows blunted cortisol reactivity among bullied children, *Journal of the American Academy of Child & Adolescent Psychiatry,* 50: 574–582.

Patchin, J. & Hinduja, S. (2010). Trends in online social networking: adolescent use of MySpace over time, *New Media and Society,* 12: 197–216.

Patchin, J. & Hinduja, S. (2012). *Cyberbullying Prevention and Response: Expert Perspectives.* New York: Routledge.

Paul, J.P. & Cillessen, A.H.N. (2003). Dynamics of peer victimization in early adolescence: results from a four-year longitudinal study, *Journal of Applied School Psychology,* 19: 25–43.

Paul, S., Smith, P.K., & Blumberg, H.H. (2010). Addressing cyberbullying in school using the quality circle approach, *Australian Journal of Guidance & Counselling,* 20: 157–168.

Paul, S., Smith, P.K. & Blumberg, H.H. (2012). Revisiting cyberbullying in schools using the quality circle approach, *School Psychology International,* 33: 492–504.

Peeters, M., Cillessen, A.H.N. & Scholte, R.H.J. (2010). Clueless or powerful? Identifying subtypes of bullies in adolescence, *Journal of Youth and Adolescence,* 39: 1041–1052.

Pellegrini, A.D. & Bartini, M. (2000a). An empirical comparison of methods of sampling aggression and victimization in school settings, *Journal of Educational Psychology,* 92: 360–366.

Pellegrini, A.D. & Bartini, M. (2000b). A longitudinal study of bullying, victimization, and peer affiliation during the transition from primary school to middle school, *American Educational Research Journal,* 37: 699–726.

Pellegrini, A.D. & Bartini, M. (2001). Dominance in early adolescent boys: affiliative and aggressive dimensions and possible functions, *Merrill-Palmer Quarterly,* 47: 142–163.

Pellegrini, A.D. Bartini, M. & Brooks, F. (1999). School bullies, victims, and aggressive victims: factors relating to group affiliation and victimization in early adolescence, *Journal of Educational Psychology,* 91: 216–224.

Pellegrini, A.D., Bohn-Gettler, C.M., Dupuis, D., Hickey, M., Roseth, C. & Solberg, D. (2011). An empirical examination of sex differences in scoring preschool children's aggression, *Journal of Experimental Child Psychology,* 109: 232–238.

Pellegrini, A.D. & Long, J.D. (2002). A longitudinal study of bullying, dominance, and victimisation during the transition from primary school through secondary school, *British Journal of Developmental Psychology*, 20: 259–280.

Penning, S.L., Bhagwanjee, A. & Govender, K. (2010). Bullying boys: the traumatic effects of bullying in male adolescent learners, *Journal of Child and Adolescent Mental Health*, 22: 131–143.

Pepler, D.J. & Craig, W.M. (1995). A peek behind the fence: naturalistic observations of aggressive children with remote audiovisual recording, *Developmental Psychology*, 31: 548–553.

Pepler, D.J., Craig, W.M., Connolly, J.A., Yuile, A., McMaster, L. & Jiang, D. (2006). A developmental perspective on bullying, *Aggressive Behavior*, 32: 376–384.

Pepler, D.J., Craig, W.M., O'Connell, P., Atlas, R. & Charach, A. (2004). Making a difference in bullying: evaluation of a systemic school-based programme in Canada. In P.K. Smith, D. Pepler & K. Rigby (eds), *Bullying in Schools: How Successful Can Interventions Be?* Cambridge: Cambridge University Press, pp. 125–139.

Pepler, D.J., Craig, W.M. & Roberts, W.L. (1998). Observations of aggressive and nonaggressive children on the school playground, *Merrill-Palmer Quarterly*, 44: 55–76.

Pepler, D.J., Craig, W.M., Zeigler, S. & Charach, A. (1994). An evaluation of an anti-bullying intervention in Toronto schools, *Canadian Journal of Community Mental Health*, 13: 95–110.

Perkins, H.W., Craig, D.W. & Perkins, J.M. (2011). Using social norms to reduce bullying: a research intervention in five middle schools, *Group Processes & Intergroup Relations*, 14: 703–722.

Perren, S., Corcoran, L., Cowie, H., Dehue, F., Garcia, D., McGuckin, C., Ševčiková, A., Tsatsou, P. & Völlink, T. (2012). Tackling cyberbullying: review of empirical evidence regarding successful responses by students, parents and schools, *International Journal of Conflict and Violence*, 6: 283–293.

Perren, S., Ettekal, I. & Ladd, G. (2013). The impact of peer victimization on later maladjustment: mediating and moderating effects of hostile and self-blaming attributions, *Journal of Child Psychology and Psychiatry*, 54: 46–55.

Perry, D.G., Perry, L.C. & Boldizar, J.P. (1990). Learning of aggression. In M. Lewis & S. Miller (eds), *Handbook of Developmental Psychopathology*. New York: Plenum, pp. 135–146.

Persson, M. & Svensson, M. (2013). The willingness to pay to reduce school bullying, *Economics of Education Review*, 35: 1–11.

Peterson, J.S. & Ray, K.E. (2006). Bullying and the gifted: victims, perpetrators, prevalence, and effects, *Gifted Child Quarterly*, 50: 148–168.

Pikas, A. (1989). A pure concept of mobbing gives the best results for treatment, *School Psychology International*, 10: 95–104.

Pikas, A. (2002). New developments of the Shared Concern Method, *School Psychology International*, 23: 307–336.

Poskiparta, E., Kaukiainen, A., Pöyhönen, V. & Salmivalli, C. (2012). Anti-bullying computer game as part of the KiVa program: students' perceptions of the game. In A. Costabile & B. Spears (eds), *The Impact of Technology on Relationships in Educational Settings*. London: Routledge, pp. 158–168.

Pozzoli, T., Gini, G. & Vieno, A. (2012). The role of individual correlates and class norms in defending and passive bystanding behaviour in bullying: a multilevel analysis, *Child Development*, 83: 1917–1931.

Pronk, J., Goossens, F.A., Olthof, T., De Mey, L. & Willemen, A.M. (2013). Children's intervention strategies in situations of victimization by bullying: social cognitions of outsiders versus defenders, *Journal of School Psychology*, 51: 669–682.

Pyzalski, J. (2011). Electronic aggression among adolescents: an old house with a new facade (or even a number of houses). In C. Hällgren, E. Dunkels & G-M. Frånberg (eds), *Youth Culture and Net Culture: Online Social Practices*. Hershey, PA: IGI Global, pp. 278–295.

Pyzalski, J. (2012). From cyberbullying to electronic aggression: typology of the phenomenon, *Emotional and Behavioural Difficulties*, 17: 305–317.

Randall, P.E. (1997). *Adult Bullying*. London: Routledge.

Reijntjes, A., Kamphuis, J.H., Prinzie, P. & Telch, M.J. (2010). Peer victimization and internalizing problems in children: a meta-analysis of longitudinal studies, *Child Abuse & Neglect*, 34: 244–252.

Renati, R., Berrone, C. & Zanetti, M.A. (2012). Morally disengaged and unempathic: do cyberbullies fit these definitions? An exploratory study, *Cyberpsychology, Behavior, and Social Networking*, 15: 391–398.

Renold, E. (2002). Presumed innocence: (hetero) sexual, heterosexist and homophobic harassment among primary school girls and boys, *Childhood*, 9: 415–434.

Renold, E. (2006). 'They won't let us play ... unless you're going out with one of them': girls, boys and Butler's 'heterosexual matrix' in the primary years, *British Journal of Sociology of Education*, 27: 489–509.

Restorative Justice Consortium (2005). *Statement of Restorative Justice Principles: As Applied in a School Setting*. London: Restorative Justice Consortium. Available at www.restorativejustice.org.uk

Reynolds, W.M. (2003). *Reynolds Bully Victimization Scales*. San Antonio, TX: The Psychological Corporation, Harcourt Assessment.

Rideout, V.J., Foehr, U.G. & Roberts, D.F. (2010). *Generation M2: Media in the Lives of 8- to 18-Year-Olds*. Washington, DC: Henry J. Kaiser Foundation. Available at www.kff.org

Rigby, K. (1997). Attitudes and beliefs about bullying among Australian school children, *Irish Journal of Psychology*, 18: 202–220.

Rigby, K. (2002). *New Perspectives on Bullying*. London & Philadelphia: Jessica Kingsley.

Rigby, K. & Griffiths, C. (2010). *Applying the Method of Shared Concern in Australian schools: An Evaluative Study*. Canberra: Department of Education, Employment and Workplace Relations (DEEWR). Available at www.deewr.gov.au/schooling/nationalsafeschools/pages/research.aspx

Rigby, K. & Johnson, B. (2006). Expressed readiness of Australian schoolchildren to act as bystanders in support of children who are being bullied, *Educational Psychology*, 26: 425–440.

Rigby, K. & Slee, P. (1991). Bullying among Australian school children: reported behaviour and attitudes toward victims, *Journal of Social Psychology*, 131: 615–627.

Rigby, K. & Slee, P. (1993). *The Peer Relations Questionnaire (PRQ)*. Adelaide: University of South Australia.

Rigby, K. & Smith, P. (2011). Is school bullying really on the rise?, *Social Psychology of Education*, 14: 441–455.

Ringrose, J. (2008a). 'Just be friends': exposing the limits of educational bully discourses for understanding teen girls' heterosexualized friendships and conflicts, *British Journal of Sociology of Education*, 29: 509–522.

Ringrose, J. (2008b). 'Every time she bends over she pulls up her thong': teen girls negotiating discourses of competitive, heterosexualized aggression, *Girlhood Studies*, 1: 33–59

Rivers, I. (2001). Retrospective reports of school bullying: recall stability and its implications for research, *British Journal of Developmental Psychology*, 19: 129–142.

Rivers, I. (2011). *Homophobic Bullying: Research and Theoretical Perspectives*. Oxford: Oxford University Press.

Rivers, I., & Noret, N. (2010). 'I h8 u': findings from a five-year study of text and email bullying, *British Educational Research Journal*, 36: 643–671.

Rivers, I., Poteat, V.P., Noret, N. & Ashurst, N. (2009). Observing bullying at school: the mental health implications of witness status, *School Psychology Quarterly*, 24: 211–223.

Rivers, I. & Smith, P. K. (1994). Types of bullying behaviour and their correlates, *Aggressive Behaviour*, 20: 359–368.

Robinson, B. & Maines, G (1997). *Crying for Help: The No Blame Approach to Bullying*. Bristol: Lucky Duck.

Robinson, G. & Maines, B. (2007). *Bullying: A Complete Guide to the Support Group Method*. Bristol: Lucky Duck.

Robinson, J.P., Espelage, D.L. & Rivers, I. (2013). Developmental trends in peer victimization and emotional distress in LGB and heterosexual youth, *Pediatrics*, 131: 423–430.

Roland, E. (2011). The broken curve: Norwegian manifesto against bullying, *International Journal of Behavioural Development*, 35: 383–388.

Roland, E., Bru, E., Midthassel, U.V. & Vaaland, G.S. (2010). The Zero programme against bullying: effects of the programme in the context of the Norwegian manifesto against bullying, *Social Psychology of Education*, 13: 41–55.

Roland, E. & Midthassel, U.V. (2012). The Zero program, *New Directions for Youth Development*, 133: 29–39.

Roland, E. & Munthe, E. (1989). *Bullying: An International Perspective*. London: David Fulton.

Ross, D.M. (2002). *Childhood Bullying and Teasing: What School Personnel, Other Professionals and Parents Can Do* (2nd edn). Alexandria, VA: American Counselling Association.

Rothon, C., Head, J., Klineberg, E. & Stansfeld, S. (2010). Can social support protect bullied adolescents from adverse outcomes? A prospective study on the effects of bullying on academic achievement and mental health of adolescents at secondary schools in East London, *Journal of Adolescence*, 34: 579–588.

RSM McClure Watters (2011). *The Nature and Extent of Pupil Bullying in Schools in the North of Ireland*, Volume 56. Bangor, Northern Ireland: Department of Education for Northern Ireland.

Rueger, S.Y., Malecki, C.K. & Demaray, M.K. (2011). Stability of peer victimization in early adolescence: effects of timing and duration, *Journal of School Psychology*, 49: 443–464.

Saarento, S., Boulton, A.J. & Salmivalli, C. (2014). Reducing bullying and victimization: Student- and classroom-level mechanisms of change, *Journal of Abnormal Child Psychology*, forthcoming.

Saarento, S., Kärnä, A., Hodges, E.V.E. & Salmivalli, C. (2013). Student-, classroom-, and school-level risk factors for victimization, *Journal of School Psychology*, 51: 421–434.

Sainio, M., Veenstra, R., Huitsing, G. & Salmivalli, C. (2010). Victims and their defenders: a dyadic approach, *International Journal of Behavioral Development*, 35: 144–151.

Salmivalli, C. (2002). Is there an age decline in victimization by peers at school?, *Educational Research*, 44: 237–245.

Salmivalli, C. (2010). Bullying and the peer group: a review, *Aggression and Violent Behavior*, 15: 112–120.

Salmivalli, C. & Isaacs, J. (2005). Prospective relations among victimization, rejection, friendliness, and children's self- and peer-perceptions, *Child Development*, 76: 1161–1171.

Salmivalli, C., Karhunen, J. & Lagerspetz, K.M.J. (1996). How did the victims respond to bullying?, *Aggressive Behavior*, 22: 99–109.

Salmivalli, C., Kärnä, A. & Poskiparta, E. (2010). From peer putdowns to peer support: a theoretical model and how it translated into a national anti-bullying program. In S. Jimerson, S. Swearer & D. Espelage (eds), *Handbook of Bullying in Schools: An International Perspective*. New York: Routledge, pp. 441–454.

Salmivalli, C., Kärnä, A. & Poskiparta, E. (2011). Counteracting bullying in Finland: the KiVa program and its effects on different forms of being bullied, *International Journal of Behavioural Development*, 35: 405–411.

Salmivalli, C., Kaukiainen, A., Kaistaniemi, L. & Lagerspetz, K. (1999). Self-evaluated self-esteem, peer-evaluated self-esteem, and defensive egotism as predictors of adolescents' participation in bullying situations, *Personality and Social Psychology Bulletin*, 25: 1268–1278.

Salmivalli, C., Lagerspetz, K., Björkqvist, K., Österman, K., & Kaukiainen, A. (1996). Bullying as a group process: participant roles and their relations to social status within the group, *Aggressive Behavior*, 22: 1–15.

Salmivalli, C., Lappalainen, M. & Lagerspetz, K.M.J. (1998). Stability and change of behaviour in connection with bullying in schools: a two-year follow-up, *Aggressive Behavior*, 24: 205–218.

Salmivalli, C. & Poskiparta, E. (2012). KiVa antibullying program: overview of evaluation studies based on a randomized controlled trial and national rollout in Finland, *International Journal of Conflict and Violence*, 6: 294–302.

Salmivalli, C. & Pöyhönen, V. (2012). Cyberbullying in Finland. In Q. Li, D. Cross, & P.K. Smith (eds), *Cyberbullying in the Global Playground: Research from International Perspectives*. Chichester, England: Wiley-Blackwell, pp. 57–72.

Salmivalli, C. & Voeten, M. (2004). Connections between attitudes, group norms, and behaviour in bullying situations, *International Journal of Behavioral Development*, 28: 246–258.

Samara, M. & Smith, P.K. (2008). How schools tackle bullying, and the use of whole school policies: changes over recent years, *Educational Psychology*, 28: 663–676.

Sapouna, M., Wolke, D., Vannini, N., Watson, S., Woods, S., Schneider, W., Enz, S. & Aylett, R. (2012). Individual and social network predictors of the short-term stability of bullying victimization in the United Kingdom and Germany, *British Journal of Educational Psychology*, 82: 225–240.

Sapouna, M., Wolke, D., Vannani, N., Watson, S., Woods, S., Schneider, W., Enz, S., Hall, L., Paiva, A., Andre, E., Dautenhahn, K., & Aylett, R. (2010). Virtual learning intervention to reduce bullying victimization in primary school: a controlled trial, *Journal of Child Psychology and Psychiatry*, 51: 104–112.

Sawyer, A.L., Bradshaw, C.P. & O'Brennan, L.M. (2008). Examining ethnic, gender, and developmental differences in the way children report being a victim of 'bullying' on self-report measures, *Journal of Adolescent Health*, 43: 106–114.

Sawyer, J-L., Mishna, F., Pepler, D. & Wiener, J. (2011). The missing voice: parents' perspectives of bullying, *Children and Youth Services Review*, 33: 1795–1803.

Schäfer, M., Korn, S., Brodbeck, F., Wolke, D. & Schulz, H. (2005). Bullying roles in changing contexts: the stability of victim and bully roles from primary to secondary school, *International Journal of Behavioral Development*, 29: 323–335.

Schäfer, M., Korn, S., Smith, P.K., Hunter, S.C., Mora-Merchán, J.A., Singer, M.M. & van der Meulen, K. (2004). Lonely in the crowd: recollections of bullying, *British Journal of Developmental Psychology*, 22: 379–394.

Scheithauer, H., Hess, M., Schultze-Krumbholz, A. & Bull, H.D. (2012). School-based prevention of bullying and relational aggression in adolescence: the fairplayer manual, *New Directions for Youth Development*, 133: 55–70.

Schuster, B. (1999). Outsiders at school: the prevalence of bullying and its relation with social status, *Group Processes & Intergroup Relations*, 2: 175–190.

Schwartz, D., Dodge, K.A., Pettit, G.S. & Bates, J.E. (1997). The early socialization of aggressive victims of bullying, *Child Development*, 68: 665–675.

Schwartz, D., Dodge, K.A., Pettit, G.S. & Bates, J.E. (2000). Friendship as a moderating factor in the pathway between early harsh home environment and later victimization in the peer group, *Developmental Psychology*, 36: 646–662.

Schwartz, D., Gorman, A.H., Nakamoto, J. & Toblin, R.L. (2005). Victimization in the peer group and children's academic functioning, *Journal of Educational Psychology*, 97: 425–435.

Schwartz, D. & Proctor, L.J. (2000). Community violence exposure and children's social adjustment in the peer group: the mediating roles of emotion regulation and social cognition, *Journal of Consulting and Clinical Psychology*, 68: 670–683.

Ševčiková, A. & Šmahel, D. (2009). Online harassment and cyberbullying in the Czech Republic: comparison across age groups, *Zeitschrift für Psychologie/Journal of Psychology*, 217: 227–229.

Shakoor, S., Jaffee, S.R., Andreou, P., Bowes, L., Ambler, A.P., Caspi, A., Moffitt, T.E. & Arseneault, L. (2011a). Mothers and children as informants of bullying victimization: results from an epidemiological cohort of children, *Journal of Abnormal Child Psychology*, 39: 379–387.

Shakoor, S., Jaffee, S.R., Bowes, L., Ouellet-Morin, I., Andreou, P., Happé, F., Moffitt, T.E. & Arseneault, L. (2011b). A prospective longitudinal study of children's theory of mind and adolescent involvement in bullying, *Journal of Child Psychology and Psychiatry*, 53: 254–261.

Shariff, S. (2008). *Cyber-bullying: Issues and Solutions for the School, the Classroom and the Home.* London: Routledge.

Sharp, S. & Cowie, H. (1994). Empowering pupils to take positive action against bullying. In P.K. Smith & S. Sharp (eds), *School Bullying: Insights and Perspectives*. London: Routledge. pp. 108–131.

Sharp, S., Thompson, D. & Arora, T. (2000). How long before it hurts? An investigation into long-term bullying, *School Psychology International*, 21: 37–46.

Shaw, T., Cross, D. Thomas, L.T. & Zubrick, S.R. (2014). Bias in student survey findings from active parental consent procedures, *British Educational Research Journal*, forthcoming.

Shaw, T., Cross, D. & Zubrick, S.R. (submitted). Testing for response shift bias in evaluations of school anti-bullying programs, *In review*.

Shaw, T., Dooley, J.J., Cross, D., Zubrick, S.R. & Waters, S. (2013). The Forms of Bullying Scale (FBS): Validity and reliability estimates for a measure of bullying victimization and perpetration in early adolescence, *Psychological Assessment*, 25: 1045–1057.

Slonje, R., & Smith, P.K. (2008). Cyberbullying: another main type of bullying?, *Scandinavian Journal of Psychology*, 49: 147–154.

Slonje, R., Smith, P.K. & Frisén, A. (2012). Processes of cyberbullying, and feelings of remorse by bullies, *European Journal of Developmental Psychology*, 9: 244–259.

Slonje, R., Smith, P.K. & Frisén, A. (2013). The nature of cyberbullying, and strategies for prevention, *Computers in Human Behavior*, 29: 26–32.

Smith, P.K. (1999). England. In P.K. Smith, Y. Morita, J. Junger-Tas, D. Olweus, R. Catalano & P. Slee (eds), *The Nature of School Bullying: A Cross-national Perspective*. London & New York: Routledge. pp. 68–90.

Smith, P.K. (ed.) (2003). *Violence in Schools: The Response in Europe*. London & New York: RoutledgeFalmer.

Smith, P.K. (2007). Why has aggression been thought of as maladaptive? In P. Hawley, T. D. Little & P. Rodkin (eds), *Aggression and Adaptation*. Mahwah, NJ: Lawrence Erlbaum, pp. 65–83.

Smith, P.K. (2010a). Bullying in primary and secondary schools: psychological and organizational comparisons. In S.R. Jimerson, S.M. Swearer & D.L. Espelage (eds), *Handbook of Bullying in Schools: An International Perspective*. New York & London: Routledge, pp. 137–150.

Smith, P.K. (2010b) (with one chapter by Y. Gosso). *Children and Play*. Oxford: Wiley-Blackwell.

Smith, P.K. (2010c). Victimization in different contexts: comments on the Special Issue, *Merrill-Palmer Quarterly*, 56: 441–454.

Smith, P.K. (2011). Bullying in schools: thirty years of research. In C. Monks & I. Coyne (eds), *Bullying in Different Contexts*. Cambridge: Cambridge University Press, pp. 36–60.

Smith, P.K. (2012). Cyberbullying and cyber aggression. In S.R. Jimerson, A.B. Nickerson, M.J. Mayer & M.J. Furlong (eds), *Handbook of School Violence and School Safety: International Research and Practice* (2nd edn). New York: Routledge, pp. 93–103.

Smith, P.K., Cowie, H., Olafsson, R. & Liefooghe, A. (2002). Definitions of bullying: a comparison of terms used, and age and sex differences, in a 14-country international comparison, *Child Development*, 73: 1119–1133.

Smith, P.K., Cowie, H. & Sharp, S. (1994). Working directly with pupils involved in bullying situations. In P.K. Smith & S. Sharp (eds), *School Bullying: Insights and Perspectives*. London: Routledge, pp. 193–212.

Smith, P.K., del Barrio, C. & Tokunaga, R. (2013). Definitions of bullying and cyberbullying: how useful are the terms? In S. Bauman, J. Walker & D. Cross (eds), *Principles of Cyberbullying Research: Definition, Methods, and Measures*. New York & London: Routledge, pp. 64–86.

Smith, P.K., Howard, S. & Thompson, F. (2007). Use of the Support Group Method to tackle bullying, and evaluation from schools and local authorities in England, *Pastoral Care in Education*, 25: 4–13.

Smith, P.K., Kupferberg, A., Mora-Merchan, J.A., Samara, M., Bosley, S. & Osborn, R. (2012). A content analysis of school anti-bullying policies: a follow-up after six years, *Educational Psychology in Practice*, 28: 61–84.

Smith, P.K., Kwak, K. & Toda, Y. (eds) (in preparation). *Reducing Bullying and Cyberbullying in Schools – Eastern and Western Perspectives*. Cambridge: Cambridge University Press.

Smith, P.K. & Levan, S. (1995) Perceptions and experiences of bullying in younger pupils, *British Journal of Educational Psychology*, 65: 489–500.

Smith, P.K., Madsen, K. & Moody, J. (1999). What causes the age decline in reports of being bullied at school? Towards a developmental analysis of risks of being bullied, *Educational Research*, 41: 267–285.

Smith, P.K., Mahdavi, J., Carvalho, M., Fisher, S., Russell, S. & Tippett, N. (2008). Cyberbullying, its forms and impact in secondary school pupils, *Journal of Child Psychology and Psychiatry*, 49: 376–385.

Smith, P.K. & Monks, C.P. (2008). Concepts of bullying: developmental and cultural aspects, *International Journal of Adolescent Medicine and Health*, 20: 101–112.

Smith, P.K., Morita, Y., Junger-Tas, J., Olweus, D., Catalano, R. & Slee, P. (eds) (1999) *The Nature of School Bullying: A Cross-national Perspective*. London: Routledge.

Smith, P.K., Pepler, D. and Rigby, K. (eds) (2004). *Bullying in Schools: How Successful Can Interventions Be?* Cambridge: Cambridge University Press.

Smith, P.K., Salmivalli, C. & Cowie, H. (2012). Effectiveness of school-based programs to reduce bullying: a commentary, *Journal of Experimental Criminology*, 8: 433–441.

Smith, P.K. & Sharp, S. (eds) (1994). *School Bullying: Insights and Perspectives*. London: Routledge.

Smith, P.K., Sharp, S., Eslea, M. & Thompson, D. (2004). England: The Sheffield project. In P.K. Smith, D.K. Pepler & K. Rigby (eds), *Bullying in Schools: How Successful Can Interventions Be?* Cambridge: Cambridge University Press, pp. 99–123.

Smith, P.K., Shu, S. & Madsen, K. (2001). Characteristics of victims of school bullying: developmental changes in coping strategies and skills. In J. Juvonen & S. Graham (eds), *Peer Harassment at School: The Plight of the Vulnerable and Victimised*. New York: Guilford, pp. 332–352.

Smith, P.K., Smees, R. & Pellegrini, A.D. (2004). Play fighting and real fighting: using video playback methodology with young children, *Aggressive Behavior*, 30: 164–173.

Smith, P.K., Smith, C., Osborn, R. & Samara, M. (2008). A content analysis of school anti-bullying policies: progress and limitations, *Educational Psychology in Practice*, 24: 1–12.

Smith, P.K. & Steffgen, G. (2013). *Cyberbullying through the New Media: Findings from an International Network*. Hove: Psychology Press.

Smith, P.K., Talamelli, L., Cowie, H., Naylor, P. & Chauhan, P. (2004). Profiles of non-victims, escaped victims, continuing victims and new victims of school bullying, *British Journal of Educational Psychology*, 74: 565–581.

Smith, P.K., Thompson, F. & Bhatti, S. (2013). Ethnicity, gender, bullying and cyberbullying in English secondary school pupils, *Psychologie in Österreich*, 1: 28–32.

Smith, P.K. & Watson, D. (2004). *Evaluation of the CHIPS (ChildLine in Partnership with Schools) Pogramme*. Research report RR570. Nottingham: DfES publications.

Smorti, A., Menesini, E. & Smith, P. K. (2003). Parents' definition of children's bullying in a five-country comparison, *Journal of Cross-Cultural Psychology*, 34: 417–432.

Solberg, M. & Olweus, D. (2003). Prevalence estimation of school bullying with the Olweus Bully/Victim Questionnaire, *Aggressive Behavior*, 29: 239–268.

Sourander, A., Helstelä, L., Helenius, H. & Piha, J. (2000). Persistence of bullying from childhood to adolescence – a longitudinal 8-year follow-up study, *Child Abuse & Neglect*, 24: 873–881.

Sourander, A., Klomek, A.B., Ikonen, M., Lindroos, J., Luntamo, T., Koskelainen, M., Ristkari, T. & Helenius, H. (2010). Psychosocial risk factors associated with cyberbullying among adolescents: a population-based study, *Archives of General Psychiatry*, 67: 720–728.

Spears, B. & Kofoed, J. (2013). Transgressing research binaries: youth as knowledge brokers in cyberbullying research. In P.K. Smith & G. Steffgen (eds), *Cyberbullying through the New Media: Findings from an International Network*. Hove: Psychology Press, pp. 201–221.

Spiel, C., Salmivalli, C. & Smith, P.K. (2011). Translational research: national strategies for violence prevention in school, *International Journal of Behavioral Development*, 35: 381–382.

Spiel, C., & Strohmeier, D. (2011). National strategy for violence prevention in the Austrian public school system: development and implementation, *International Journal of Behavioral Development*, 35: 412–418.

Spriggs, A.L., Iannotti, R.J., Nansel, T.R. & Haynie, D.L. (2007). Adolescent bullying involvement and perceived family, peer and school relations: commonalities and differences across race/ethnicity, *Journal of Adolescent Health*, 41: 283–293.

Stevens, V. & Van Oost, P. (1994). *Pesten op school: Een actieprogramma* [Bullying at school: An action programme]. Kessel-Lo: Garant Uitgevers.

Stevens, V., Van Oost, P. & De Bourdeaudhuij, I. (2004). Interventions against bullying in Flemish schools: programme development and evaluation. In P.K. Smith, D. Pepler & K. Rigby (eds), *Bullying in Schools: How Successful Can Interventions Be?* Cambridge: Cambridge University Press, pp. 141–165.

Strohmeier, D. & Noam, G.G. (eds) (2012). Evidence-based bullying prevention programs for children and youth, *New Directions for Youth Development*, 133, Spring (whole issue).

Sullivan, K., Cleary, M. & Sullivan, G. (2004). *Bullying in Secondary Schools*. London: Paul Chapman.

Sutton, J. & Keogh, E. (2000). Social competition in school: relationships with bullying, Machiavellianism and personality, *British Journal of Educational Psychology*, 70: 443–456.

Sutton, J. & Smith, P. K. (1999). Bullying as a group process: an adaptation of the participant role approach, *Aggressive Behavior*, 25: 97–111.

Sutton, J., Smith, P.K. & Swettenham, J. (1999a). Bullying and 'theory of mind': a critique of the 'social skills deficit' view of anti-social behaviour, *Social Development*, 8: 117–127.

Sutton, J., Smith, P.K. & Swettenham, J. (1999b). Social cognition and bullying: social inadequacy or skilled manipulation?, *British Journal of Developmental Psychology*, 17: 435–450.

Tani, F., Greenman, P.S., Schneider, B.H. & Fregoso, M. (2003). Bullying and the Big Five: a study of childhood personality and participant roles in bullying incidents, *School Psychology International*, 24: 131–146.

Tapper, K. & Boulton, M.J. (2002). Studying aggression in school children: the use of a wireless microphone and micro-video camera, *Aggressive Behavior*, 28: 356–365.

Tattum, D. (1989). Violence and aggression in schools. In D.P. Tattum & D.A. Lane (eds), *Bullying in Schools*. Stoke-on-Trent: Trentham Books.

Tattum, D. & Lane, D.A. (eds) (1989). *Bullying in Schools*. Stoke-on-Trent: Trentham Books.

Tellus 4 National Report (2010). Research Report DCSF-RR218. London: DCSF.

Thompson, F., Robinson, S. & Smith, P.K. (2013). Il cyberbullismo nel Regno unito: valutazione di alcune procedure di intervento [An evaluation of some cyberbullying interventions in England].

In M.L. Genta, A. Brighi & A. Guarini (eds), *Cyberbullismo: Ricerche e Strategie di Intervento* [Cyberbullying Research and Intervention Strategies). Milano: Franco Angeli, pp. 136–153.

Thompson, F. & Smith, P.K. (2011). *The Use and Effectiveness of Anti-bullying Strategies in Schools.* DFE-RR098. London: DfE.

Thurlow, C. (2001). Naming the 'outsider within': homophobic pejoratives and the verbal abuse of lesbian, gay and bisexual high-school pupils, *Journal of Adolescence*, 24: 25–38.

Tippett, N. & Kwak, K. (2012). Cyberbullying in South Korea. In Q. Li, D. Cross & P.K. Smith (eds) *Cyberbullying in the Global Playground: Research from International Perspectives.* Chichester: Wiley-Blackwell, pp. 202–219.

Tippett, N. & Smith, P.K. (submitted). Is cyberbullying changing? Findings from a 3-year longitudinal study. *In review.*

Tippett, N., Wolke, D. & Platt, L. (2013). Ethnicity and bullying involvement in a national UK youth sample, *Journal of Adolescence*, 36: 639–649.

Tokunaga, R.S. (2010). Following you home from school: a critical review and synthesis of research on cyberbullying victimization, *Computers in Human Behavior*, 26: 277–287.

Toomey, R.B. & Russell, S.T. (2013). The role of sexual orientation in school-based victimization: a meta-analysis, *Youth & Society*, 45: 500–522.

Totura, C.M.W., Green, A.E., Karver, M.S. & Gesten, E.L. (2009). Multiple informants in the assessment of psychological, behavioural, and academic correlates of bullying and victimization in middle school, *Journal of Adolescence*, 32: 193–211.

Townsend, L., Flisher, A.J., Chikobvu, P., Lombard, C. & King, G. (2008). The relationship between bullying behaviours and high school dropout in Cape Town, South Africa, *South African Journal of Psychology*, 38: 21–32.

Tremblay, R.E. (2003). Why socialization fails: the case of chronic physical aggression. In B.B. Lahey, T.E. Moffitt & A. Caspi (eds), *The Causes of Conduct Disorder and Juvenile Delinquency.* New York: Guilford.

Troop-Gordon, W. & Quenelle, A. (2010). Children's perceptions of their teachers' responses to students' peer harassment: moderators of victimization–adjustment linkages, *Merrill-Palmer Quarterly*, 56: 333–360.

Ttofi, M.M. & Farrington, D.P. (2008). Reintegrative shaming theory, moral emotions and bullying, *Aggressive Behavior*, 34: 352–368.

Ttofi, M.M., Farrington, D.P. & Baldry, A.C. (2008). 'Effectiveness of Programs to Reduce School Bullying: A Systematic Review'. Report prepared for The Swedish National Council for Crime Prevention. Västerås, Sweden: Edita Norstedts.

Ttofi, M.M. & Farrington, D.P. (2011). Effectiveness of school-based programs to reduce bullying: a systematic and meta-analytic review, *Journal of Experimental Criminology*, 7: 27–56.

Ttofi, M.M. & Farrington, D.P. (2012). Bullying prevention programs: the importance of peer intervention, disciplinary methods and age variations, *Journal of Experimental Criminology*, 8: 443–462.

Ttofi, M.M., Farrington, D.P. & Lösel, F. (2011). Do the victims of school bullies tend to become depressed later in life? A systematic review and meta-analysis of longitudinal studies, *Journal of Aggression, Conflict and Peace Research*, 3: 63–73.

Ttofi, M.M., Farrington, D.P. & Lösel, F. (2012). School bullying as a predictor of violence later in life: a systematic review and meta-analysis of prospective longitudinal studies, *Aggression and Violent Behavior*, 17: 405–418.

Ucanok, Z., Smith, P.K. & Karasoy, D.S. (2011). Definitions of bullying: age and gender differences in a Turkish sample, *Asian Journal of Social Psychology*, 14: 75–83.

United Nations (1991). *United Nations Convention on the Rights of the Child.* Innocenti Studies, Florence: UNICEF.

Vandebosch, H. & van Cleemput, K. (2008). Defining cyberbullying: a qualitative research into the perceptions of youngsters, *CyberPsychology & Behavior*, 11: 499–503.

Vandebosch, H. & van Cleemput, K. (2009). Cyberbullying among youngsters: profiles of bullies and victims, *New Media & Society*, 11: 1349–1371.

Van IJzendoorn, M.H. & Tavecchio, L.W.C. (1987). The development of attachment theory as a Lakatosian research program: philosophical and methodological aspects. In L.W.C. Tavecchio & M.H. van IJzendoorn (eds), *Attachment in Social Networks*. North-Holland: Elsevier, pp. 3–31.

Van Kaenel-Platt, J. & Douglas, T. (2012). Cybermentoring. In A. Costabile & B.A. Spears (eds), *The Impact of Technology on Relationships in Educational Settings*. London: Routledge, pp. 151–157.

Van Roekel, E., Scholte, R.H.J. & Didden, R. (2010). Bullying among adolescents with autism spectrum disorders: prevalence and perception, *Journal of Autism and Developmental Disorders*, 40: 63–73.

Veenstra, R., Lindenberg, S., Zijlstra, B.J.H., De Winter, A.F., Verhulst, F.C. & Ormel, J. (2007). The dyadic nature of bullying and victimization: testing a dual-perspective theory, *Child Development*, 78: 1843–1854.

Volk, A.A., Camilleri, J.A., Dane, A.V. & Marini, Z.A. (2012). Is adolescent bullying an evolutionary adaptation?, *Aggressive Behavior*, 38: 222–238.

Von Marées, N. & Petermann, F. (2009). The bullying and victimization questionnaire for children (BVF-K): construction and analysis of an instrument for the assessment of bullying in kindergarten and primary school, *Praxis der Kinderpsychologie und Kinderpsychiatrie*, 58: 96–109.

Wachs, S. (2012). Moral disengagement and emotional and social difficulties in bullying and cyberbullying: differences by participant role, *Emotional & Behavioural Difficulties*, 17: 347–360.

Walsh, C.A., D'Aoust, G. & Beamer, K. (2011). Elder abuse and bullying: exploring theoretical and empirical connections. In C. Monks & I. Coyne (eds), *Bullying in Different Contexts*. Cambridge: Cambridge University Press, pp. 185–210.

Wang, J., Iannotti, R.J., Luk, J.W. & Nansel, T.R. (2010). Co-occurrence of victimization from five subtypes of bullying: physical, verbal, social exclusion, spreading rumors, and cyber, *Journal of Pediatric Psychology*, 35: 1103–1112.

Wang, J., Iannotti, R.J. & Nansel, T.R. (2009). School bullying among adolescents in the United States: physical, verbal, relational, and cyber, *Journal of Adolescent Health*, 45: 368–375.

Whitney, I., Smith, P.K. & Thompson, D. (1994). Bullying and children with special educational needs. In P.K. Smith & S. Sharp (eds), *School Bullying: Insights and Perspectives*. London: Routledge, pp. 213–240.

Willard, N.E. (2006). *Cyberbullying and Cyberthreats*. Eugene, OR: Center for Safe and Responsible Internet Use.

Williams, K., Chambers, M., Logan, S. & Robinson, D. (1996). Association of common health symptoms with bullying in primary school children, *British Medical Journal*, 313: 17–19.

Williams, S. (2013). Sexual bullying in one local authority. In I. Rivers & N. Duncan (eds), *Bullying: Experiences and Discourses of Sexuality and Gender*. London: Routledge, pp. 60–74.

Wolak, J., Mitchell, K. & Finkelhor, D. (2006). 'Online Victimization of Youth: Five Years Later'. Report to National Center for Missing & Exploited Children. http:www.missingkids.com/en_us/publications/NC167.pdf

Wolfe, D.A., Crooks, C.C., Chiodo, D. & Jaffe, P. (2009). Child maltreatment, bullying, gender-based harassment, and adolescent dating violence: making the connections, *Psychology of Woman Quarterly*, 33: 21–24.

Wolke, D., Copeland, W.E., Angold, A. & Costello, E.J. (2013). Impact of bullying in childhood on adult health, wealth, crime and social outcomes, *Psychological Science*, 24: 1958–1970.

Wolke, D. & Samara, M. (2004). Bullied by siblings: association with peer victimisation and behaviour problems in Israeli lower secondary school children, *Journal of Child Psychology and Psychiatry*, 45: 1015–1029.

Wolke, D., Woods, S. & Samara, M. (2009). Who escapes or remains a victim of bullying in primary school?, *British Journal of Developmental Psychology*, 27: 835–851.

Wong, D.S.W., Lok, D.P.P., Lo, T.W. & Ma, S.K. (2008). School bullying among Hong Kong Chinese primary schoolchildren, *Youth & Society*, 40: 35–54.

Woods, S. & Wolke, D. (2003) Does the content of anti-bullying policies inform us about the prevalence of direct and relational bullying behaviour in primary schools?, *Educational Psychology*, 23: 381–402.

World Health Organisation. See www.who.int/violenceprevention/approach/definition/en/

Ybarra, M., Boyd, D., Korchmaros, J. & Oppenheim, J. (2012). Defining and measuring cyberbullying within the larger context of bullying victimization, *Journal of Adolescent Health*, 51: 53–58.

Ybarra, M. & Mitchell, K.J. (2004). Online aggressor/targets, aggressors, and targets: a comparison of associated youth characteristics, *Journal of Child Psychology and Psychiatry*, 45: 1308–1316.

Ybarra, M. & Mitchell, K.J. (2007). Prevalence and frequency of Internet harassment instigation: implications for adolescent health, *Journal of Adolescent Health*, 41: 189–195.

Ybarra, M., Mitchell, K.J. & Korchmaros, J.D. (2011). National trends in exposure to and experiences of violence on the internet among children, *Pediatrics*, 128: 1376–1386.

Young, S. (1998). The Support Group approach to bullying in schools, *Educational Psychology in Practice*, 14: 32–39.

Youth Justice Board (2004). *National Evaluation of the Restorative Justice in Schools Programme*. Youth Justice Board Publication, Number D61.

Yuile, A., Pepler, D., Craig, W. & Connolly, J. (2006). The ethics of peeking behind the fence: issues related to studying children's aggression and victimization. In B. Leadbeater (ed.), *Ethics in Community-based Research*. Toronto: University of Toronto Press, pp. 117–150.

Zapf, D., Einarsen, S., Hoel, H. & Vartia, M. (2003). Empirical findings on bullying in the workplace. In S. Einarsen, H. Hoel, D. Zapf & C.L. Cooper (eds), *Bullying and Emotional Abuse in the Workplace: International Perspectives in Research and Practice*. London: Taylor and Francis, pp. 103–126.

Zwierzynska, K., Wolke, D. & Lereya, T.S. (2013). Peer victimization in childhood and internalizing problems in adolescence: a prospective longitudinal study, *Journal of Abnormal Child Psychology*, 41: 309–323.

Index

Stability of bully and victim roles 93–95
Stammer 56, 89–90
Stereotypes 61, 85–86
Suicide, suicide attempt, suicidal ideation 4, 6, 104, 116–119, 134, 138, 170, 187
Support Group Method 152–155, 169
Survey of Bullying at Your School 49
Sweden 13, 36, 89, 100, 115, 125, 136, 143, 151, 181, 191
Switzerland 110, 114, 159–160

Teachers 24–25, 39–41, 56, 64–65, 68, 77, 79, 106, 114, 131–134, 140–142, 144–145, 152, 156–157, 160, 172, 176–178, 181–183, 189
Temperament 104, 107–108, 125, 138, 186
Thailand 26
Theory of mind 111–112, 186
Toronto project 174
Transactional model 105, 110–111, 119–120, 128–129
Transitions 76, 95–96, 129, 143, 162
Trends over time 69, 97–100, 188–189
Turkey 27, 83, 136
Types of bullying 43–44, 51–52, 74–76, 78–80, 87, 141, 179, 191
Types of informant, *see* Informants, types of

UK 30–32, 54, 56, 85–87, 92, 110, 120, 130, 136–137, 150, 157, 166, 185, 187–189, *see also* England, Great Britain, Northern Ireland, Scotland, Wales
UK Household Longitudinal Study 86

Ukraine 69
Unjust use of power, unjustified aggression 11, 17–18, 35, 101–102
United Nations, UNESCO 6, 33
USA 12, 25, 30, 32, 34, 38–41, 45–48, 54, 60–61, 64, 67–70, 80, 83, 86, 89, 93–96, 98–99, 105, 108, 110, 117–120, 124–126, 128–129, 132, 134–136, 143, 154, 159, 173–174, 180, 183, 188

Validity 44, 49, 64, 66, 161
Vietnam 16, 142–143
Violence 11, 20–21, 29–30, 162, 187
Virtual Learning Environment 158, 177–178, 184, 190
ViSC 159
Visual impairment 89–90

Wales 40, 54, 72–73, 78–79, 86–87, 91, 97, 106, 112, 116, 124, 134, 155–156, 180
Wang-ta 101
Welsh Assembly Government 72
Whole-school policy on bullying, *see* School anti-bullying policies
Witnesses, of bullying 2, 77, 82, 135, 164, 186
Workplace bullying 28, 101
World Health Organisation 20–21, 29, 68

Youth Internet Safety Survey 99

Zero programme 172, 175–176